Transnational Classes and International Relations

D1552614

Transnational Classes and International Relations presents an original analysis of class formation in the global political economy. It deals with the growth of an integrated, transnational capitalist class and provides the student and academic reader with the first systematic overview of the theory and concepts developed in the Research Centre for International Political Economy at the University of Amsterdam. Among its many areas of focus are:

- the processes of commodification and socialisation
- class formation under the discipline of capital
- international relations between the English-speaking heartland of capital and successive contender states
- transnational integration of the capitalist class in historical perspective

The author develops an understanding of class, by discussing such notions as the 'imagined-community' nature of class, *Vergesellschaftung* (socialisation), fractions of capital, comprehensive concepts of control, the Lockean heartland versus the Hobbesian contender states and the cadre stratum as a lever of socio-political transformation.

With its broad scope and thorough examination of the agents actively involved in the process of globalisation, this study offers researchers and advanced students, in addition to its own findings, a treasure trove of research hypotheses.

Kees van der Pijl is Reader in International Relations at the University of Amsterdam.

RIPE series in global political economy

Series editors: Otto Holman, Marianne Marchand
and Henk Overbeek

Research Centre for International Political Economy, University of Amsterdam

The *RIPE series in global political economy*, published in association with the *Review of International Political Economy*, provides a forum for current debates in international political economy. The series aims to cover all the central topics in IPE and to present innovative analyses of emerging topics for students and specialists alike. The titles in the series seek to transcend a state-centred discourse and focus on three broad themes:

- the nature of the forces driving globalisation forward;
- resistance to globalisation;
- the transformation of the world order.

Forthcoming titles in the series:

MONEY AND NATION-STATES

The past, present and future of national currencies
Edited by Emily Gilbert and Eric Helleiner

IDEOLOGIES OF GLOBALISATION

Mark Rupert

Transnational Classes and International Relations

Kees van der Pijl

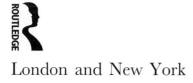

London and New York

337
P634t

First published 1998
by Routledge
11 New Fetter Lane, London EC4P 4EE

Simultaneously published in the USA and Canada
by Routledge
29 West 35th Street, New York, NY 10001

© 1998 Kees van der Pijl

Typeset in Baskerville by
The Florence Group, Stoodleigh, Devon

Printed and bound in Great Britain by
Redwood Books, Trowbridge, Wiltshire

British Library Cataloguing in Publication Data
A catalogue record for this book is available from the British Library

Library of Congress Cataloguing in Publication Data
Pijl, Kees van der.
    Transnational classes and international relations / Kees van der
Pijl.
        p. cm. — (RIPE (Series) : 1)
    Includes bibliographical references and index.
    (alk. paper)
    1. International economic relations—Social aspects. 2. Social
classes—History—20th century. 3. Capitalism—History—20th
century. I. Title. II. Series.
HF1359.P54   1998
337 – dc21   98–17032 CIP
JK
ISBN 0–415–19200–5 (hbk)
ISBN 0–415–19201–3 (pbk)

To Joyce and Gabriel Kolko
committed scholars, generous friends

Contents

Series editors' preface

The *RIPE series in global political economy* aims to make innovative contributions to key debates in the burgeoning field of international political economy. As series editors, we are especially keen to develop the series by addressing a wide audience made up of not only academic specialists but also students in a variety of related fields, policy makers, trade unionists and other activists in non-governmental organisations.

The series aims to present books that move beyond the traditional concerns of state-centric analysis, to address emerging issues in the global political economy and to present original accounts that synthesise work being done in the different core areas of IPE. *Transnational Classes and International Relations* fulfils these aims.

Central to our understanding of the process of global restructuring is the recognition of the dialectic of contradictory forces and processes at work. Global restructuring is driven by structural processes (such as the transnationalisation of production and the globalisation of financial markets) and by the agency of strategic actors such as transnational corporations, the competition state and globalising élites.

At the same time, globalisation produces new forces, forms and sites of resistance worldwide. In spite of the universalising tendencies of globalisation, new forms of particularism are emphasised and old forms acquire a new significance. Also, the new roles of transnational NGOs and the impact of new information and communications technologies have led to an increasing literature on the emergence of a global civil society harbouring the seeds of counter-hegemonic forces.

Transnational Classes and International Relations by Kees van der Pijl presents the first comprehensive and synthetic statement of the contribution of the Amsterdam group to international relations theory. The work of this group of IPE scholars departs from mainstream approaches to international relations on at least three central issues.

First, in the debate between neo-realist and pluralist approaches on the relevance of non-state actors, the ontological primacy of the state is not in question. In that sense, both main currents of IR thinking can be said to be state-centric. The analysis of world politics presented in this book clearly moves beyond state-centrism by identifying state formation and interstate politics as moments of the transnational dynamics of global capital accumulation and class formation.

Second, in the structure–agency debate the Amsterdam approach rejects the reductionism implied both in structuralist as well as in actor-oriented approaches. It advocates a historically grounded conception of the *dialectic totality* of structure and agency, as a neo-marxist would phrase it, or the *duality of structures*, as a structuration theorist would prefer.

Third, it argues that the national/international dichotomy no longer contributes to an understanding of world politics (if it ever did).

The Amsterdam group strives to salvage historical materialism from the rubbish heap of history by rigorously applying Marx's theory of historical change and class formation to the global level. This rejuvenated historical materialism, which in a sense brings to life themes that were central to the debates on imperialism in the early years of the twentieth century but have since been forgotten, shares many concerns with what has come to be known as the neo-Gramscian approach as manifested in the work of Robert Cox, Stephen Gill and Craig Murphy amongst others. The analysis of the *fractionation* of capital and the related strategic divisions within the bourgeoisie, however, sets out the Amsterdam approach as distinct. The situation of ideology and the political articulation of (fractional) class interests in the context of the dynamics of capital accumulation in a non-reductionist manner through the elaboration of the analytical tool of 'comprehensive concepts of control' enable these authors to escape the trappings both of deterministic reductionism and of voluntarism.

In this book, Van der Pijl presents a succinct and thought-provoking restatement of the essential ingredients of the Amsterdam project. But he does more. In his presentation, he also breaks new ground both in developing the method of historical materialism and in contributing, from that background, to the reinterpretation of inter-state relations.

First, Van der Pijl gives a fresh and novel meaning to two concepts that were central in Marx's analysis of the accumulation of capital and the emergence of bourgeois society, namely the concept of *socialisation* (or *Vergesellschaftung*) and the notion of capital as a *discipline* that exhausts the social and biospherical substrata of human life. These two concepts play a central role in Van der Pijl's resurrection of historical materialism, and provide the structure on which his analysis of world politics is based. Moreover, the treatment of the process of fractionation of capital and the distinction between the money capital concept and the productive capital concept throws new light on recent discussions on different 'models of capitalism' (such as the Rheinland and the Anglo-Saxon models of Michel Albert). Van der Pijl follows this through with a closer look at the cadre class, the embodiment of transnational socialisation in the contemporary epoch. The book ends with a discussion of the dilemmas of global governance and the potential for transformative action of the transnational cadre class.

Second, directly relevant to theories of international relations in the traditional sense, this study offers an original reinterpretation of the dynamics of the state system through the introduction of the distinction between what Van der Pijl calls the expanding Lockean heartland of capitalism and the rise of Hobbesian contender states on the perimeters of this heartland. From there, the author turns to a discussion of the mechanisms of hegemonic integration within the Lockean heartland. Van der Pijl examines how the dynamics of capital accumulation, institutional developments and ideological processes combine to produce a truly transnational society in which what used to be called international politics has largely become 'domestic' politics. Finally, it is worthwhile to call attention to Van der Pijl's analysis of the ways in which the state classes of Hobbesian contender states are integrated into the transnational structures of hegemony in specific historical periods.

The editors of the *RIPE series in global political economy* are proud to present *Transnational Classes and International Relations* to the readers as the series' first volume. We hope and expect that the series will become a popular and important focal point in the fields of international relations theory and international political economy.

Otto Holman
Marianne Marchand
Henk Overbeek
Amsterdam, May 1998

Tables and figures

Tables

Figures

Acknowledgements

In writing this book I have been helped – by getting either comments on parts of the manuscript, suggestions for further reading, or other forms of support – by Mehdi Amineh, Melanie Comman, Robert Cox, Stephen Gill, Henk Houweling, René Hulst, Gerd Junne, Isam al-Khafaji, Samuel Knafo, Ans Kolk, Joyce and Gabriel Kolko, Marcel van Maastrigt, Marianne Marchand, Arthur Mitzman, André Mommen, Arjen Nijeboer, Ronen Palan, Stephan Raes, Frank Schröder, Susanne Söderberg, Ellen Meiksins Wood and Hans van Zon. I also want to thank the two anonymous reviewers whose criticism forced me seriously to rethink the original manuscript. Through the years, IR students in Amsterdam have been a constant source of inspiration; earlier versions of the present study were discussed by graduate students in the Research Centre for International Political Economy, always to my benefit. In July 1997, I had the opportunity to present an outline of chapter 5 to colleagues and students at the Social Faculty of Frankfurt University, and of chapter 4 to an audience at Marburg University. On both occasions, I received valuable comments which I used in finalising the manuscript.

I am also grateful to the editorial team at Routledge, in particular to Martin Barr and Goober Fox, for their efficient handling of the book and for valuable suggestions. Most of all, I have to thank my friends and colleagues Henk Overbeek and Otto Holman for their close support and criticism as well as Magnus Ryner, who made important suggestions for recasting the original draft. It goes without saying that none of the above can be blamed for any remaining deficiencies in the text, for which I alone am responsible. Unless stated otherwise, quotations from non-English-language sources have been translated by myself.

Permission to reproduce pictures herein is gratefully acknowledged from Beeldrecht Amstelveen. Every effort has been made to contact copyright holders, and apology is made for any inadvertent omissions. If any acknowledgement is missing, it would be appreciated if contact could be made care of the publishers so that this can be rectified in any future edition.

Abbreviations

AFL–CIO	American Federation of Labor and Congress of Industrial Organizations
BCSD	Business Council for Sustainable Development
BW	*Business Week*
CED	Committee on Economic Development
CEO(s)	chief executive officer(s)
CFR	Council on Foreign Relations
CIA	Central Intelligence Agency
CIO	*see* AFL–CIO
COMECON	Council for Mutual Economic Aid
CPD	Committee on the Present Danger
EBRD	European Bank for Reconstruction and Development
Ec	*The Economist*
EC	European Community
ECE	Economic Commission for Europe
ECSC	European Coal and Steel Community
EEC	European Economic Community
ELEC	European League for Economic Cooperation
EMU	economic and monetary union
ESID	European Society for Industrial Development
EU	European Union
Euratom	European Atomic Energy Community
ExCom	executive committee
FCF	Free Congress Foundation
FDI	foreign direct investment
FT	*Financial Times*
G-7	Group of Seven
GDP	gross domestic product
GNP	gross national product
GST	General System Theory
IBRD	International Bank for Reconstruction and Development
ICC	International Chamber of Commerce
IEA	Institute of Economic Affairs

IEC	International Electrotechnical Commission
IHT	*International Herald Tribune*
ILO	International Labour Organization
IMD	Institute for Management Development
IMF	International Monetary Fund
IPE	international political economy
IR	international relations
ISO	International Standards Organization
ITU	International Telecommunications Union
MD	*Le Monde Diplomatique*
MEW	*Marx–Engels Werke*
MIT	Massachusetts Institute of Technology
MPS	Mont Pèlerin Society
MRA	Moral Re-armament Movement
NAFTA	North American Free Trade Agreement
NATO	North Atlantic Treaty Organization
NCF	National Civic Federation
NERO	National Economic Research Organisations
NGO	non-governmental organisation
NIEO	New International Economic Order
NRC	*NRC-Handelsblad*
Nw	*Newsweek*
OECD	Organization for Economic Cooperation and Development
OEEC	Organization for European Economic Cooperation
OMGUS	Office of the Military Government for Germany, United States
RIIA	Royal Institute of International Affairs
SDI	Strategic Defense Initiative
SI	Socialist International
SIFI	Stratégies Industrielles des Firmes Internationales
SIGINT	signal intelligence
TC	Trilateral Commission
UN	United Nations
UNCED	United Nations Conference on Environment and Development
UNESCO	United Nations Educational, Scientific and Cultural Organization
Vk	*De Volkskrant*
WACL	World Anti-Communist League
WCC	World Council of Churches
WEF	World Economic Forum
WEU	Western European Union
WTO	World Trade Organization

Introduction

This study seeks to present, in a concise format, an outline of critical international relations (IR) theory that builds on insights developed in the International Relations Department of the University of Amsterdam, currently the *Research Centre for International Political Economy*. My aim is to highlight the conceptual aspects of this theory rather than presenting an integral historical narrative.[1]

The Amsterdam International Political Economy project dates back to 1974–75, when a group of staff and students embarked on an integrated research–teaching programme entitled 'Social Forces in Western European Integration'. This project was intended to investigate the origins of that integration process in the immediate post-war period and its antecedents. It coincided in time with other developments widening the field of IR to include economic questions – notably, the shift from Cold War IR realism to a neo-realism which sought to deal with stable patterns of co-operation between states, 'regimes'; and world-systems theory which proposed a comprehensive historical analysis building on the development/underdevelopment thesis originally developed by André Gunder Frank.

At the time, these approaches were not directly pertinent to our research concerns. Our inspiration instead came from the work of Alfred Sohn-Rethel (1975, 1976) on the class structure of German Nazism; Joyce and Gabriel Kolko's *The Limits of Power. The World and United States Foreign Policy, 1945–1954* (1972); the collective work on European integration by a study group led by Professor Frank Deppe of Marburg University in West Germany (Deppe 1975) in addition to Ernst Haas's *Uniting of Europe* (1968); as well as the analyses on the internationalisation of capital by Christian Palloix of the University of Grenoble, France, and his team of researchers (Palloix, 1973, 1974a/b, 1976; Maurino 1974), and Paul Sweezy's *Theory of Capitalist Development* (1972). This literature, too, reflected the opening up of traditional and behavioural IR discourse to insights emerging from social and economic history and to Marx's critique of economic theory. In that sense, our work fitted into the broader tendency towards an inclusive international political economy (IPE), which hitherto had been a term confined to Marxist discourse (see also Chattopadhyay 1974). And although we criticised mainstream theories for glossing over the dynamics of capital accumulation and class conflicts structuring the political arena, we also aimed at re-evaluating a (neo-) Marxism which in our view failed to take class formation and politics into account as instances mediating and structuring capital accumulation nationally, transnationally, and internationally.

The project evolved to its present outlook in three steps. We began by studying the differences in the *social labour process* in the United States and Europe. The crisis of 1929 and the early 1930s, when the industrial labour process in the US was geared to a system of demand-led mass production of consumer durables (Fordism), did not produce a comparable restructuring in Europe. Only after the war, following the Marshall Plan and the establishment of the European Coal and Steel Community (ECSC), did Western Europe start to catch up with, while simultaneously being integrated into, the American pattern. The thesis of Dietmar Goralzcyk (in Deppe 1975), that the Second World War functioned as a 'crisis of restructuring' in Europe because those in power in the 1930s had successfully resisted a transformation along US/New Deal lines, was extended to include the Marshall Plan and the ECSC. These structural transformations, and hence, European integration, were then interpreted as a belated adjustment of the Western European labour process to an emerging North Atlantic pattern modelled after Roosevelt's New Deal.

As one can now establish, this emphasis on the labour process that was our point of departure, already put the Amsterdam project on a different track from the parallel development of neo-realism and world systems theory. In neo-realism, labour processes were not and are not considered as constitutive of regimes. Regimes are the product of agreement between states or of one state's hegemony, past or present (Keohane 1984). In the 1971 special issue of *International Organization*, 'Transnational Relations and World Politics', which may be considered the watershed publication in the shift to IPE as far as mainstream IR is concerned (Keohane and Nye 1973), only one contribution took labour relations into account. But this article, by Robert Cox, charted a course different from the emerging neo-realism – eventually, towards a Gramscian approach which meanwhile has become a major strand in the field (see also Cox 1971, 1987; Gill 1993; Gill and Mittelman 1997). As far as world systems theory is concerned, its structural approach rests on patterns of unequal exchange between regions first of all. 'Modes of Labor Control' as they are called by Wallerstein, are functionally determined by these exchange patterns. 'Free labor is the form of labor control used for skilled work in core countries whereas coerced labor is used for less skilled work in peripheral areas. The combination thereof is the essence of capitalism' (1974: 127). Clearly, in such a perspective, struggles over the rate of exploitation by capital cannot be the mainspring of social and political development (see Brenner 1977; Palan 1992).

As a second step, research in the Amsterdam project focused on the *relations between the different industries* in the 'Fordist' restructuring of Atlantic capital between 1929 and the 1950s. One aspect of the crisis of the 1930s had been the subordination, by market or political mechanisms, of industries in the sector producing means of production (investment goods) to industries producing consumer durables. The Coal and Steel Community was the specific form of this subordination in Western Europe. In Britain, nationalisation served a comparable purpose (Overbeek 1980). This conclusion expanded on the findings of other authors, notably Sohn-Rethel, who explain German fascism in terms of a reverse movement, i.e. the stifling of the growth of internationally oriented, high productivity industries by the autarkic Ruhr barons.

At the theoretical level, the understanding of 'pre-political' economic blocs operating behind and within the actual political parties and other legitimate actors, led to renewed attention for Marx's concept of *fractions of capital*. Fractions of capital are functional divisions within total capital (notably money, commodity, and productive capital); around which, at a more concrete level and in historically specific combinations, *class fractions* take shape. This concept of fraction makes it possible to reconstruct the historical growth of capital in terms of a pluralism (or better, 'polyarchy', since the range of options remains within narrow limits) of class strategies which articulate, ultimately, empirical constellations of particular fractions. Now if, for instance, mass-production industry under state-monitored demand management replaces the *haute finance* and international capital markets as the nodal points of overall capital accumulation (as it did in the 1930s and 1940s), this of course does not mean that only a part of capital is functioning. It only means that a certain fraction, and the historical perspective this fraction has developed on capitalist relations of production in their entirety, guides the action of the state and other instances of the general capitalist interest. In this way, the fraction concept can help to connect economics and politics in a way which cannot be achieved by either a monolithic concept of capital with a big 'C' (prevalent in much modern Marxism, say Mandel 1972, or *Collectif PCF* 1971, as well as looming behind much American Elitism – Mills 1959; Domhoff 1978, and others); or the politicism of mainstream IR, in which states are the privileged or even exclusive actors.

The next step taken to arrive at a more complete analysis, involved the historical processes of transnational class formation in which the link between economic structure and interest articulation, and political action, is made actual. Gramsci's 'Americanism and Fordism' (in Gramsci 1971) and Poulantzas's (1971, 1976) analysis of an international fraction of capital in Europe seeking to insert itself into circuits of capital centring on the USA, showed that understanding the relation between structural changes in production and the political struggles through which they take shape, requires a *historical* as well as a *transnational* analysis. Only when the space in which economy and politics interact is extended to cover entire historical eras and larger-than-national complexes of states and society, can the cohesion underlying such interaction be defined in terms of the rise and decline of social classes.

This problem – how economics and politics become fused in transnational and historical processes of *class formation* – was addressed by Ries Bode's notion of *comprehensive concepts of control (globale beheersconcepties*, Bode 1979). This notion seeks to capture the unity (again, a broader, mediated historical/transnational rather than immediate unity) of the interests of fractions of capital and the need to impose the discipline of capital on society at large. What is it that unites the different social forces to which we refer by the term 'class fractions' and fractions of capital in their relation with other social strata, over longer periods and larger-than-national spaces – and which is not a unified, all-powerful 'capital' in the singular?

This question was answered, first by Bode, by showing how 'fractions of the bourgeoisie', configured around specific combinations of capitals and fractions of capital, continuously seek to approximate a general interest which they and their allies define in terms different from their *specific* needs yet satisfying these needs. The capacity to transcend the immediacy of particular, 'fractional' interests and cast a wider net by organising a coalition of interests around a historically concrete definition of the *general* interest, qualifies social forces to effectively enter the contest for power. But this contest is *decided* by the question which fractional élites are strengthened more than others by the current tendency of capital accumulation and social development (towards industrial expansion, towards liquidation of a given industrial pattern, etc., etc.) – if also, in the final analysis, by the purely political qualities of those élites in mobilising the passions and aspirations of the population at large.

Concepts of control, then, are the projects of rival political alliances which on account of their appropriateness to deal with current contradictions in the labour, intersectoral/competition, and profit distribution processes, as well as with broader social and political issues, at some point become *comprehensive*, crowding out the others by their greater adequacy to a historically specific situation – until they themselves unravel in the course of further development and struggle.

What is at stake here can be easily understood if we think of 'Keynesianism' or the 'welfare state' as belonging to a concept which until the mid-seventies was generally accepted in the Atlantic political economy, although it was *also* the special interest of mass-production industry and organised labour, interfacing with a state apparatus committed, in a Cold War context imposing a specific class discipline on it, to full employment and demand management. Today, the self-evidence of this concept has evaporated. The metropolitan mass-production industry is considered a 'rust belt', while organised labour has suffered severe setbacks. Along the escape routes out of a seemingly deadlocked socio-economic configuration (through accelerated internationalisation, 'liquidation' of assets into financial ones, individualisation, etc.) new social forces are articulating and propagating a different concept. This concept stresses the market as the sole arbiter of social life, replacing the state-monitored social compromises of the previous one. But, like its predecessor two or three decades ago, the new concept was until recently broadly seen as an almost natural, self-evident truth rather than as the ideological programme of 'particularly interested' financial specialists and individual entrepreneurs.

Now the alternation of fractions of capital and the successive configurations of class forces galvanised by specific concepts of control takes place, as indicated, in a transnational setting. That is, concepts of a class/fraction origin seek to be adequate to realities that never are confined to a single state, but occur in several of them – if perhaps in different forms. The awareness of this fact and the quest for a comprehensive strategy to deal with those realities in part relies on transnational channels. Networks of multiple directors of international corporations and banks, planning groups of various sorts, and international media play their part here. But since different states, on account of the very differences that make up their specificity as historically separate units, are unequally affected, and resources are, of course, unequally distributed to begin with, the spread of a specific concept of control nearly always assumes the form of a dominance of a particular state or combination within the group of states that together constitute the field of action of capital. Thus, both the Keynesian ('corporate liberal') and the newer market ('neo-liberal') concepts achieved their comprehensive, *hegemonic* status through a victorious reassertion of American and, in the second case, Anglo-American power in the world political economy. Accordingly, we may understand the *Pax Americana*, both in its 1945–1971 and in its more recent, Reaganomics/'New World Order' editions, as the expression of the hegemony of a transnational ruling class unified behind a concept of control reflecting a particular configuration of capitalist forces.

Of course, 'regimes' in the neo-realist approach broadly denote what we term concepts of control. Thus, in Stephen Krasner's study on the struggle over world order in the 1970s, *Structural Conflict*, the struggle was between two rival concepts of global political economy, one guided by the principle of 'authoritative allocation' (a sort of generalised state-monopolistic concept), the other a 'market-oriented regime' of the corporate liberal or neo-liberal type (Krasner 1985: 5). However, it makes quite a difference whether one considers these regimes as having been put in place by states, and as being dependent on the continued observance by states alone, or whether one sees them as ultimately expressing dominant patterns of exploitation in production, mediated by class and state relations. In neo-realism, state power is a self-explanatory category while states are endowed with rationality and other psychological characteristics (Palan 1992: 23). The origins of the historical hegemonic cycle, and the distribution of power among candidates for hegemony, are endogenous, essentially political–military. As to the 'core' states, Wallerstein takes the same position (1984: 49). In our view, however, struggles in production constitute the inner tension propelling societies forward. They engender conflicts that force change on the entire constellation of historical structures in which, on a global scale, humanity's capacity to determine its own existence is contained. As Mark Rupert writes (1993: 83),

> Both the system of sovereign states and the global division of labour, taken as ontologically primitive units by neo-realism and world-system

theory, respectively, – may instead be understood as aspects of the historically specific social organisation of productive activity under capitalism, as embodying relations of alienation, and as potentially transcendable.

The concepts of control which we have distinguished, and which in a most general sense (allowing for regional and sectoral variations) have guided transnational class formation over a period of three centuries, are liberal internationalism; a state monopoly tendency; corporate liberalism, and neoliberalism. In a gradually expanding capitalist heartland evolved around Great Britain and the English-speaking settler colonies and today comprising the OECD area broadly speaking, the hegemony of these concepts has expressed the ascendancy of consecutive configurations of capital, indeed 'generations' in the capitalist class in their relation to others and to other social strata.

'Ascendancy', as well as the fact that stages of development covered by these concepts overlapped, imply that we are dealing with an *evolving, and contradictory, totality*. Thus, forces committed to liberal internationalism in the *Pax Britannica* at its meridian already faced the countermovement of state monopolists both from within and from abroad; while the American New Deal and its extrapolation to Western Europe through the Marshall Plan was driven by the liberals' hope to overcome the self-encapsulation of class relations within the separate states. (Neo-)liberalism all along was a counterpoint within the class compromises of corporate liberalism, and emerged only when the crisis of 1974–75 (others would perhaps point to May 1968) definitively derailed the Keynesian programme. The crisis of US-led Cold War imperialism marked by Vietnam, Portuguese Africa, and *détente*, complemented the demise of Keynesianism, while mobilising the neo-liberals also into foreign policy militancy. Indeed, war and the threat of war have always been an integral part of the historical restructuration processes underlying the shift to new definitions of the general (imperial, 'Western', 'World') capitalist interest which concepts of control represent.

The continuous infighting of new fractions of the ruling and governing classes, united behind concepts striving for comprehensiveness, has to be stressed to underline the open-ended nature of the process. At all levels (labour process to world politics), 'strategy' encounters unexpected obstacles, 'planning' lacks sufficient information, 'will' stumbles on what Braudel has termed the limits of the possible (quoted in Gill 1993: 9). There *is* structure in the action of social forces (classes, fractions of classes, transnational coalitions of classes . . .), but not in the 'system' sense of functionality/teleology in a self-sustaining totality, or series of such totalities, but only within 'limits of the possible' defined by contradictions.

Let me now briefly sum up the contents of the five chapters of the present study. The first chapter treats two processes basic to capital accumulation and class formation: *commodification* and *socialisation* (German *Vergesellschaftung*, literally, 'societisation'). The second in particular (which should not be confused with/reduced to the sociological concept of transmitting social norms and habits) is relevant not only to describe the particular forms of social organisation under capitalist conditions, but also refers to the moment of transformation towards a new type of society maturing in the context of the old.

Chapter 2 discusses the processes of class formation driven by capital accumulation in greater detail. It argues, first, that all class formation is structured by a historical social topography which reaches back to the earliest phases of human existence and accordingly is shaped by long chains of locally and temporally specific events. It then distinguishes the different forms in which the discipline of capital is imposed and resisted, so that ruling and subordinate social groups tendentially become part of a specifically capitalist class constellation. Finally, the chapter outlines how the capitalist class develops its own unity through different historical phases, expressed in successive concepts of control.

Before elaborating how these concepts and the class constellations supporting them have evolved historically, chapter 3 deals with the political geography of capitalist expansion. Here, I argue that capital originated in England, partly due to the particular, and unique, state/society configuration we have labelled Lockean. This Lockean pattern expanded by colonial settlement to North America and elsewhere to constitute a relatively integrated 'heartland', unified against successive *contender states*. These contender states represent a 'Hobbesian' state/society configuration (from France through the USSR to the Asian NICs today) in which the social basis is still being unified and demarcated by the state in order to challenge and catch up with the heartland.

In chapter 4, the analysis turns to the actual channels of transnational class formation which historically have emanated from the heartland and partly have been absorbed into the contender states by *passive revolutions*. Three themes will concern us specifically: first, the origins of bourgeois transnationalism in specific 'imagined communities' such as Freemasonry; second, the emergence of planning groups acting as collective intellectuals for the wider class – of which the Rhodes–Milner Group was the prototype; finally, this chapter investigates the process of hegemonic integration of contender state classes into the transnational bourgeoisie, in which a new type of transnational planning group has played the role of a synthesising force.

Chapter 5 deals with an important aspect often overlooked in IPE analysis – the new social strata generated by *Vergesellschaftung*/socialisation. These strata – to which some observers have lent, and others denied, the status of a class (new middle class, managerial class, cadres, etc.) – in the author's view constitute a critical factor in the evolving contradiction between the private and the social, which today takes the form of the evident inappropriateness of the 'private' for dealing with the planetary challenges facing humanity. Socialism in the twentieth century all along was a political project of particular tendencies within this managerial or cadre stratum, and since this class continues to grow, no transition to a sustainable society can be imagined in which this stratum would not play a crucial role.

1 Commodification, socialisation and capital

> The connection of the individual with all, but at the same time also the inde-
> pendence of this connection from the individual, have developed to such a
> high level that the formation of the world market already at the same time
> contains the conditions for going beyond it.
>
> Karl Marx

In this chapter, we will introduce the most abstract, general determinants of
capitalist development, the inner structure of what is called 'capital-in-general'.
The above quotation from Marx's *Grundrisse* (1973: 161) in fact refers to three
of these in a nutshell.

First, the process of *commodification*. This means that the lives of ever
more people are determined by tendentially world-embracing market relations ('the connection of the individual with all'). Goods produced, services
rendered, but also the raw material of nature and human beings as such, are
thus subjected to an economic discipline which defines and treats them as
commodities.

Second, the elementary exchange relations by which a market connection
is established, in the course of their development create webs of complex,
quasi-organic interdependence in which the initial division of labour implied
in exchange becomes objectified in knowledge, machinery, and organisation
('the independence of this connection from the individual'). This refers to the
process of *socialisation*. Socialisation (*Vergesellschaftung*) comes about either by
capital accumulation or by state action. However, under a commodity
economy (ultimately, the capitalist economy), the growth of an interdependent, global social system remains subject to competitive strategies for profit
and control. The planning of a partial structure of socialisation – say, a firm,
or a social security system – cannot be generalised for the world economy as
a whole, because it continues to be mediated by market relations and private
appropriation. (Hayek's claim in *The Road to Serfdom* (1985) that large-scale
economies cannot be planned at all due to lack of knowledge implies that,
even within a single firm or state institution, internal exchanges should be
of a market type.) Clearly, the system of multiple state sovereignty, which

historically has emerged along with the world market, also rebels against unified direction.

Yet (and this is the third element), the ever-tighter imbrication of technical labour processes as a consequence of competitive profit strategies exerts a continuous pressure towards transcending the limits of the separate structures of socialisation. The more the particularity of separate firms ('particular capitals') is suspended by generalising the nature of the labour process towards the exploitation of abstract, polytechnic labour (which is one way of saying that particular capitals conform to capital-in-general), the greater the potential advantages of eliminating the waste of resources implied in head-on competition. In this sense, the world market 'at the same time contains the conditions for going beyond it'. Social dislocation and the ongoing destruction of the biosphere must be expected to activate this potential at some point in the future. But there is no historical necessity which will assure that this will usher in a functioning new order to replace the old, or that it will do so in time. Powerful ideological processes such as fetishism, which turns the capitalist economy into a quasi-natural phenomenon that cannot be interfered with, stand in the way of democratic regulation. Likewise, pressures to integrate state functions run upon the reality of the unique ways in which countries and regions have historically developed sources of authority and internal cohesion and in that context, deal with the class conflicts provoked by the imposition of the discipline of capital.

All this will be worked out below. We begin with commodification as a historical process in its own right, without for the moment concerning ourselves with its dialectical opposite (which is socialisation).

Commodification and community

Our starting point is that commodification begins on the limits of hitherto closed communities, at their points of contact with other communities or members of other communities (by 'community', we mean the web of reproductive/affective relations crystallising around the household; see also Weber 1976: ch. 3). This applies to primitive, feudal, or patrimonial society, but also to e.g. state socialism. The idea can be found in Marx (*MEW* 23: 102), Weber (1976: 383), and Polanyi (1957: 58). Trade according to the latter is intimately bound up with adventure, hunting, and piracy, so that the 'economic' is in reality embedded in patterns of behaviour highly charged with symbolic meaning; while geographic conditions and pre-existing patterns of sexual and age-related division of labour already determine who *can* be a hunter, adventurer, and hence, a trader, long before anything like a market economy has come into existence.[1]

As commodification proceeds, ever more aspects of community life are restructured by free, equivalent exchange relations. These in turn presume private property, the full ownership of the item to be exchanged. Thus one after another, qualities of people and of goods and services are turned into marketable items to be sold and bought, ultimately in the world market. The consequences for the cohesion of the community were analysed by Marx and Engels in the *Communist Manifesto* in terms of the destruction of idyllic and patriarchal community relations and their tendential replacement by the only remaining social bond, the cash nexus (*MEW* 4: 465). In Polanyi's words, the commodity form 'was to annihilate all organic forms of existence' and the freedom of contract 'meant that the noncontractual organizations of kinship, neighborhood, profession, and creed were to be liquidated' (1957: 163).

Now, even apart from a consciously protective reaction of society to this trend, human beings will never entirely be substituted by what Marx and Engels in an earlier work called 'world-historical, empirically universal individuals' (*MEW* 3: 35) as a consequence of commodification. There remains a community substratum on which commodified relations continue to rest, even if much of the actual community has become an 'imagined' one, such as nationality (Anderson 1983). Henri Lefebvre's notion of 'everyday life', by which he means the set of relationships and popular notions which most directly relate to natural/organic existence, such as living space, family and sexuality, the temporality of life, etc., also refers to this (quasi-) community substratum (Leithäuser 1976). Economically, this is the sphere of use values, ordered by their own logic of material and mental *reproduction* rather than by the (market) logic of exchange value, which is the vantage point of commodification. Here the regeneration of humanity takes place in all its aspects; it is the source of energies and potentialities which are subject to commodification and, eventually, to exploitation and appropriation. Hence everyday life contains an economy, too – one which Polanyi (1957: 47–53) describes by such terms as reciprocity, redistribution, and householding. Commodification, however, tends to progressively stifle the instincts and emotions that structure everyday life, resulting in alienated, externally controlled, 'functionalised' behaviour and objectively pauperised human relations (Leithäuser 1976: 52–3).

Still it is important to logically distinguish (quasi-)community relations from the commodity relations by which they are penetrated and transformed (but never entirely negated). The separation of private from public space in the nineteenth century, which demarcated the bourgeois home as a refuge from the harsh world of work and business, can be seen as an attempt to draw a line in this respect (Saisselin 1984: 29). But psychoanalysis, too, has been interpreted as an attempt to rediscover intimacy, self-knowledge, sensuous and emotional satisfaction in a context of social relations one-sidedly moulded by commodification (Zaretsky 1977: 102–3). In the 1970s, 'flower power' and Eastern religions performed a comparable function, and today, we may think of 'New Age' in the same way. Inevitably, however, such countermovements remain within the coordinates of the general trend. As Seeley (1962: 198) rightly observes in his essay on the 'Americanization of the Unconscious', 'the threats of manipulation from without are countered but fatally compounded by self-manipulation'.

While the subordination of social relations to the cash nexus, and the parcellisation of people's lives and capacities into marketable items, thus develop in a dialectical fashion, the unity of productive and reproductive existence is by and by destroyed. Wage labour may be employed per hour (or at piece-rates, which is an attempt to outpace the sixty-minute hour) – but whether this hour is embedded in a working life balanced by other concerns of human existence, care for the future, provision for childbirth, illness or retirement, is not necessarily part of capitalist calculation. The contemporary worker, Rosenstock-Huessy writes (1961: 473–4), can no longer relate the contents of a job in any way to his/her personal life, or even to the notion of a life-work. He/she is forcibly disinherited from reproductive responsibilities, which may be reconquered by forms of socialisation (welfare state or self-help arrangements), but which are not part of, and even are in principle at odds with a fully commodified existence and the tendency towards a twenty-four hour economy.

Commodified reality and fetishism

The spectre of an atomised society composed of disoriented, dehumanised individuals, obtained ample representation in the arts, especially in the early twentieth century. In Cubist painting and sculpture, human beings are depicted as robot-like recompositions of machine parts, cloth, and straight lines, from which organic vitality seems to have been removed (see Figure 1.1). In James Joyce's 1922 novel *Ulysses*, a kaleidoscopic panorama of the inner world of a group of Dubliners merges into snapshots of their aimless wanderings through the city. Is this really the human condition? Indeed, isn't it a miracle that there exists a mechanism by which the fragments of humanity are connected again into a functioning whole?

Here precisely the magical connotations of the market enter the picture. It is the market which supposedly reunites the fragmented human particles, whose inner world is as disjointed as their appearance, into a functioning totality. But the very fact that it is an *invisible* hand that supposedly brings order to life, if it is not the arbiter of life altogether, reveals the profound alienation underlying the market ethic and the implicit abdication of conscious direction of social reproduction at large. In this respect, contemporary society retains a primeval helplessness in relation to what it treats as forces of nature. As a result, even the wealthiest and most powerful inhabitants of the developed capitalist world, who have at their disposal all the accumulated technology of past centuries, turn into fearful, superstitious primitives when confronted with the vacillations of the Dow Jones index.

This phenomenon in which modern society resembles the most primitive community, is called *fetishism*. Fetishism is the ascription of animate spirit and magical powers to dead objects. It is a particular form of alienation – the process by which mental and material products are exteriorised and separated from the producers in such a way as to confront them as alien forces rather than as things or ideas of their own making (*MEW* 23: 85; Hinkelammert

Figure 1.1 Fragmented humanity: *Soldiers Playing at Cards* (1917) by Fernand Léger (1881–1955). © 1998 Fernand Léger, c/o Beeldrecht Amstelveen.

1985). Commodity relations presuppose the separation of the product from concrete social relations, disarticulating the commodities from the relations of production that still were largely transparent in earlier types of society. Commodities (consumer goods first of all) travel apparently on their own account, carrying with them certain qualities which evoke admiration and associations of happiness and fulfilment – rather than the traces of how and under which particular conditions they have been produced. But fetishism is not just mirages and miracles. It is also rational in the sense of clinging to the only acknowledged regulator of commodified society, the market mechanism. There is, in other words, a logic to economic orthodoxy which is however compounded by superstition.

Fetishism in cultural anthropology belongs to a complex of phenomena of which two are of particular importance for understanding the 'magical', fetishistic quality of commodity circulation (and, ultimately, of capital as its most developed form): *mana* and *taboo*. *Taboo* means that if there is direct contact with what is sacred, feelings of awe and fear will be awakened which narrowly circumscribe the behaviour that is considered appropriate (van Baaren 1960: 123). In dealing with the world economy, governments and government officials indeed approach the swings of capital and commodity markets as tokens of the gods, which one may hope to placate but never should challenge. Those closest to the supernatural world even claim to speak in its name, as when the president of the German central bank, Tietmeyer, in a comment on EU countries trying to manipulate the books in order to qualify for monetary union, warned that they would be 'heavily punished' by the markets and that if a country were to sneak out of EMU later, 'the markets will not forget that for a long time' (*FT*, 8 October 1996).

Although the increasing concentration of capital renders the real players in the world economy perfectly visible (and Keynesian counter-orthodoxy of the 1950s and 1960s pioneered a managerial attitude to it), the taboo on imposing any form of regulation has been reaffirmed in the more recent period. The incantations of today's professional economists serve to keep alive the idea that the workings of the market economy are only interfered with at one's peril. Even obviously inhuman conditions of production, such as child labour, are declared beyond regulation in the name of the free market (e.g. by the current head of the World Trade Organisation, Ruggiero, *FT*, 31 May 1995).

Mana refers to a magical, supernatural force operative in things and persons because they have been touched by a holy spirit. Things or people which contain mana become 'effective, true, real, remarkable, special' etc., and exert a magical attraction as a consequence (van Baaren 1960: 120). This should not be thought of as something which exists only in remote, unexplored outposts of civilisation. Secularisation, which we take for granted when it comes to contemporary society, in fact has redefined rather than obliterated the metaphysical. Today, the sphere of the magical and of aesthetic illusion ('aura') is increasingly functionalised to foster ostentatious, intensive consumption by means of advertising and life-style reporting (Saisselin 1984: ch.3; Debord 1967: 17). Thus aestheticised and sanctified (but also, as we shall see presently, eroticised), commodities carry the spark of the divine to the consumer, bestowing mana on whomever owns an object marked by the right sign.[2]

People accordingly tend to view themselves as commodities in all respects, not just as labour power. Shaping their identity by what may be termed *commodification of the self*, they become the conscious subject of their own individuality, defined entirely from the viewpoint of its success in the universal marketplace that is life. In the spirit of Cubist painting, they are living assemblies of fashionable cosmetics brands, dress and dress-related attributes, means of transport, etc. Ultimately the commodity economy in this way encourages every individual to become a living advertisement of him/herself as a marketable item.[3] The elementary life-cycle indeed is turned into a series of marketing events altogether. Thus a Dutch newspaper, commenting on the veritable advertising campaigns that increasingly replace the simple birth announcement, headlines its story as 'A baby is no longer born, but launched into the marketplace' (*Vk*, 29 September 1995). An advertisement in the same newspaper a few days later depicts a swarm of spermatozoa, one of which is highlighted in a different colour, with the caption 'A career cannot start early enough', etc.

Apart from the mana bestowed on the wearer of Nike shoes, Levi jeans, etc., the element of sexuality here deserves special mention. As Saisselin notes

(1984: 55), luxury, and the act of buying generally, in the nineteenth century became associated with sexuality. But with the penetration of the commodity form (itemisation, separation, sharp distinction between property and non-property in every sphere of life) and the stripping bare of community life, *all* the instincts increasingly have been elevated, apparently unmediated, to the surface of civilised life. The will to live, *eros*, the impulse to dominate, as well as the sexual instincts proper, are becoming one more axis on which the commodified universe revolves (Harvey 1995: 287). Ogburn's appreciative claim that rapid social change 'helps to shape a culture more in conformity with biological nature' than a stationary, heavily institutionalised one (1964: 54) cannot account for today's suspension of all sense of history by the short-circuiting of human instincts and market economy.

It is therefore not intended as moralism if we speak here (still pursuing the theme of commodification in the abstract, as if no countertendencies were operative) of a tendency towards universal prostitution. As elementary vital energies become available for commercial exploitation through a combination of magical attraction and sexual symbolism, while community bonds are simultaneously atrophied, the instincts directly connect into the cash economy. Of course, the female half of humanity was cast as the public object of desire first. 'Woman became the rival of the work of art,' Saisselin writes of the Paris *demi-monde* of the late nineteenth century (1984: 62): 'She turned into a bibelot herself . . . an expensive object of desire, to be possessed and cherished, but also exhibited.' With emancipation and individualisation, the female role acquires a new autonomy, on a par with the male, without shedding the commodity association. Thus a British tabloid approvingly writes of the pop artist, Madonna, that 'she looks like a whore and thinks like a pimp' (quoted in *Vk*, 21 August 1987). Not just selling, but exploiting oneself as an object of lust thus becomes the ideal propagated by a thoughtless commercialism.

Taken together, these effects of commodification should be understood as the supposition of the globalisation of capital. 'Americanisation', the hegemony of things associated with the USA, which was such a powerful weapon in e.g. the Cold War (Menand 1990: 106), cannot be understood without the magical and erotic associations of a range of brand names and idols. That this is not the real America, but the fetishised universe of things 'Made in America' (or not even 'made', but merely associated with the 'USA', like tennis socks with stars and stripes made in Portugal or elsewhere), is only a paradox, because what counts is the illusion.

Concepts of socialisation

To Karl Polanyi, commodification is a process which in the course of its development encounters its own limits. There are in his view three elements of social reality which are emphatically not commodities and can only be considered so at the risk of injuring social cohesion: labour, land, and money. They are, by the logic of market economy, fictitious commodities at best: for 'the postulate that anything that is bought and sold must have been produced for sale is emphatically untrue in regard to them' (Polanyi 1957: 72).

As production becomes more complex, the supply of these elements, which the discipline of the market presumes are forthcoming by the same mechanisms as other commodities, has to be safeguarded by certain interventions meant to curb the destructive effects on the social and natural substratum of the market economy (as well as on its monetary system). Hence,

> Social history in the nineteenth century was ... the result of a double movement: the extension of the market organization in respect to genuine commodities was accompanied by its restriction in respect to fictitious ones. While on the one hand markets spread all over the face of the globe ..., on the other hand a network of measures and policies was integrated into powerful institutions designed to check the action of the market relative to labor, land, and money (Polanyi 1957: 76).

This is the principle of *social protection* which according to Polanyi is mobilised time and again to keep the dislocating effects of market economy in check, and which in the 1930s assumed the proportions of a sea-change, the 'Great Transformation'. However, it is our contention that Polanyi's social protection is only *one* modality of a more fundamental process of socialisation – other modalities being, e.g. corporate planning, education, or international integration.

By socialisation, *Vergesellschaftung*, we understand the planned or otherwise normatively unified interdependence of functionally divided social activity. It should not be confused with or reduced to the sociological concept of transmitting culture (see Broom and Selznick 1970, ch. 4; or, in international relations, Ikenberry and Kupchan 1990). Before developing this definition by reference to its authors' specific use of the term, let us take an example from industrial organisation. In Figure 1.2, the steps taken by a British machine tool company to prepare for the conversion of its product line to the metric system, in conformity with the 1965 British adherence to the international measurement standard, are depicted graphically (a few machine tool operations are also shown, to give an idea of what machine tools are; they are the machines with which to make machines). The objective here is that a German or Brazilian lathe operator would have no trouble using a lathe made in Great Britain, given the precision requirements of machine tools. As can be seen in the figure, the steps taken involve a division of tasks within a single company ('prepare design drawings', 'make and test prototype', various training activities, etc.), but also relations with other companies ('make or procure special tooling and gauges'). Ultimately, these various activities inside the company or with specified partner companies relate to the wider setting of all countries using the metric system (the 'world market').

The conversion example highlights how one *structure of socialisation* (the machine tool corporation) is embedded in another (the British national

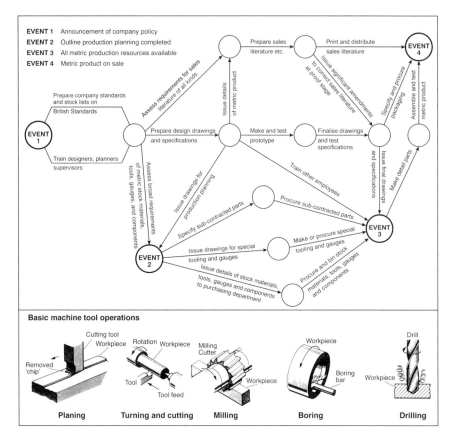

Figure 1.2 Socialisation: conversion of machine tool production to the metric system.
Source: Charnley 1973: 162, 164.

economy) and again in a further, in this case the ultimate one (the world market), and drives towards the latter as part of its development. If we think back to Marx's claim that the world market contains the conditions for going beyond it, the step to conform to international product standards is particu-larly meaningful.[4] Indeed, when looking at this particular conversion operation, the commodity form (of the eventual metric machine tool, of the services and products from external suppliers, and of the labour power entering into the various stages of its being produced) seems rather contingent to what is going on and may even come to be perceived as a positive obstacle. What is at stake in the situation depicted in Figure 1.2 is not a question primarily of markets and prices, but of *organisation*, combining the different activities; *plan-ning* their availability and conjunction at the right moment; and keeping *control* of the process in its entirety.

This applies to any system of production beyond the most primitive one. Yet the fact that socialisation under capitalist conditions is necessarily mediated by commodification (in the diagram, there are several market relations between Events 2 and 3, and at Event 4 the product itself appears on the market), also inherently limits the comprehensiveness of organisation, planning, and control in the case of any structure of socialisation. Confining ourselves to *control* (in the double sense of effective management and coercive power), on which organisation and planning are predicated, and taking the single company as our starting point, we can distinguish a series of 'control dilemmas' facing every firm (Ruigrok and van Tulder 1995: 37). 'Make *or procure* special tooling and gauges', etc. In the first case, a company department provides the necessary tools, which implies full control; in the second, they are bought from a different firm, in which case there must be a cost or time advantage offsetting the loss of control. The same for financing, raw material supplies, etc.

If we move up one notch, to the level of the British national economy, of which the machine tool company is a part, there are comparable dilemmas – for instance, encouraging national production of the elements of a product chain or importing; printing or borrowing money; and so on. Clearly, 'control' here is much less stringent, at least in Britain as a capitalist state. But even if the British national economy were a planned economy in which every possible material element could be procured without any exchanges between privately owned firms entitled to making their own choices (a fully *de*-commodified economy in other words), at Event 4 (Figure 1.2) the product still would enter the world market. At this supreme level, which, as such, represents a structure of socialisation, too, control is necessarily absent, and a very loose form of coordination is the best that e.g. a cartel of machine tool producers can hope to obtain in terms of control, organisation, and planning.

Although each of these instances, national economies and firms or groups of firms, represents a structure of socialisation (in the sense of a unified entity cutting across previous autonomies and exerting a degree of control), this does not by itself imply that their controlling action is already an instance of social protection in Polanyi's sense. Thus as long as the company is a private company, its control strategies must be subordinated to the competitive quest for profit; it usually will not be concerned with the overall condition of the social and natural substratum which Polanyi argues is threatened by the fiction of a self-regulating market economy. Only when this substratum, too, is made subject to some form of coordinated management, tasks are parcelled out and integrated again with an eye to the functioning of the whole; in other words, only if the overall *re*production of labour is socialised, too, can we speak of social protection in Polanyi's sense. In that case the control aspect of socialisation is directed against the disruptive effects of commodification.

Contemporaries often perceived the drift towards socialisation and standardisation in the 1930s and 1940s which underlay Polanyi's 'Great Transformation' as anything but protective. Novels such as Aldous Huxley's *Brave*

New World of 1932 and George Orwell's *1984* of 1948 equated capitalist social-isation with Soviet socialism (a viewpoint which was also propagated, with an eye to restoring *laissez-faire*, by men like Hayek and Popper – see chapter 4, this volume). In Huxley's sombre picture of a society mass-producing its own citizens in public hatching complexes, the reference to Henry Ford (the equiv-alent of Orwell's 'Big Brother' in *Brave New World* is called 'Our Ford' and the sign of the 'T', after the T-model, has replaced the sign of the cross) mixes with proper names derived from Marx and Lenin. In either book, men steeped in the traditions of British nineteenth-century individualism denounce, in a broader existential rather than political sense, the stifling of freedom by unre-strained socialisation. In the visual arts, fear and fascination evoked by the organisation, planning and control aspects of advancing socialisation were conveyed by films such as Fritz Lang's *Metropolis* of 1927 and Chaplin's *Modern Times* of 1936. The collage, in which separate images are pasted together into a representation of modernity in which humanity seems lost, combines the logic of the organisation chart with the multiple images of the motion picture, or indeed the view from the train window, as in Paul Citroen's *Métropolis* (Figure 1.3).

Let us now reconstruct our definition of socialisation by reference to Marx and the Marxist tradition, Weber, and Habermas.

Socialisation in Marxism

With Marx, *Vergesellschaftung* has its roots in production. By combining elements ('productive forces') from the biological and natural substratum, productive activity (initially, human labour pure and simple) imposes its own order on them. It integrates them into a new unity which is 'social' (*gesellschaftlich*) rather than 'communitarian' (*gemeinschaftlich*).

As production becomes more complex by introducing co-operation and division of labour, the social nature of the productive process is enhanced. Once certain qualities of the productive forces become recognised (say, the iron content of ore, the method of obtaining it, the use of iron in making a tool, etc.), they are objectified into standardised knowledge, which in turn is 'applied' to the labour process, yields new knowledge, and so on. Parallel to this cumulative aspect of socialisation, there develops a division of labour (mental/manual, parcelling of tasks in both domains), which builds not only on parallel tasks but also on the objectified, standardised knowledge and the tools and patterns of organisation in which it is embodied. Work no longer requires the integral mobilisation of the capacities of design and execution; it becomes social in the sense of partial – shared with present and past social labour (Marx 1973: 832).

The shift from individual, self-sufficient work to participation in collective labour processes implies that the specific craft of the artisan is tendentially replaced by abstract, general labour (Gorz 1982: 31). Such labour is not neces-sarily 'degraded', unskilled labour (as Braverman – 1974 – implies); it may

Figure 1.3 Humanity lost in the thick of organised urban life: *Métropolis* (1923) by Paul Citroen (1896–1983). © 1998 Paul Citroen, c/o Beeldrecht Amstelveen.

involve highly qualified types of 'polytechnic' work. But at any rate it can only function if it is combined with the objectified properties of past craft labour – objectified as machinery, work rules, or otherwise. They allow the operation of what Marx calls the *collective worker*, to which one may belong without necessarily working with one's hands: 'it is enough to be an organ of the common labour, to fulfill one of its subfunctions' (Marx quoted in Wijmans 1987: 40; see also Garaudy 1971). Taken together, socialisation includes, in Marx's own words,

The conscious technical utilisation of science, the planned exploitation of the earth, the economisation of all means of production by their use as means of production of combined, social labour, the devouring of all peoples in the net of the world market and with it, the international nature of the capitalist regime (*MEW* 23: 790).

The notion of *control*, planning, direction, implying the combination of power and management, is a crucial ingredient in Marx's concept of socialisation (Fennema 1976: 3). On each of the dimensions summed up in the above quotation, commodification, and the alienation it implies (fetishism etc.), intersects with socialisation. Since firms take part in mutual exchanges in a market setting, the control aspect of socialisation beyond the confines of the firm is correspondingly alienated. Ideally, it is entirely surrendered to the abstract, aggregate dynamic of exchange value expanding and accumulating by the competitive appropriation of unpaid labour – in other words, to capital. However, all across the expanding productive grid, socialisation tends to challenge the market logic. It pushes the logic of control, organisation and planning further into the sphere of the market, even imposing it on capitalist relations of production as such.

Thus in the joint stock company, Marx argued in *Capital* Vol. 3 (*MEW* 25: 452), 'capital itself already assumes the form of social capital in contradiction to private capital – *it is the transcendence of capital as private property within the limits of the capitalist mode of production itself*' (emphasis added). In the relations between different joint stock companies that form a financial group (Menshikov 1973: 205–6), a comparable – if always partial – transcendence can be said to take place. As Fennema argues (1982: 43), we should understand the form of socialisation embodied in networks of joint directorates as in between market and hierarchy: 'The market relationships of the interlocked firms are not nullified, yet interlocks impose some hierarchy. It therefore implies competition and co-operation as well as control.'

As the contradictory counterpart and potential negation of commodified production, certain aspects of socialisation can be seized upon to provide democracy with the levers of control, but this has too often been interpreted as if these levers existed outside of concrete class relations. Lenin, in his study on imperialism, even assumed that in the 'monopoly stage' of capitalism, private capital would become constricted in socialisation to such an extent that the entrepreneurial, innovative moment would be squeezed out and that socialisation through cartels, state-supported division of markets, centralised bookkeeping by the banking system, and so on, would drive to the very threshold of actual socialism by its own momentum (*Coll. Works* 22: 205).

Socialisation has its roots in the labour process, however, and its forms and extent are shaped by class struggles on the shop floor. The socialisation of labour at the plant level, especially in large-scale production, may create a system of technical equations which tendentially unhinges commodity relations between various parts of the social labour process. Such structural socialisation of labour reaches a point 'where the reintegration of atomised labour into production processes follows economic laws of its own, not derived from the value standards of commodity exchange' (Sohn-Rethel 1976: 29). But the tendency of socialisation to assume a dynamic of its own, notably by creating cumulative contexts of social protection (see also Basso 1975), is always under pressure to be replaced again by commodity relations in order to extend the workings of the market as widely as possible. Therefore even the 'Great Transformation' which resulted from the general crisis of markets in the 1930s, was partly reversed by a neo-liberal restructuring of society away from social protection and socialism in the 1970s and 1980s (precisely when it seemed as if Sohn-Rethel's and Basso's refinements/restatements of Lenin's argument were coming true).

A parallel counterthrust to restore and deepen the commodification of capital's social substratum has been directed at the state. Historically, it was the state which assumed tasks that fall under the heading of the *socialisation of reproduction*. 'Social protection' in Polanyi's sense largely equals this form of socialisation of labour, i.e. the collective organisation of its regeneration. This includes both day-to-day and generational reproduction of labour power – the physical, psychological, and qualification requirements which the family and other community forms cannot (fully) provide any more and which are accordingly taken up by the state (Fennema 1976: 6–7). Under neo-liberalism, this has been attacked and partly privatised again, to the effect, as Gill notes, of a 'reduction of the socialisation of risk provision for the majority of the population – and thus as greater privatisation of the risk calculus at the level of the individual' (1995: 21).

Summing up, the Marxist concept of *Vergesellschaftung* includes the sociali-sation of labour and the productive forces, both in the plant and in the wider, eventually world economy; the parallel, tendential socialisation of property forms and capital itself; and the socialisation of reproduction including the state apparatus. Socialisation is premised however on commodification and develops only through class struggles in which the coordinates of their mutual relation are constantly redefined, an aspect to which we will return in chapter 2.

Weber and Habermas: elements of synthesis

In Weber's use of the concept of socialisation in *Economy and Society* (1976), the historical perspective of a community legacy carried over from the past and a transformative potential of socialisation projected into the future are replaced by an analytical use of the two as parallel aspects of social action (by individuals). This is in line with the subjective praxeology Weber shares with the marginalist economists (see also Burnham 1994: 223 and Bukharin 1972: Introduction). Social phenomena in this view are additive, statistically totalised summations of individual actions. But then, Weber does not look at history through the prism of dialectics, but through an evolutionist lens focused on intellectual élites – a sociology which Gramsci criticises but which he himself is surprisingly close to (Levy 1987: 398; see also Gramsci 1971: 426).

Building on Tönnies's typology of community and society (*Gemeinschaft* and *Gesellschaft*), Weber distinguishes between 'communitisation' and 'socialisation'. Socialisation to Weber equals interdependence and (a degree of) awareness of it, expressed in certain forms of collusion. Thus, in contrast to 'communitisation' (*Vergemeinschaftung*), based on affective or traditional feelings of community (as when a family is founded, but also professional *esprit de corps*), socialisation is defined as a social relation in which either rationally motivated compromise, or joint articulation of interests is achieved (Weber 1976: 21). *Vergesellschaftung* and *Vergemeinschaftung* are not mutually exclusive, though. As Bendix (1969: 19) notes, 'the constant interweaving of economic utility and social affinity . . . represents *one* recurrent theme in Weber's work' (the other being 'a belief in the existence of a legitimate order').

The market in Weber's view brings about socialisation between exchange partners, and, indirectly through competition, creates a need for market parties to acknowledge each other's existence and activities. A further, important aspect of Weber's interpretation of *Vergesellschaftung* concerns the centrality of *law* as the regulator of market socialisation. In his own words,

> Rational goal-oriented interests determine market proceedings to a particularly high degree, and *rational legality*, more specifically: formal inviolability of something promised, is the quality which is expected from exchange partners and which constitutes the contents of the market ethic (Weber 1976: 383, emphasis added).

Thus the requirements of a contract society tend towards regulation, making the original Protestant ethic superfluous by rational bureaucratisation. In this respect, as Kolko argues (1959: 27), Weber was a precursor of the managerialist theses of Adolf Berle and James Burnham, to which we will return in chapter 5.

Weber's attention for the normative structure of socialisation (rational–legal, as socialisation develops), and the imbrication of communitisation with socialisation he assumes, resonate in the concept of socialisation developed by Jürgen Habermas (1973: 21–3). Habermas conceives of *Vergesellschaftung* as the collective, social appropriation of *nature* and distinguishes between three forms:

1   the socialisation of *external nature* (the labour process and the entire material political economy surrounding it); this summarily denotes the same area as the Marxist concept of socialisation discussed above;
2   the socialisation of *internal nature*. This refers to the development of normative structures which exteriorise the organic substratum of biological human beings, their 'inner world'. Here Weber's notion of a specific normative structure accompanying the development of socialisation reappears. Normative structures, by which needs are interpreted and actions

legitimated, develop from the conformity of the traditional community member, to the internalised norms imposed by the 'imagined' community (religion or nation; see Anderson 1983). Finally, it is the drift of opinion as such which guides people's value orientations. Socialisation here expresses itself in other-directedness in David Riesman's (1950) sense, with society providing the collective conscience previously provided by traditional community. Habermas has indicated that such a normative structure is itself a class-transcending reality (see Greven 1974: 224). This also refers to what we have already encountered above, namely, the fact that somehow, forms of community (transformed, mutated, etc.) are dragged along in the comprehensive transformation to fully socialised relations and globalisation: a combination acknowledged by Weber without the chronological dimension. This connotation of Habermas's second form of socialisation becomes particularly relevant concerning the following;

3   the socialising action of *different units of social cohesion* upon each other. This refers to a spatial/temporal dimension concretising the two prior forms of socialisation that is of particular importance to the analysis of the international political economy. We will term this, in the absence of a label (or an elaboration) offered by Habermas, *inter-community socialisation*. It can perhaps be understood in a historical perspective as follows. Primitive communities experience each other as part of external nature while their mental worlds are mutually closed. War, growing out of hunting and involving the capture of slaves, is their natural mode of contact (Marx 1973: 474). With the development of piracy and plunder into commerce, and the crystallisation of mobile wealth, the mercantilist state begins to develop. While fostering commodification, this state simultaneously provides a context for socialisation, at first primarily internally. However, foreign trade also exposes the different states to each other. Market exchanges (and here we may follow Weber's lead) give rise to certain common expectations, the need for contracts to be upheld, and so on – in brief, a common normative structure (see also Kant 1953). But although commerce paves the way in important respects, the real mutual exposure occurs through the revolutionary transformations by which peoples constitute themselves as nations, lending substance to the unit of social cohesion which the state formally represents. These revolutions because of their international ramifications (civil war, counter-revolutionary emigration and inter-state war) literally drive into other areas, provoking, on the one hand, the assertion of their particularity as units of social cohesion, too; but on the other, drawing them into the widening circle of a common civilisation (see Rosenstock-Huessy 1961 and my 1996b).

In this way, the process of inter-community socialisation, although still bounded by war-like confrontations, begins to demarcate areas within which a common normative structure keeps the simultaneous assertion of specificity within certain limits. Therefore, as Bettelheim (1972: 295) puts it, the 'socialization of labor on the international scale takes place through a structure of specific complexity, embracing the structure of each social formation and the world structure of the totality of social formations' – or, as an advertising agency predicted for the decade now closed, that people 'may eat globally-marketed products, but the style of preparation will reflect local tradition' (*FT*, 9 October 1986).

The reproduction of commodified social relations, which (if considered in the abstract) results in the progressive atomisation of the community, in fact takes place through successive *contexts of social cohesion*. These have their origins in, and in part are carried over from prior community bonds, traditional or 'imagined'. But increasingly, they assume a socialised form, that is, commodification and individualisation are made subject to collective arrangements of a secular nature. Social cohesion becomes increasingly abstract from personal peculiarities and ever more dependent on largely invisible (at least indirect) forms of mutual dependence and routinised organisation. Interchangeability of personnel, complementarity of tasks, regulation and planning, are all aspects of this. Occasionally, there may be dramatic reversals on this trajectory of increasing secularisation. Especially when certain particularly sensitive areas of community life are threatened (be it family, religion, or nation), a 'tribal' reaction may throw back the apparently rationalised social order to the level of the primitive group, or worse, combine the capacity for planning engendered by a high degree of socialisation with certain features of a primitive order, as in Fascism, or Muslim fundamentalism.

In all cases of *Vergesellschaftung*, division of labour and separation of tasks, driven by commodification directly or indirectly, are reintegrated into collective arrangements under (different degrees of) capitalist control or normatively connected to it. The objective integration of a patchwork of overlapping units of social cohesion structured around units of socialised labour exists in a tension with the commodity form of social relations, requiring constant mutual readjustment through struggle. Therefore, the effects of commodification, as discussed on pages 11–14, are not only partly compensated for by persisting forms of (imagined) community; but also, if always incompletely so, by structures of socialisation. The phenomena belonging to each set – commodification, (imagined) community, and socialisation – will all be observable in a real situation, because none of them cancels out the others completely, although their relative weight may vary considerably.

The discipline of capital

As we have seen, the contradictory processes of commodification and socialisation, mediated by social struggles in which their mutual relation is arbitrated, can be understood as forces constantly restructuring a prior (imagined) community substratum without entirely obliterating its reproductive/affective core. Such transformed communities exist, as units of social cohesion, in a wider arena which is tendentially subject to the same, mutually conflicting pressures of commodification and socialisation. Let us now pose the question how social cohesion is maintained at all under the strain of these contradictory forces. This brings us to the role of the state as the source of authority and discipline, on which an actual discipline of capital is grafted at a later stage of development.

In chapter 3 we will investigate the state in a more concrete, historical sense as a succession of specific state/society complexes and state forms. At the level of abstraction we are dealing with here, however, a state can be said to emerge, either on the foundations of an imagined community such as the nation (which is shaped in one of the world revolutions summed up by Rosenstock-Huessy 1961, see also my 1996b); or, in an act of mimicry (Gramsci's 'passive revolution') from international relations as such. In this case, the state relates to its social base differently, as a creative instance shaping its own (multi-)national substance from above. In all cases in between and including the two extremes, however, the state acts as a quartermaster of capitalist relations. As Marx notes, 'war developed earlier than peace; . . . certain economic relations such as wage labour, machinery etc. develop earlier, owing to war and in the armies etc., than in the interior of bourgeois society' (1973: 109; see also 893, and Krippendorf 1973).

The theme of institutions such as armies and workplaces as well as prisons imposing a corporeal discipline on people has been elaborated by Foucault. Foucault argues that 'discipline increases the forces of the body (in the sense of raising their economic utility) and simultaneously diminishes these forces (in the sense of increasing political obedience)' (Foucault 1981a: 589). The role of the various disciplinary spaces on the habits of diligence, precision and regularity in the seventeenth and eighteenth centuries, their contribution to a new sense of rhythm and measured time, all worked towards shaping 'modernity' as we know it – and not just in the political economy strictly speaking, but also, e.g. in music (Rich 1995: 22). But however broad our inclusion of social forms which together constitute the setting in which capital crystallised, the disciplines emerging along with it and permeating it should not be reduced to 'power' as such, but to capital and the state(s) clearing the terrain on which it is operative. Otherwise, the 'microphysical' omnipresence of power is turned into an uncontestable, general condition of human existence, and hence, a superfluous, *meta*physical principle (Bartels 1991: 92; see also Foucault 1981b).

As to commodification and socialisation, the state initially relates to these by demarcating a provisional structure of socialisation for commodity production. It provides, as Hirsch explains (1973: 202), 'a contradictory and illusory form of the general' to a world of small producers. The state takes care of the general conditions of production and reproduction that are beyond the reach of the individual producers (just as money provides social unity to the individually parcelled labour process), and which remain so due to competition (van Erp 1982: 102). The idea of an abstract universality represented by the state (abstract because its unity covers a totality riven by competition) sustains the specific notion of a *general interest* into which particular interests must inscribe themselves to be heard at all. 'In a true state,' Marx wrote in an early work, 'there is no landed property, no industry, no material substance, which can . . . reach an agreement with the state; there are only *spiritual powers*, and only in their resurrection at the level of the state, in their political reincarnation, the natural powers are entitled to vote in the state' (*MEW Ergänz.band* 1: 419). These spiritual powers are not random. They are the fractured expression of the commodity and money economy, and eventually, of developed capital. 'Individuals are now ruled by *abstractions*, whereas earlier they depended on one another. The abstraction, or idea, however, is nothing more than the theoretical expression of those material relations which are their lord and master' (Marx 1973: 164).

To the degree that these material relations crystallise in fixed capital and the world of finance arbitrating between its various branches, the state loses its semblance of an independent power (see also Hirsch 1973: 205). But even now that capital has fully developed and is perceived, in its self-movement, as the supreme life-giving force, the 'world economy' to which even the state must bow, it cannot do without state support. To ensure the availability and supply of Polanyi's 'fictitious commodities' – labour power, money, and land – the state continuously has to suspend or modify the operation of the market mechanism in these areas. It must articulate the outcomes of social struggles in each of them into a coherent policy, shaping, as de Brunhoff puts it (1976: 53), 'new class compromises which the capitalists cannot realise themselves directly', but on which continued capital accumulation depends. In the process, states have most visibly functioned as structures of social cohesion and social protection, bending socialisation towards the sustenance of everyday life and the maintenance of the territory, as well as defending, through the value of the currency or otherwise, the position of the national economy against others (Knieper 1976: 45–7). Finally, the need for means of coercion and violence, internally and externally, means that capital continues to rely on the visible, and in principle, accountable, political power of the state.

Capital and society

A key difference between Hegel's and Marx's views of the relation between state, economy, and society (and Polanyi's approach here may be considered an explicit reformulation of what remains implicit in Hegel) is that Hegel still proceeds on the assumption of a society of small commodity producers. His philosophy of history (Hegel 1961), in which he traces the march of freedom from its earliest beginnings, might be decoded as a chronicle of the extent to which the specific subjective individuality required for commodity production, is able to spread and structure consecutive types of society. In each of these, a specific form of state confronts the citizens' spiritual aspirations for freedom (the market economy itself to Hegel remains a sphere of historically unstructured randomness waiting to be tamed). Ultimately, a state emerges (in Europe) which is entirely rational in that it is strong in itself but allows the realisation of its subjects' interests as well, 'the one finding satisfaction and realisation in the other' (1961: 68; Fukuyama's attempt to rephrase the same argument so that it ends with a *Lockean* state may be left aside here; see also Pierre Hassner's comment in Fukuyama 1989, and Fukuyama's response, 1992: 144).

To Marx, Hegel's 'World Spirit' driving forward this historical development to its logical conclusion by working through people's subjective quest for freedom, should be reunified with its material counterpart, the real movement of humanity 'as a presupposed subject' (*MEW Ergänz.band* 1:570). In his analysis, it is *capital* which as the objectified result of the social labour process, confronts society as a quasi-natural force. Thus he can also interpret Hegel's 'Spirit', to quote Helmut Reichelt, as 'the idealism of capital, in which a derivative becomes the original and unfolds its own law of motion' (in Hegel 1972: xxx; see also van Erp 1982: 58). This spirit mutates with every major turning-point in the history of capital, expressing a changing class configuration in a different balance of forces. In every age, 'reason', i.e. capitalist rationality, accordingly has a different content – from nineteenth century liberal internationalism, to state monopolism and corporate liberalism in the twentieth, up to contemporary neo-liberalism – thus testifying to its own historicity and that of its material foundations.

From this perspective, the state is seen as a mediation between society and total capital, a structure of socialisation and social cohesion by which a given society is subordinated to capital. Hegel's idea that at every juncture, one particular state rises to become the privileged embodiment of the World Spirit, even obtains an echo in Marx's claim that one state (we may think of, for example, the state performing the role of the world's banker) 'represents capital *par excellence*' (1973: 449) in its relations with other states. Neither the state nor capital, however, can ever reach a stage in which the tension with the social foundations of which they are excrescences, objectifications living a life of their own, is suspended (again the reference should be to Fukuyama's claim to the contrary). Society, and all that it contains in terms of relations, capacities, resources, etc. (the productive forces), remains logically separate both from the state and from capital – a fact perhaps obscured by the term 'capital*ism*' (introduced by authors like Weber and Werner Sombart, not by Marx), which suggests a comprehensive, closed totality that can only be replaced by another.

Capital, then, should be understood as a historical regime imposing rules of behaviour on its individual particles, the separate firms (rules which are enforced in competition) and on society at large; while projecting a universe of meanings and associations reaching into the subconscious of those under its spell. One of the illusions capital evokes is that of its own comprehensiveness, its self-idealisation as consummate economic rationality – obscuring

the fact that it is historically rooted in a process of violent appropriation/
expropriation (van Erp 1982: 58). If an economics textbook pays attention to
the prehistory of the capitalist ('market') economy at all, this is usually by way
of a 'Robinsonade' (after Crusoe), a narrative of abstract, free individuals some
of whom start a company. But capital 'did not begin the world from the
beginning, but rather encountered production and products already present,
before it subjugated them beneath its process,' Marx writes (1973: 675).
Neither, he explains elsewhere, is capital

> as the economists believe, the *absolute* form for the development of the
> forces of production . . . it is a discipline over them, which becomes super-
> fluous and burdensome at a certain level of their development, just like
> the guilds etc. (ibid.: 415).

If looked at in this way, capital cannot ever reach the stage where it really
establishes itself as the comprehensive form of social life, containing all
commodity chains and structures of socialisation within itself. Capital accumulation rather is a continuous coming together of the material elements to
be transformed, turned into *value* (use value/exchange value), and the discipline which supplies the particular, historic form of this transformation. As
Jessop puts it in a seminal article (1983: 95), 'The interests of capital even at
the most general level of abstraction consist in the reproduction of a contradictory and ambivalent nexus of value *and non-value* forms whose reciprocal
effects can sustain capital accumulation.'

The disciplines of the state, increasingly functionalised by a more comprehensive, 'world market' discipline of capital (Gill 1995), in this process
serve to prioritise the process of capital accumulation over any inherent
(re)productive functions or needs of society – to the point of abolishing disciplines which have become superfluous or dysfunctional, and hence antiquated,
in this respect. This in turn enhances the modernisation dynamic suggested
by capital accumulation, as testified by certain aspects of 'Americanisation'
such as egalitarian behaviour against, say, European 'class' prejudice.

The limits to capital

The above throws a different light on the limits of the capitalist order than
a theory which is cast entirely in terms of the internal contradictions of capital.
Certainly, there exists a whole system of equations which capital must keep
within certain limits if it is to continue in operation. But authors such as Baran
and Sweezy (1968), and Mandel (1972), have often tended to concentrate
entirely on these internal balances to explain the movement and crisis of
capital. In this respect, they have approached the problems of capitalist society
in a spirit close to that of Keynes, but also to that of a much older strand of
underconsumptionist analysis in the Second International (Clawson 1976:

71–2). In fact, capital has usually weathered this type of crisis relatively easily, by technical or spatial restructuring, or, less 'easily' of course, but not different logically, by massive devalorisation of existing capital through war. Whereas these equilibrium models concentrate on the circulation aspect of capital, Marx seeks to analyse the discipline of capital by reference to the labour process, society's metabolism with nature on which capital imposes a specific form. It is the penetration of the commodity form into the labour process itself which constitutes the starting point of capital; the progress of commodification therefore is the best measure of the development of capital as such.

Rainer Funke (1978: 223) has argued that this development indeed must be measured in terms of the 'unfolding of capitalist principles of organisation, in particular the tendential realisation of the commodity form of all social relations' (the term 'unfolding' should be understood as a metaphor, because our central idea here is that both the commodity form and capital crystallise as forms/forces *outside* the community and are not in any sense inherent to it). Hence, rather than viewing capital as something which existed in a pure form in nineteenth-century Britain but in the twentieth century already had to compromise with more advanced forms of social organisation (leading to qualifications such as Mandel's 'late capitalism' and the 'state monopoly capitalism' of communist party theory – Inosemzev *et al.* 1972; *Collectif PCF* 1971 – each of which suggests a declining capitalism), the comprehensive imposition of the discipline of capital over world society is still in progress. Therefore,

> If one proceeds on the assumption that contemporary ('developed') capitalist societies are – still – characterised by the rise to *dominance* of capitalist principles of organisation – in general: the spread of the commodity form of social relations; negatively: the breakdown of traditional immobilities . . . – then a new analytic and crisis-theoretical perspective (but one elaborating on Marx) emerges. The starting point for the analysis [would then be] . . . the *growing incapacity of capitalism to 'grow into' an existing infrastructural basis*. Economies must grow into societies or be able to remodel them after their own requirements (Funke 1978: 227–8).

This perspective, which we can also find in Giddens's work (1973: 22; 1992: 133), on the one hand throws light on the particularities of capital's expansion, that is, its spread across the globe; while on the other, it raises the issue of the limits of what society and nature can sustain. For, as we argued already, commodification penetrates the pre-existing community and society, to a point where it *exhausts* this substratum.[5] Society and nature together constitute the source of capital's productive performance, they are the locus of the forces of production. The action of capital, which is driven by the quest for unpaid labour, and which in its constant return to itself (as capital in money form invested in production, 'realised' as enlarged money capital again, etc., $M \ldots P \ldots M'$) indeed requires a whole complex of balances to remain within certain limits if it is to survive market crises. But in the longer term, it tends to exhaust both the community/society and the natural substratum on which it feeds, the productive/reproductive nexus on which it imposes its specific discipline.

In chapter 2, we will look at the ways the discipline of capital is imposed and resisted and how, on the resulting front lines, class relations crystallise.

2 Capital accumulation and class formation

In a commercial country like England, every half century develops some new and vast source of public wealth, which brings into national notice a new and powerful class. A couple of centuries ago, a Turkey Merchant was the great creator of wealth; the West India Planter followed him. In the middle of the last century appeared the Nabob. These characters in their zenith in turn merged in the land, and became English aristocrats; while, the Levant decaying, the West Indies exhausted, and Hindostan plundered, the breeds died away, and now exist only in our English comedies. . . . The expenditure of the revolutionary war produced the Loanmonger, who succeeded the Nabob; and the application of science to industry developed the Manufacturer, who in turn aspires to be 'large-acred'.

Benjamin Disraeli

In this chapter, we ascend to a more concrete level of analysis. Here we introduce the concept of class. Class denotes the aspect of agency producing and reproducing the structures of a society based on exploitation; put otherwise, by embodying the structural inequalities of the social order, classes constitute the living reality of these structures. Yet class is still a relatively abstract concept. It manifests itself usually in mediated forms, through all kinds of 'imagined communities' (see also Anderson 1983). In chapter 4, we will discuss some of the concrete, transnational forms of class. Here, we shall investigate the structural determinants of capitalist class formation including the ideological universes it has given rise to.

Speaking generally, class formation springs from the exploitative social relations through which humanity's metabolism with nature develops. Every advance in the capacity to create wealth, shapes new opportunities for appropriating unpaid labour; hence a new relationship between exploiters and exploited, which is superimposed on those already in existence. As the exploiters across all historical experience have sought to consolidate their privileged access to society's wealth by symbolic and material means of power (ultimately concentrated in state power), we may speak of ruling and subordinate classes.[1] In this broad sense, all past history is the history of class struggles, as Marx and Engels claimed in the *Communist Manifesto* (*MEW* 4: 462; see also de Ste Croix 1985).

However, we must proceed to a more specific understanding of class formation and struggle if we want to analyse capitalist society. The twin concepts of commodification and socialisation and the understanding of capital as a discipline over society will help us here. Some authors indeed argue that we should speak of 'class' only in capitalist society, or even in one, restricted phase of that society's development – the period from the late nineteenth century to the immediate post-World War II period (Pakulski and Waters 1996: 26). Our position will be that class is a phenomenon of all past history but that it acquires a specific meaning in a capitalist context. We will briefly look at the prehistory of capitalist class formation and then concern ourselves with the ways the discipline of capital is imposed and resisted, and how class rule is structured by capital accumulation.

The historical topography of class society

Any discussion of class formation must take into account the sediments and living remnants of past history, which remain relevant to the structure of a society subjected to the discipline of capital. As Freud observes, 'humanity never entirely lives in the present. . . . The past – the tradition of race and people – lives on in the ideologies of the Super-Ego and is replaced only gradually by the influences of the present and new changes' (quoted in Zaretsky 1977: 107–8). Likewise, all class formation and social differentiation in general is premised on prior patterns of structuration. Thus Schumpeter writes (1951: 145),

> Any general theory of classes and class formation must explain the fact that classes coexisting at any given time bear the marks of different centuries on their brow, so to speak – that they stem from various conditions. This is in the essential nature of the matter, an aspect of the nature of the class phenomenon. Classes, once they have come into being, harden in their mold and perpetuate themselves, even when the social conditions that created them have disappeared.

Classes crystallise on a highly differentiated terrain shaped by successive transformations from group and community life to early society, and so on. The particular conditions under which bands of hominids took to the steppes, began to walk upright and developed the use of weapons and tools, already determined the ways in which leaders related to followers, the old to the young, men to women, etc. However specific in each case, there are some general observations to make on how the powerful have been able to keep their distance from the rest of the community and consolidate their privileged position over time.

The first concerns the magical connotations of *authority* and the sacrosanct stratification of society it implies. Since the primitive community exists in a state of war with the outside world, but also faces the overwhelming power of the forces of nature, authority from the outset is usually claimed by those capable of negotiating both the physical and the spiritual, supernatural forces perceived as threatening the community. Power accordingly is adorned with magic, and commonly entitles warriors and magicians/priests to an exemption from physical labour (van Baaren 1960; see also Veblen 1994: 2). On this basis, an entire system of worthy and unworthy occupations develops for each particular social group. The Indian caste system is perhaps the most explicit form of such a pyramid of occupations invested with the power of the sacred and ultimately sanctioned by political authority. Yet as testified by processes such as Sanskritisation and casteism, this system, too, develops its inherent responses to changing circumstances (see also Carstairs 1957).

All patterns of rule retain their references to this aspect of authority and are mediated by them. Lefebvre (1976: 66) writes in this connection that bourgeois rule is sustained by the sacrality of all past forms of rule, by the entire catalogue of magic, the power over life and death, etc. Thus even EU leaders on a short working visit still meticulously inspect each other's guards of honour, a gesture of recognition of their sovereignty. No ruling class has ever entirely done away with the material and symbolic spoils of its past victories – which is why religious ritual, monarchs in gold chariots, diamond crowns and the like continue to adorn the ceremonies by which in even the most advanced capitalist state, new leaders are sworn in, or annual budgets are presented.

Language constitutes a repository of the symbols of which we are speaking here. It also contains, e.g. in proverbs and popular sayings, the myths in which their supposed origin is explained. As a means of communication, too, every distinct language is necessarily permeated with references to this sacrosanct structure of authority. By assigning meaning and validity to people's experiences, language codifies a social construction of reality which simultaneously is a force conserving it. Yet the language and the system of meanings are also a terrain of struggle, since even if there is a common normative structure, it is approached from different angles and levels of comprehensiveness and elaboration (Topitsch 1971: 92–3; Bourdieu 1979: 490–3). As McNally writes (1995: 18),

> There is no one master discourse which permeates all contexts, although those who exercise power may try to impose a single discourse upon their subordinates. . . . Ruling classes aspire to depict a single worldview through discourse; as a result they try to assert a unified set of meanings and themes as the only possible way of describing things.

Different languages and systems of meaning, including religion, thus codify implicit structures of authority and orders of stratification, prefiguring class relations.

In their mutual confrontation and interpenetration, language/religious groups living side by side also may constitute a caste-like hierarchy, sometimes coinciding with the urban/landed divide. If we remember what was said in chapter 1 on the origins of exchange at the limit of the original community, then often, this 'limit' was a social one in the sense of particular groups of trading/plundering people entering the area of a sedentary community (as what Marx calls 'living money', 1973: 858). Different attitudes to objects in relation to signs, to nature in relation to ideas, to self and others, individual and community, already crystallise on these boundary lines. Just as a language registers differences in the level of objectification, self-objectification, the place of the sacred in daily life, etc. (Whatmough 1956: 52–3), a religion may allow for the separation of man from nature and its subordination by society to varying degrees. In this respect the Semitic religions (Judaism, Christianity, and Islam) are in a separate category from Confucianism and Hinduism, and herald Enlightenment materialism, positivism, etc. (Amin 1977).[2]

The intermingling of different religious, language, and ethnic groups has always implied a social hierarchy laying the groundwork for exploitative relations. Although colour hierarchies had been operative before, in India for instance, nineteenth-century imperialism inserted the new element of European racial superiority into the emerging global social structure. Europeans saw themselves as Christians against heathens, but the discoveries confronted them with civilisations for which they often were no match. Following the industrial revolution and European expansion, however, the evolutionary, Darwinist view became fashionable, which again placed Europeans at the pinnacle of a pyramid of living creatures (Curtin 1971: xv). This racially charged view of civilisations, in line with older European conceptions of status now projected on the globe at large (Kiernan 1972: xvi; Nederveen Pieterse 1990, ch. 11), has persisted, from implicit apartheid barring immigrant groups from social advance to self-congratulatory racist discourse dressed as scholarship (e.g. de Benoist 1983).

Magic and religion and the structures of authority and hierarchy they define and reproduce, different language groups and their implicit normative structures, national and ethnic divisions thus constitute an age-old social topography, on which all classes form, of which they represent the further concretisations defined by a particular mode of exploitation. As we argued in chapter 1, the unifying and synchronising aspects of more comprehensive structuring forces, such as global capital, can never entirely obliterate this particularity. Concrete ruling classes cannot therefore be equated with the functionaries of capital, because they carry on a historical consciousness and posture derived from their confrontations and clashes with subordinate classes and many more 'others'; but also from the conditions under which they won power from previous ruling classes, domestic and foreign. Violence and war are essential constitutive aspects of rule (Moore 1981) and also of capital, so that every particular enterprise and its owners are ultimately bound up with the unique history of the country and only in the mirror of monetary validation are momentarily abstracted from it as a particle of collective capital.

Kinship and gender

Social power relations also are rooted in the reproductive/affective life of the community. In the earliest types of human community, which were kinship-based, division of tasks rested principally on gender differences and age categories; the marriage system in such communities constitutes the essential source of power and privilege (Rey 1983: 591). Given biologically differential gender roles in procreation and child-bearing and -rearing, women usually were relegated to a logistical, subordinate position in the community. With the development of the division of labour and commodification, the family ceded aspects of reproduction, such as education including apprenticeship, as well as health and child-care to the community/society, but gendered connotations for these activities persist. Also, the reality of household work, however compressed by paid work in or outside the house, continues to be associated with the female condition first.

As with household tasks, certain patriarchal/male leadership roles, originally associated with hunting and war-making, have likewise, as a consequence of the break-up of the extended patriarchal family, been turned into particular practices of the larger unit and the 'male condition' generally. The charismatic leader (in Weber's nomenclature, 1976: 140) perhaps can be considered such an 'imagined' patriarch, but power in general has definite male connotations. Lionel Tiger's (1970) notion of 'male bonding' as a pervasive and persistent set of practices and rituals with its roots in a protracted prehistory of hunting and war-making, must be considered a crucial variable in generalising the male/female divide and the corresponding development of gender ideal-types that enter class relations. As Ken Post writes (1996: 125), 'male dominance became *structured into* class societies through gender ascriptive roles and relations as part of their total linkages'.

The major national revolutions which shaped, by their impact on world civilisation, the modern world, have further differentiated and historicised gender-ascriptive roles, too. Thus Rosenstock-Huessy argues that the French Revolution confirmed a new type of relationship between the sexes. This pattern, exemplified by the hostesses of the famous *salons*, replaced the pattern of outright exclusion of women from public affairs typical of English society after the Puritan revolution, by a more equitable relationship in which women combined a cultivated eroticism with intellectual qualities (Rosenstock-Huessy 1961: 348–9). The avenues thus opened to women (of course, a minority, but providing a role model to a nation asserting itself in the Revolution) allowed them to give an intellectual expression to their emancipatory strivings, whereas the English suffragettes had to throw themselves before the racehorses at Ascot to draw attention to their cause. In the Russian Revolution, another pattern emerged in the 'comrade', the woman who spoke at her exiled husband's grave and was a revolutionary in her own right (ibid.: 452).

The family all along was the setting for household work as a substructure of social exploitation and a last resource of unpaid labour. Within it, people could reproduce their human existence in a bond of mutual love and obligation (Horkheimer 1970: 76–7). By several intermediaries (and likewise complicated by exploitation), this complex of attachments and feelings has been socialised to apply to the larger unit of social cohesion as patriotism (Doob 1964: 181–4). It can be argued, therefore, that if the structure of power and authority as embodied in the state retains strong male (patriarchal) connotations on anthropological/ethnological grounds, the imagined community that is the nation, by its backgrounds in kinship and quasi-kinship networks and reproduction, carries a parallel female/motherly connotation. When state power is asserted *vis-à-vis* society, or certain social values are on the contrary upheld in the face of state repression, the class element crystallising in political struggles may well be modulated, in membership and/or means of expression, by such 'gendered' dividing lines.

Having indicated that in no society, capitalist class formation can possibly begin abstractly, 'economically', let us now turn to the different ways in which the discipline of capital is imposed on its social substratum.

Capital as discipline and class struggles

The discipline of capital does not emerge spontaneously, from the inner recesses of society. It is imposed by a social force which owes its apparent autonomy to commodification and alienation, the breaking of elementary community bonds. Resistance therefore always includes the quest for a restoration of some sort of community against this disruptive, alien force. Capital is in constant quest for unpaid labour in its social substratum, and once a major 'deposit' is found and incorporated, it seeks to raise the rate of exploitation in the actual labour process; until at some point the social and natural substratum on which capital accumulation feeds, which it penetrates and transforms, begins to show signs of exhaustion. From this sequence we can deduce three terrains on which capitalist discipline is imposed, and where it can and usually will be resisted. The first is *original accumulation* – the process in which, by imposing the commodity form on social relations including productive relations, capital itself crystallises as a relatively autonomous social force. The second is the capitalist *production* process, the exploitation of living labour power, in which the technical labour process and all that it implies in terms of human autonomy and creativity has to be subordinated to the process of expanding value, the valorisation of capital invested. The third is the process of social *reproduction* in its entirety, the exploitation of the social and natural substratum, which likewise has to be made subject to the requirements of capital accumulation.

Although these three forms of imposing the discipline of capital are intricately connected, and the struggles they elicit often overlap (if they can be distinguished along these lines at all), their main impact follows a chronological order. Obviously, original accumulation is a phenomenon of the early history of the capitalist mode of production. As to the other two, the subordination of the labour process to capital and the subordination of the process of social *re*production mutually condition each other, but the deep penetration of capital into the latter sphere is the more recent phenomenon. For whereas under *formal* subordination of labour to capital, the worker still commutes between the job and a relatively intact, non-commodified reproductive sphere close to nature, to recover from the effort of work, under conditions of what Marx (1971) calls *real* subordination of labour to capital, this reproductive sphere, too, has become subject to profit strategies of capital at best partially compensated by socially protective, collective arrangements. Under these conditions, recovery/regeneration itself becomes subject to commodification and exploitation, and this leads to the eventual exhaustion of the social and natural substratum sustaining reproduction.

Here we encounter the limit to capital highlighted by Funke (1978: 227–8) and referred to in chapter 1. The struggles which are the result of the resistance to this exhaustion, have occurred before, e.g. in early industrialisation and absolute surplus value production (in which exploitation assumes the form of lengthening the work day and intensifying work). But on a global scale, they are a recent phenomenon and signal the passing of an industrial age in which the preservation of the integral human/social substratum (though not the natural one) also represented a certain interest to capital.

Now why we may qualify these three types of struggle as *class* struggles is because the imposition of the discipline of capital inevitably serves the interests of those who are its owners or controllers and who can draw on the power resources carried over from pre-existing social and political hierarchies and consolidated in state power. To the degree socio-political authority and domination become imbricated with, back up and sustain the discipline of capital, the bourgeois element associated with the capitalist mode of production moves into the forefront of the ruling class. It modifies its nature and orientation in the process to the point where the former ruling classes may serve as a governing class, but no longer can lead social development.

On the other hand, the resistance to the discipline of capital inevitably brings forth experiences and insights challenging/scattering fetishistic notions about capital as 'modernity', 'the economy', etc.; thus shaping the contours of an alternative perspective which is likewise collective and based in social practice. The cohesion of these forces of resistance is much more fragile and fleeting, and as we will see, resistance displays different accents under the three modes of imposing capitalist discipline to begin with.

Original accumulation and proletarianisation

The primordial process in which capital itself crystallises as a quasi-independent social force, imposing its discipline on a pre-existing social infrastructure by penetrating and transforming it, is commodification (privatisation, commercialisation). This implies that the use value aspect of an element or item of social production (its quality to satisfy a need and be consumed) has to be subordinated to the exchange value aspect (the quality of being a commodity sold at a price realising socially necessary labour time, which presupposes private property and a market). The main form of this is the incorporation of previously non-commodified goods and services in a setting only now coming within the reach of capital or giving rise to it itself (hence, *original* accumulation). Here items hitherto circulating within other types of economy than market economy, are turned into commodities for the first time, ultimately (when labour power itself is commodified) engendering a sea-change in social relations altogether (see Rosa Luxemburg 1966: 290 on the subordination of the 'natural economy').

The conflicts involved in original accumulation constitute a first, and usually violent, form of social struggle elicited by capitalist discipline. Rosenstock-Huessy (1961: 404–5) even argues that not regularised wage bargaining, but this struggle of expropriation/appropriation is the only real class struggle under capitalist conditions – conditions, moreover, which still lack their eventual magical–naturalistic self-evidence. The very fact of being disinherited from one's more or less independent means of subsistence and the destruction of the entire life-world with which they are entwined, with its natural/traditional time-scales and rhythms, drives people to resistance. The actual historical processes do not concern us here, although it is important to recognise that a proletariat may form also under conditions where the entrepreneurial role is assumed by a state class. The English enclosures and Stalin's collectivisation campaign, but also the contemporary 'opening' of Brazil's Amazon region, in this sense belong to the same category (Moore 1981; Kolk 1996). The assassinations of the Brazilian rubber tapper Chico Mendez and of Iqbal Masih, a 12-year-old boy who was organiser of some of the estimated 10 million child workers under fifteen years of age in Pakistan (*FT*, 28 March 1995), and many other instances of extreme 'disciplinary' violence illustrate the severity of the clashes involved.

In terms of its effects on the formation of classes, original accumulation may be a phased phenomenon in which different stages of expropriation and expulsion, appropriation and occupation, can be distinguished. On the side of capital, it may be a land-owning class adopting a commercial perspective as in England or, elsewhere, *merchant capital*, which is the paramount social force in this context. On a global level, it is this, antediluvian form of capital which 'contribute[s] to organizing economic space and exchange in a way that permit[s] the eventual emergence of a fully developed capitalist system' (Genovese 1989: 291). The advance of capital into uncharted territory takes place in a temporal sequence, but also on a concentric, spatial dimension so that even today, there are processes of original accumulation going on. In its real-life appearance, merchant capital often will assume piratical, criminal forms – the 'robber baron' of old, or the contemporary ex-Komsomol functionary privatising the organisation's real estate.

On the side of the workers, the varying degrees to which the commodity form is imposed on labour relations yields a highly differentiated picture of semi-proletarianised people, hired hands, etc. Thus wage workers may be employed in a family setting (putting-out systems), recruited as vagrants into work-house labour forces, or be former artisans and their apprentices dislocated by new forms of factory organisation of work, and so on. The destruction of the autonomy of artisans which often provoked trade unionism, the Luddite revolt against early mechanisation and the laws against combination to quell it (Thompson 1968: 543), or the resistance to the introduction of Taylorism and Fordism in Europe under the Marshall Plan (Carew 1987: 209), testify to the phased process of original accumulation and the corollary deepening of the control of capital at each juncture. While the aspect of violence may gradually recede (although even at the time of the Marshall Plan, the introduction of American work methods was accompanied by violence against non-cooperative segments of the labour force by the CIA and allied underworld elements in Europe), there always occurs what sociologists call anomie among those put under the new discipline – the loss of normative coherence which creates a susceptibility to new forms of collective consciousness (Vieille 1988). Thus the Islamist doctrine that triumphed in the 1979 Iranian revolution carries a 'proletarian' connotation because, in the words of Nima (1983: 142), 'Islamic ideology became a substitute for the lost communality of the oppressed masses'; indeed the Iranian revolution has been compared to the Bolshevik revolution in that both found their mass base among 'former peasants streaming into the city' (Hough 1990: 48). The fact that the intellectual moment of resistance here still is concentrated in a small vanguard occupying the normative vacuum, to some extent explains the radically different outcome of the two revolutions apart from obvious historical differences, as such vanguards in the circumstances have a disproportionate effect on the movement's orientation.[3]

Struggles in production and the historical proletariat

The development of capital beyond its prototypical, mercantile form into fully-grown *industrial* capital interacts with the generalisation of the commodity form and the wage relation. Having imposed *formal* discipline (and continuing, as we saw, to deepen it), the drive of capital now coming into its own is towards raising the rate of exploitation. The discipline of capital here means that behind a veil of commodity relations, the technical labour process is subordinated to the process of *value expansion* or valorisation (German *Verwertung*). Human labour power exists as part of the natural/social substratum on which the mode of production rests. It is the human capacity to produce tools and food, to have ideas, etc., but it is also treated as a commodity (labour power) which forms part of the material inputs of the process of capitalist production and accumulation. This contradictory unity requires a constant reimposition of the capitalist discipline on the human reality, comparable to stamping the commodity form on the product as such.

Capitalist social development here has its mainspring, the contradiction in which its self-movement originates. As Sohn-Rethel writes (1976: 27), 'the basic and decisive impulses to social change must be seen as emanating, not from the economics of the profit making process, but from the developments of the labour process evolving under the impact of the profit making process'. The replacement of living by dead labour, that is, machinery and work organisation, and the changing technical aspect of society which is its result, cannot be understood without understanding this fundamental tension. Workplace conflict is not just an aspect of early, extensive accumulation characterised by incomplete, formal subordination of labour to capital (i.e. relatively independent workers working *for* capital rather than being set to work as a particle of socialised labour, an extension of machinery). It also applies to contemporary work situations. In the words of Elger (1979: 70),

> The continually revolutionised character of modern mechanised production persistently renders 'incomplete' the subordination of labour to capital. . . . On one hand it creates new skills, competencies and other opportunities for bargaining leverage arising from the complex co-ordination and interdependence of the collective labourer; on the other hand, in phases of rapid accumulation unaccompanied by massive displacement of living by dead labour, it depletes the reserve army of labour and provides the basis for powerful worker organisation.

The same process has been observed in e.g. computer programming (Greenbaum 1976) and office work generally (Doorewaard 1988).

Struggles in production clearly are *internal* to the established capital relation – workers do not fight to resist subordination altogether and to retain their independent means of living, or remnants of it. Rather, having lost these and conscious of it, they try to evade the discipline of work because it does not fit with their bodily rhythms and mental make-up. Or, more positively (but also reflecting a more commodified understanding of work), they seek to improve their bargaining position over wages. Weber remarks in this respect that the better the freedom of contract in the labour market is observed (i.e. no unionisation), the greater the discipline of capital on the shop floor (1976: 440). Hence the interaction of the two spheres both in imposing and resisting discipline. But once trade unions succeed in securing a degree of regularisation of negotiations (which can be understood as the socialisation of the sale/purchase of labour power), they will seek to monopolise their relationship with the employers. These in turn prefer to make concessions in the wage sphere rather than loosening workplace discipline, especially once relative surplus value production allows them to reduce the cost of the reproduction of labour power by raising productivity in the sector producing wage goods, or by shifting to industrially produced wage goods to begin with (Maurino 1974: 54–5).

Class struggles, then, tend to become manifest in the labour market, but often express workplace resistance and in extreme circumstances, are taken back to the shop floor (factory occupations, sit-down strikes). The trade unions as organisations for defending the workers and advancing their interests in this sense are 'class' organisations. However, as structures of socialisation embodying a particular dimension of social compromise basically shaped by the requirements of the mode of production, they simultaneously give rise to a relatively distinct stratum of cadres, professional intermediaries comparable in many respects to hired managers working for capital, or state personnel concerned with the reproduction of complex social relations. One perennial problem of the cadre trade unionists is to relate back to the workplace, maintain a union presence there, and anticipate conflict; hence an institution such as shop stewards, or, discarding the union, the direct self-organisation of the workers (Bologna 1976). This tension also creates possibilities for Communist vanguard parties to go on organising disaffected workers beyond the pre-industrial workforce in agriculture, construction, mining, dockworkers etc., to which their influence has been traditionally confined.

Employers' organisations, as indicated already, reciprocate worker unionisation. Around these two poles, an entire superstructure of negotiation and regularised conflict and compromise crystallises (sometimes, adapting to an antecedent social topography, further differentiated into confessional organisations as in the Netherlands). Pakulski and Waters (1996: 98) call this the 'corporatization of class'. This process extends into politics as party formation. The complex in its entirety, especially as long as it is contained within a single state, brings forth a cumulative process of class compromises in which socialisation tends to crowd out straight market relations at the local and intermediate, and even the national level, leaving only the formal property rights of capital intact (in the 1970s, several European Social Democratic-governed states entertained plans for the socialisation of 'super-profits' though).

It is our thesis that the historical *proletariat* emerged (and continues to emerge) in a setting in which the first form of class struggle (resistance to proletarianisation, or any struggle accompanying original accumulation) overlaps with or still strongly resonates in the second (shop-floor resistance/labour market bargaining). In other words, at the juncture where the initial commodification and subordination to capital, involving a degree of anomie, via the experience with the socialisation of labour, still allows the self-assertion of the workers *against* capital as an alien, hostile force – rather than as a comprehensive, inescapable but fetishised reality which is socially amorphous: the 'economy', the 'market'. 'Class', at least in the case of the working class, under these specific conditions belongs to a category of forms of imagined community like religion and nation in the sense that it is shaped by settings absorbing dislocated/disoriented people into a new unit of social cohesion, or structure of socialisation. The overview of 'communities of fate' given by Pakulski and Waters (1996: ch. 5) is instructive here.

Filling the normative void that characterises anomie, proletarian millenarianism in socialist thought and propaganda defined the workers as a collective actor capable of forcing the transition towards an integral socialist society for which the material preconditions were shaped by industrial capital itself.

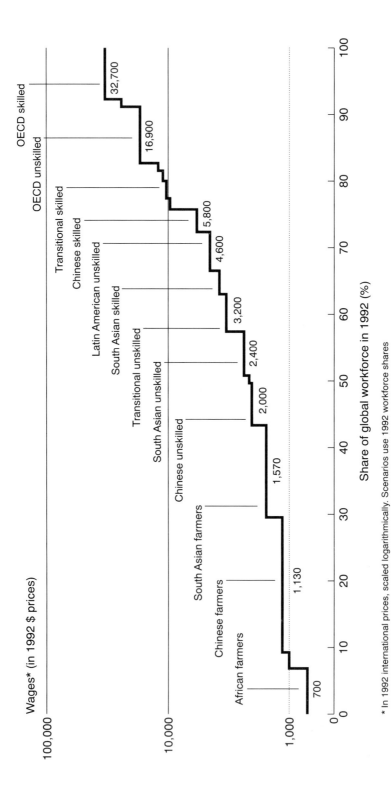

Figure 2.1 Structure of the global labour supply, 1992.

* In 1992 international prices, scaled logarithmically. Scenarios use 1992 workforce shares

Source: World Development Report, reprinted in the *Financial Times*, 24 July 1995.

The most important of these preconditions was the development of the social-isation of labour already referred to: the crystallisation of the 'collective worker' eventually assuming a social, indeed global dimension. But the prime mover was the anger of the disinherited on whom the discipline of capital had been imposed and who now sensed a new strength in their being thrown together in vast factories, working-class neighbourhoods, or shanty towns. Of course, today, this experience has been robbed of its millennarian socialist perspec-tive by the collapse of a Soviet state socialism identified with Marxism. Yet wherever first and second-generation factory workers are brought together under the discipline of capital, drawn into collective living conditions, etc., certain features of the 'proletarian spirit' will be sure to emerge and class struggles in the sense of mass movements for the improvement of living condi-tions will be among them. In Figure 2.1, the 'proletarian range' can be thought of as lying somewhere between 'Chinese unskilled' and 'Transitional skilled' – thus, very roughly, demarcating the zones in which proletarian mass move-ments are to be expected and have an obvious function, namely that of reducing the differential with the OECD level.

On the side of capital, it is *industrial* capital which imposes its discipline on the workers. More specifically, the moment of national concentration of industry and labour that accompanies the shift from a local/world-market-driven food and textile industry to heavy industry (iron and steel, railway equipment, shipbuilding) would mark the threshold beyond which the prol-etariat and the capitalist class become susceptible to 'corporatisation' – especially as the state at this point tends to become involved to sustain the structures of socialisation growing up around this generation of industry.

Struggles for survival

The third way in which the discipline of capital is imposed and resisted concerns the capacity of the social and natural substratum in its entirety to sustain developed, comprehensive capital accumulation. This can be approached from the angle of the *reproduction* of labour power in the broadest sense. Whereas in the earlier forms of imposing the discipline of capital, the need is to obtain a hired work-force first and then to have it perform its tasks according to the required job descriptions, on time-scales decreed by manage-ment, etc., in light of this third mode we are speaking of the conditions – in a fully developed capitalist economy – under which labour power will be avail-able at all in the longer run. Parallel to this comes the question of the limits of the earth's resources and the life-sustaining capacity of the biosphere at large. Therefore we may postulate a process of *exhaustion* on three dimensions.

First, the effort of work itself can already lead to such exhaustion that there is no chance for recovery to begin with. Shortening the working week for people with skills/tasks that are so specialised that free time loses its value, in practice leads them to take a second job especially if wages erode and consumption standards keep rising under the continuing bombardment of advertising. In the US, 'moonlighting' as well as overtime contributed to an effective lengthening of working time so that in the early 1990s, workers on average worked 164 extra hours compared to twenty years earlier, the equivalent of a month's work (Gorz 1982: 167; Schor 1992). Over roughly the same period, average hours of *sleep* in the main industrial countries have been reduced by half an hour as a consequence of shift labour and irregular working hours, late-night television broadcasting, and the use of medicine (*Vk*, 20 June 1997).

Japanese production methods in particular have tended to stretch to the extreme the total occupation of the personality by the labour process. As Hoogvelt and Yuasa write (1994: 293), 'the collective work in teams is a method to harness peer pressure to the point of nightmare surveillance'. *Karoshi*, dropping dead on the work floor, is the ultimate consequence of this particular way of organising the labour process, which replaces direct management supervision by 'teamwork' to achieve the near-impossible. Phrases like 'Toyotisation of the banks' and 'McDonaldisation of PTT-Telecom' indicate how these patterns are generalised throughout the economy (W. Buitelaar and P. Vos in *Vk*, 20 July 1996). In the office, 'technological advances – modems, laptops, faxes, cellular phones, and voice mail – have all but erased the boundaries around work. It is now possible, and thus increasingly expected, for employees to be accessible and productive any hour, any day' (*BW*, 17 February 1992 in a review of Schor 1992). As a consequence, time pressures generalise to the point where a single person no longer is capable of adjusting the body rhythm to the requirements of the task.

This leads us to the *second* form of exhaustion of the substratum on which capital accumulation rests, that of the reproductive sphere properly speaking. The new office technologies also allow the progressive reorganisation of the reproductive sphere where labour power is supposed to obtain its necessary qualifications and to be regenerated. Schools, hospitals, and the public sector in its entirety all are compelled, by budgeting techniques and straight cutbacks, to match standards of work organisation and profitability set by the most advanced firms. After having been standardised by processes of socialisation, often under state auspices and in a spirit of social protection, the qualification/reproduction of labour power, too, has become subject to cost-cutting and profit maximation strategies copied from or directly applied by private capital. Usually, the introduction of industrial, 'lean/mean' production methods can only be achieved at the expense of the substance of the historic social function. The transfer and development of culture and learning or the provision of necessary public services and socialised forms of care, thus are functionalised in a context shaped by economic competition and ultimately, private enrichment. The atomisation inherent in commodification in this way is no longer compensated by socialisation, and the state itself is losing credence as a source of social regeneration. According to a recent opinion poll, the US, for instance, has become 'a nation of suspicious strangers, whose mistrust of one another is exceeded only by their distrust of the federal government' (*FT*, 30 January 1996).

The cultural and emotional wasteland which is the result of the imposition of the discipline of capital on socialised reproduction tendentially aggravates the condition of the private reproductive sphere, too. Already in the 1970s, it was noted that married women in the US increasingly were drawn into the labour process to compensate wage erosion due to inflation (Stover 1975: 54–5). Although the causes have shifted to other forms of wage erosion and higher costs of living (in combination with a more commodified consciousness of what constitutes an acceptable standard of living), the mobilisation of the reserve army of labour hidden in the household has proceeded in all capitalist countries. As a consequence, the reproductive function of care and the transfer of social skills comes under pressure. Thus, the per centage of children having to cook their own meals in the US has risen to 36 per cent of *all children* in 1993 (from 13 per cent as late as 1987; *Nw*, 10 January 1994). Neglect of children but also juvenile crime (three out of four juvenile homicides today take place in the US, *IHT*, 8 February 1996) may be taken as a clear sign of society's failure to perform its reproductive function.

The combination of exhaustive outside work, reduced social care and the concomitant compression of household work and caring functions also affects the reproductive/affective core of community by the break-up of the elementary household bond. This instance of the atomisation of everyday life is illustrated in Table 2.1 below. Especially in the countries which belong to the original English-speaking heartland of capital and which experience an advanced stage of commodification and individualisation (see also Albert 1992), the rise of single-parent households ('single parent' for all practical purposes meaning female-headed families) has been strong between the early 1970s and mid-1980s, whereas the corporate–liberal welfare states on the heartland's rim have been less affected. To give an idea of the degree to which this corresponds with the reduction of social relations to the cash nexus by

Table 2.1 Parents living without partners, early 1970s/mid-1980s: negative community attitudes among managers. (Figures expressed as percentages)

			Managers	
	Single parent, mid-1980s	*% Change from early 1970s*	*Negative on family wage*	*Profit the only goal of corporation*
United States	24	84	95	40
United Kingdom	14	79	96	33
Australia	15	62	92	35
West Germany	11	43	90	24
Sweden	17	13	89	27
France	10	7	88	16
Japan	4	14	32	8

Sources: *Newsweek*, 12 June 1995; Hampden-Turner and Trompenaars 1994: 168, 32 [N=15,000 (1986–93)].

managers, we have added the percentages of managers rejecting responsibility for their employees' families and considering profit the only goal of the corporation.

The exhaustive effects of the discipline of capital on the reproductive sphere do not include the exhaustion of the supply of labour, on the contrary. Parallel to the overexploitation of those employed (including about 250 million children, *FT*, 12 November 1996), there is a growing under-utilisation of the global labour force. This is one sign that capital as such has become the main obstacle to development (M. Nicolaus in Marx 1973: 49). Some 820 million people of working age, 30 per cent of the world's total, are unemployed or underemployed, the highest figure since the Great Depression of the 1930s, according to the first annual employment report of the ILO (*FT*, 22 February 1995). The discipline of capital is total only in the sense that there is no alternative left to the worker but to sell his/her labour power to capital.

The traditional measurement of unemployment as a percentage of the labour force meanwhile tends to obscure its social effects. If we look instead at *households* with labour and households without, the trend is towards a bifurcation of society away from the traditional one-earner pattern. Developments rather seem to head towards a two-thirds of households in which both partners work (from half in 1983) and a bottom segment of varying proportions without any work. This trend is most pronounced in the US and the UK, and least in Southern Europe where the single-earner household remains prominent (Gregg and Wadsworth 1996; see also *FT*, 8 January 1997). This would suggest that where the discipline of capital has become most comprehensive, we find a cumulative exacerbation of social exhaustion by: (a) the concentration of work and compression of household functions; (b) the concentration of poverty and dependency; and (c) the break-up of families.

Hence we can understand the poverty and destitution of inner cities of the United States and Britain as the other side of the coin of Schor's 'overworked American'. Both are subject to a particular aspect of social exhaustion. Although the trend is everywhere in the same direction, the US leads the way here. The degradation of an American inner city is of a qualitatively different kind from, say, Calcutta or any other Third World concentration of poverty, because it is the result of extreme commodification and the destruction of, first, the family and related community structures of reproduction and next, the compensatory, socialised infrastructure on which people relied instead. This tearing down of the welfare infrastructure is not a matter of neglect but an aspect of the imposition of the discipline of capital, actively championed by its ideologues on the grounds of progress (de Goede 1996). Capital accumulation, in a world market context at that, then links up to the last source of purchasing power, the destitute drug addict.

Finally, the tightening discipline of capital on the reproductive sphere also implies the destruction/exhaustion of the biosphere. This is the *third* dimension on which exhaustion of the reproductive sphere can be observed. The record rate at which e.g. forests are being destroyed world-wide can be directly related to structural support for the major timber and paper groups. As a recent report observes, 'The handful of companies controlling the timber trade have the economic and political might to log wherever they want. Once forests are exhausted in one region, companies simply move elsewhere' (quoted in *FT*, 10 September 1996; see also Kolk 1996). Need we repeat here that the world's food supply is being endangered by the steady exhaustion and poisoning of fresh water, soil and sea; by the warming of the atmosphere and destruction of the ozone layer; that by subordinating life itself to capitalist cost accounting, new diseases are generated and spread, antibiotics are used in a way undermining future defence against epidemics, and so on?

Summing up the forms of capitalist discipline in the contemporary period, Stephen Gill (1995) calls the straitjacket in which the world is being forced on this suicidal course, and which today, as an apparently inevitable 'globalisation' is applied on a planetary scale, *disciplinary neo-liberalism*. The segment of capital most prominently involved here is financial, or *money capital*, the circuit M ... M'. It has meanwhile become a platitude to expound on the hypertrophy of this circuit relative to productive capital and trade.[4] The requirements dictated by a capitalist order geared one-sidedly to financial enrichment are translated into guidelines for economic policy by the IMF, the World Bank, OECD, WTO, and regional bodies such as the EU; and subsequently are adopted, with few exceptions, by states acting as intermediaries of the global capitalist constraint, precluding and often overruling national democratic procedure and sovereignty. Hence Gill's parallel notion of the *new constitutionalism* to highlight the political implications of disciplinary neo-liberalism. Guarding conformity here are the major rating agencies (Moody's or Standard & Poor) which by their credit ratings feed information on credit-worthiness and investor-friendliness back to capital markets, potential investors, etc. (Sinclair 1994). Often, the leverage created by states' indebtedness (debt, too, is rated and traded) is sufficient reason to comply with any guideline issued.

This apparently all-powerful, tightly integrated system of controls does not mean that the discipline of capital over the entire reproductive system is beyond resistance. The many different forms in which society and nature are subjected to the discipline of capital do produce anger and discontent, often exacerbated by the 'politics of unpopularity' of governments confronting their own populations in the name of 'the economy'. Under conditions of extreme commodification and individualisation, such discontent easily assumes apparently personal, non-political forms. In chapter 1, we already referred to what extreme commodification does to the personality. Many of the 'new social movements' that emerged in the late 1960s and 1970s built on aspects of defending and enhancing the sovereignty of the personality in a commodified context – the new feminism and the gay rights movement can be thought of here. But the squatters' movement, too, by challenging real estate speculation defended an aspect of the immediate, personal sphere of life. The same applies to the campaigns against torture of Amnesty International. Still other movements of resistance and emancipation, such as black liberation, combined a class with a communitarian dimension.

Now the element of backlash provoked by such movements, say, white supremacist attitudes (or male chauvinism in the case of feminism/gay rights), often has been fed back into the evolving popular resentment over the disruption of social life by neo-liberal economic development. As a result, neo-fascism is able to mobilise segments of a defeated working class behind xenophobia and anti-immigrant sentiment. The social movements, on the other hand (including the mass movements against the new round of nuclear armament initiated by NATO after 1978) and the Green political parties and activist groups such as Greenpeace, until recently seemed comparatively 'middle class' in orientation, and certainly were not yet ready to challenge the global discipline of capital frontally. Moreover, as resistance to disciplinary neo-liberalism is imbricated with a *recherche du temps perdu*, a nostalgia for everyday life as people knew it, there is another window through which the neo-fascist element can climb in.

Yet, although this cannot of course be satisfactorily argued in the abstract, resistance to the penetration of the reproductive sphere by capital must at some point overcome these internal contradictions between 'sectoral' social movements and other forms of resistance to the exhaustion of the social and natural substratum of the mode of production. As more and more aspects of life are invaded by the logic of exploitation and profit, the cumulation of moments of resistance cannot, in the longer run, be undone by resentment among different groups of victims – especially not when these victims leave 'victimisation' behind and in the act of resistance take on the forces of capital. The struggles for the defence of human dignity and self-determination, against the destruction of the biosphere, and all the terrains on which the corrupting influences of money and profit are souring the joys and quality of life – from sports and leisure to art, education and health – even a funeral today is part of a fiercely contested field of capital accumulation – in our era are converging on a common pattern. In these struggles, society literally fights for survival, rather than mounting, in the tradition of left vanguardism or proletarian mass politics, an offensive aiming at the revolutionary transformation of society. Yet they constitute a class struggle against capital precisely because they are no longer waged from a narrow, corporatist definition of class, but as popular struggles uniting a broad array of social forces seeking 'the fulfilment of tasks set by interests wider than their own' (Polanyi 1957: 152). The issue is no longer that 'capitalism' is showing signs of collapse, and 'socialism' is around the corner. *What is failing today is not capital but the capacity of society and nature to support its discipline.*

The December 1995 mass movement against the disciplinary neo-liberalism imposed on France by a government committed to meeting the entry requirements of the projected EU monetary union, may be considered the landmark event in the development of this type of struggle to maturity (see *MD*, January 1996). The French movement followed on other movements against aspects of neo-liberal 'reform' and commodification/exhaustion – against government corruption and moral decay in Italy and Belgium, against agrobusiness practices in India and ecological destruction by Shell in Nigeria's Ogoniland, the Chiapas revolt against NAFTA, etc. (J. Vidal in *Vk*, 18 November 1995). Although highly varied and complex, and always including both resistance against original accumulation and workplace resistance, still it would seem that the resistance to the exhaustion of the human and natural substratum increasingly is the overdetermining, synchronising aspect, subsuming the others into a broader struggle.

As the inherent legitimacy of a movement to restore and defend social protection and implicitly, democracy and popular sovereignty is necessarily superior to a socialist project *per se*, and its appeal proportionally broader, the struggle for survival stands in the tradition of '1935' (the antifascist, Popular Front orientation of the 7th Comintern Congress) rather than in that of '1917'. Its advance would accordingly require, to use Gramsci's typology (1971: 108–10), a 'war of position' strategy of piecemeal progression with a pronounced element of ideological persuasion, instead of an insurrectionary 'war of movement'. However, we can develop this argument on the prospects for democracy and, if properly understood as a society 'richer in collective values', socialism, only on the basis of a more concrete understanding of the actual configuration of class forces. In this perspective, we now turn to the capitalist class properly speaking.

Fractions of capital and concepts of control

Class struggle as conducted by capital, in which the formation of the bourgeoisie as a class for itself comes about, must concretely be understood, first, as embedded in a historically contingent social topography (as discussed on pp. 32–6); and second, as flanked/compounded by the two other modes of imposing the discipline of capital besides the immediately productive one. Concrete class struggles revolve around the imposition of the discipline of capital in production, but in real life are entwined with struggles on the two other dimensions (original accumulation, reproduction) and by the community legacy bequeathed by the past to modern society. This does not mean that every particular social conflict can be *reduced* to imposing/resisting the discipline of capital in production, but rather that in the developed capitalist world, specific conflicts necessarily are part of a structure of socialisation of which the ramifications ultimately relate to this central dimension of exploitation. This, then, warrants the theoretical construction of a referential structure along which we can arrive, step by step, and moving from the abstract to the concrete (in the sense of composite), at the understanding of a given bourgeoisie (see also Ritsert 1973: 10; *MEW* 23: 11–2).

The labour process and class fractions

In the relationship with living labour power, the bourgeoisie develops its primary consciousness of itself as a class (historically, this consciousness first took shape in its democratic struggle against the aristocracy and European absolutism; but here we are still abstracting from chronological history). In the struggle for shop floor control of the workforce, labour market struggles, and their dealings with trade unions and labour parties, as well as in their attitude towards the infrastructure of reproductive social welfare, different tendencies in the bourgeoisie take shape over time. Basically, this difference relates to the conjunctural shifts between innovative, rapidly accumulating capitals, and others whose rhythm of accumulation has slowed down. The former, anticipating productivity rises and expanding market shares, are in a position to make concessions if pressed to do so; whereas the stagnating sectors will tend to confront the working class frontally from their basically defensive position. Lenin distinguished between these different orientations of the capitalist class (flexible 'liberalism' versus the 'method of force') in a pamphlet of 1910 (*Collected Works* 16: 350–1). They mirrored, in his view, two possible attitudes of the workers: reformism reciprocating the flexible–'liberal' bourgeois posture, anarcho-syndicalism the method of force.

To the bourgeoisie, such rival options as flexibility and the method of force cannot be applied locally, in surgical doses, without undermining its own position in the longer run. The ultimate stakes of class struggle are political, related to the contest for power in the state. The bourgeoisie as a ruling class accordingly must express a particular class posture in terms of the *general interest*, as 'a spiritual power'. In the process of defining a particular definition of this general interest, which in a developed capitalist state involves the activities of organic intellectuals and planning bodies as well as professional politicians, the different perspectives vie for leadership. Hence, at the level of the class as such, the bourgeoisie is continuously engaged in building coalitions transcending the particularity of 'special interests'. But the uneven development of the productive forces by capital, resistance to its discipline, and the centrifugal force of competition, work against a once-and-for-all comprehensive formula, so that the struggle for political leadership, *hegemony*, never ends.

Particular capitals participate in the process of interest aggregation along the lines of functional and historical *fractions*, say, as money capital, or more concretely, as City merchant banks, or late nineteenth-century German heavy industry, etc. From their particular vantage point, they seek to build the momentum to direct the course of society at large. As Hickel writes (1975: 151), 'the actual relevance of the fractioning of the bourgeoisie resides in the continuous attempt (which itself is the result of competition) of the individual capitals to make their specific interests appear as the general interest at the level of the state'. Therefore, fractions can only be observed *in action* – the notion as such is 'indeterminate and must be complemented by strategies that impart some substantive coherence to what would otherwise remain formal unities' (Jessop 1983: 89).

In the case of the contradiction between capital and labour, the strategy of a certain fraction of the bourgeoisie may involve (once a shortage of labour power leads to a slackening of shopfloor discipline and/or stronger trade union bargaining power and, eventually, worker resistance) the mechanisation or reorganisation of the labour process. In the case of the electrical engineering industries Siemens and AEG in Weimar Germany (or parts of the chemical industry), capital in this way sought to sustain a class compromise with the workers by making concessions (Sohn-Rethel 1975). Capital can also try to evade the present workforce by relocating production to areas or countries where the discipline on the workers can be imposed on more favourable conditions. The opposed strategy (represented in Weimar Germany by the coal and parts of the iron and steel industries), was to entrench and try to intensify work, lengthen the work day, etc. At first sight, it would seem as if this second option simply 'won', but this has to be made more concrete.

Ultimately, class strategy through a multi-layered process transcends its fractional origins, merging into what Ries Bode has termed *comprehensive concepts of control* (Bode 1979). Concepts of control are frameworks of thought and practice by which a particular world view of the ruling class spills over into a broader sense of 'limits of the possible' for society at large. Adding the dimension of (international) politics and (transnational) class struggle to what Aglietta and others call 'mode of regulation' (Aglietta 1979), a concept of control strategically articulates the special interests of a historically concrete configuration of classes and states with the management requirements of the order with which those interests are most immediately congruent. Remaining largely implicit as long as it is actually hegemonic, a concept of control turns a particular interpretation of capitalist development into orthodoxy. It offers a language in which interests can be legitimately put forward, while galvanising the self-consciousness of the bourgeoisie and its allies.

The analysis of successive concepts of control allows us to see that 'capitalism' has only existed in historically bounded, transient forms; what was 'normal' in one age, say, the welfare state, is anathema in another. Such codes of normalcy in practice appear subject to change, along with the shifts in labour processes and modes of accumulation, the widening and/or deepening of commodification and the discipline of capital, the changing forms of state/society relations, world politics, etc.

Let us now return to the intermediate level of determination of such concepts, that of circulation relations.

Circulation relations and fraction perspectives

As Marx argues in *Capital*, vol. II, 'Capital as expanding value does not only include class relations, a definite social nature which rests on the existence of labour as wage labour. It is a movement, a circulatory process through different stages, which itself includes three different forms of the circulatory process again' (*MEW* 24: 109). Each single, competing capital has to go through these transformations in order to relate to others in terms of the technical division of labour. Firms and sectors producing for each other or for each other's workers must deliver goods or services; hence capital necessarily assumes a *commodity form*. In the process of value expansion, in order to make profit available for new accumulation, capital must appear in *money form*. In other words, although the notion of industrial capital usually evokes its *productive form* first, these other forms, contain, as capital, the metamorphosed value equations of the elements actually engaged and obtained in the productive synthesis. Accordingly, they should be understood as equally part of it, in a constant movement.

Now this movement, which is composed of innumerable single capitals going through the successive transformations, has historically come about as the integration of previously independent activities (money-lending, trade and transport) into the circuit of industrial capital, and remains subject to the reality of particular capitals in competition with each other. It is thus that Marx arrives at his concept of capital fraction, of which we can speak 'to the degree that a function of capital operative in the circulation process is autonomised into a special function of a special capital at all and crystallises as a function assigned by the division of labour to a particular kind of capitalist' (*MEW* 25: 278). Fractions of capital based on this functional division would then be, for instance, bank and insurance capital; various forms of commercial capital such as wholesale and retail or import/export capital; as well as productive capital properly speaking (which includes, on account of its real value-adding rather than merely distributive function, transport). At this level of abstraction, however, we still speak of money, commodity and productive capital. In the previous discussion (pp. 37–49), we already loosely referred to these fractions in relation to their role in imposing the discipline of capital: merchant (commodity) capital in original accumulation, productive capital in production, money capital in reproduction. But in the overall circuit of capital, both at the collective and the particular level, value first assumes its money form, M; then a commodity form, C (at this point subdivided into means of production and labour power); and then submerges into the actual productive process, in which circulation is suspended and surplus value is added. This is denoted by P, which is set to eventually become P', productive capital on an expanded scale. Before P reaches this stage, however, value first resumes its commodity form (a given output serving as input for other cycles or the reproduction of labour power). This C' contains the metamorphosed value increment. Finally, output must be sold at a price realising surplus value in money form, M'. Around each of these forms, *fractions* crystallise to which we can ascribe a certain ideal–typical perspective which will make itself felt in the formulation of class strategy.

Indeed at the entry point at which an autonomised functional fraction is routinely inserted into the composite circuit, the process in its entirety is perceived from the particular angle of that fraction – money capitalists fix their gaze on the circuit $M \ldots M'$, commodity capitalists on $C \ldots C'$, and productive capitalists on P ... P′. Looking over the shoulder of an imaginary entrepreneur engaged in one of these circuits, one can hypothesise a specific phenomenology. The perspective of the trader, which prioritises the profitable movement of goods and compares potential markets in terms of their capacity to absorb particular commodities; the *rentier* perspective of money capital, for which the money return is the sole decisive reference and which also, on account of its capacity to 'totalise' and arbitrate competing productive and commercial ventures, redistributes capital between them; and finally, the productive capitalist, concentrated on securing the specific human and material inputs of the next, expanded round of production (see also Shortall 1986). Ultimately, the different orbital movements making up the composite circuit of industrial capital relate to each other also as part of a structure of socialisation, which involves division of labour and parcellisation of functions and, at a higher level, reintegration and mutual adjustment of the separate activities, the crystallisation of a directive element, and ultimately, a moment of control.

Therefore, the collective decision to either accommodate or confront the workers in a situation such as in the Weimar Republic, is not necessarily taken at the level of production directly. Rather, such a strategic decision comes about through a more complex, mediated configuration of interests in which alternative options are arbitrated at various 'fractional' levels to obtain a momentary optimal solution. In Kurt Gossweiler's analysis (1975: 344), the dividing line between new industries (electrical, chemical, automobile) in favour of a flexible solution, and the old, entrenched industries (coal and steel), was in fact cut across by a second dividing line separating rival constellations of money capital connected with industry in *financial groups* – clusters of finance capital in Hilferding's sense (interpenetrated and officer-interlocked banks and industrial corporations, 1973), usually but not always configured around a major bank (Menshikov 1973: 205). These financial groups, depicted in Figure 2.2, articulated the alternative options for dealing with the working class with their international orientations – the Dresdner/Danat bank group (penetrated by Anglo-American capital) preferring a radical liberal, Atlantic strategy; the Deutsche/Disconto Bank group a state-monopolistic, corporatist strategy with a European accent. The dead weight of what Sohn-Rethel (1975) calls the 'bankrupt' fraction of industry and the failure of German bank capital and the modern industrial fractions to overcome Germany's lack of capital and market access mutually reinforced each other. The eventual recourse to fascism was then decided at the level of key investment banking houses such as Stein (depicted in Figure 2.2 as the axis around which the entire constellation revolves) acting as the embodiment of total capital in dialogue with Hindenburg, Papen and others in the conservative bloc, the Nazi party, the army, etc. This interpretation has been criticised on factual grounds (Stegmann 1976), but the methodology as such, which primarily concerns us here, remains valid if we concentrate on capitalist structures (see also Abraham 1981).

Generally speaking, the question how rival options are transmitted through the fractional structure of socialisation and become strategy in the context of

Figure 2.2 Fraction structure in Weimar Germany.
Source: Gossweiler 1975: 344.

a particular concept of control, can be related to: (a) the moment and conditions of the insertion of circuits of capital into an overall world market movement of capital; and (b) the relative prominence of fractions and particular forms of capital accumulation at any given time.

As to the first, the three functional circuits we have distinguished according to Palloix (1974 a/b) also represent three consecutive moments in the emergence of a world market movement of capital. The internationalisation of the circuit of commodity capital was characteristic for the *Pax Britannica*; the circuit of money capital also assumed international dimensions in the era of imperialist rivalry; while in the twentieth century, productive capital was internationalised through direct manufacturing investment in the *Pax Americana*. The hypothesis would then be that each of these periods would typically bear the marks of the internationally ascendant circuit also in terms of prevailing outlook. Thus Polanyi's distinction between two 'organising principles' in the double movement on the threshold of the twentieth century: liberalism/*laissez-*

faire, and 'social protection aiming at the conservation of man and nature as well as productive organization' (1957: 132), would broadly correspond to the perspectives of, respectively, nineteenth-century money and commodity capital engaged in international circulation, and productive capital still predominantly entrenched nationally.

As to the second question (relative prominence), the distinction between *departments of production* supplying themselves and each other in the enlarged reproduction of total capital (*MEW* 24: ch. 21) likewise has been the point of departure for analyses of internationalisation. As Palloix has done in the case of the separate functional circuits, these 'departments', too, have been directly projected on history, in this case by Rosa Luxemburg in her analysis of imperialism (1966). In fact, in both cases, we are dealing with a set of structures still conceived at an intermediate level of abstraction (*SIFI* 1974; see also my 1975). An elaboration of Marx's analysis of departments (I, means of production, 'capital goods'; II, wage goods; and III, luxury goods) which takes this into account can be found, though, in Wladimir Andreff's work (1976).

Articulating labour process determinants with circulation determinants, Andreff distinguishes between three differently defined departments, or *sectors*, which each represent a particular *mode of accumulation* and one after another determine a composite *regime of accumulation* (see also Andreff 1982). Placing these in a historical perspective, he arrives at three eras. We have added two further determinants to arrive at a more concrete profile of capital and the prevailing, or at least ascendant ideology in each era: one, the circuit internationalising in the same period (Palloix's scheme); two, the *paradigmatic scale of operation* referring to the spatial coordinates of the mode of accumulation. By this we mean the gradually widening scale on which production has been organised, from local to national to global (money capital all along has been cosmopolitan in outlook, but in the 'Great Transformation' was subordinated to nationally operating productive capital) (see Overbeek and van der Pijl 1993: 7, Figure 1.1). By serving as a general frame of reference in the outlook of industrial entrepreneurs, paradigmatic scales have further determined the strategies pursued by ascendant fractions of the ruling class. Of course, this remains a schematic presentation which will have to be elaborated. The expanded periodisation, however, would comprise the following stages:

A. *extensive accumulation*, originating with the industrial revolution itself and dominant until well into the nineteenth century. Production is characterised by a low organic composition of capital (high labour-intensive); output consists of means of consumption mainly. The textile and food industries are the historical sectors in which this mode of accumulation originated, and in which it to a certain extent persists as a 'Sector A'. As to the paradigmatic scale of operation, the industries mentioned typically operated on a local scale, 'distributed in much the same way as population itself', although textiles was already more regionally concentrated than food and construction (Estall and Buchanan 1966: 142). At the same time, products of these industries, textiles first of all, were inserted into commercial circuits flung far and wide (captured by Palloix's internationalisation of C . . . C′). Industry was entirely dependent on this global commercial circuit – through the eighteenth century, already, British production for export grew by 544 per cent against domestic market production's 152 per cent (Palloix 1971: 54, table 3) – so that we may assume that the cosmopolitan vision of the world market traders also coloured the outlook of the producers in England and in those countries seeking to compete with them in world markets. In the course of the nineteenth century, however, this complex of forces encountered a new configuration based on

B.   *intensive accumulation*, characterised by high organic composition ('capital-intensive') and primarily supplying producer goods. The nineteenth/early twentieth-century metals, oil and engineering industries are the examples of this 'Sector B'. Expressing also the rise of rivals to British supremacy who resorted to trade protectionism, B industries' paradigmatic scale of operation was typically *national*, often imbricated with the Hobbesian state/society configuration we will discuss in the next chapter. This does not mean that these industries were literally contained within and coextensive with national borders, but that they were typically state supported and their foreign activities intertwined with foreign policy (Estall and Buchanan 1966: 166; see also Martinelli *et al.* 1981: 39–40). Cartelisation therefore went hand in hand with protectionism and reinforced the identity of industry with a particular national economy. Also, there occurred a marked nationalisation of social relations in response to the rise of the organised labour movement and the reciprocal self-organisation of employers. Yet at first, the parallel internationalisation of the circuit of money capital still masked the countermovement to cosmopolitan liberalism. Until World War I, and again in the 1920s, 'high finance' (meaning the complex of central banks and key investment banks) operated as a transnational force mediating between national industrial blocs (Polanyi 1957: 10). Only after the Great Crash of 1929 and the subsequent banking crisis did the skyline of discrete national industrial systems emerge in full. The emergency tutelage under which bank capital was placed by governments and the policy of the 'euthanasia of the *rentier*' prescribed by Keynes (1970: 376) then inaugurated a period in which the productive–capital perspective, summed up in Polanyi's concept of social protection and reflecting the high level of socialisation typical of an economy centring on the production of investment goods, reigned supreme. The international circuit of money capital virtually collapsed. In the United States, however, the same period witnessed the ascent of what Andreff calls

C.   *progressive accumulation*, combining labour and capital-intensive processes and producing 'mixed goods' as far as their destination is concerned. The twentieth-century automobile, chemicals and electrical engineering industries are typical of this 'Sector C', which is also a highly innovative, research-intensive sector. If the rise of the latter two can still be partly related to the preceding period, the car industry, both by reference to the revolutionary labour process set up by Ford and in terms of actual internationalisation of production really heralded a new era (Ferguson 1984: 53ff). In terms of scale of operation, 'C' industry in this period combined a concern for secure national markets with active internationalisation (Lipietz 1982). Banks on the other hand often operated as relays of monetary authorities and, as with US banks in Europe, supported internationalising C industries from a subordinate position – at least until the lifting of restrictive bank legislation in the late 1960s and after (Koszul 1970; Weston 1980).

Science-related growth (which as we saw is one aspect of the socialisation of labour) meanwhile has become the overriding quality of the contemporary accumulation regime in the form of the introduction into all sectors of what van Tulder and Junne (1988: 14) term 'core technologies'. The producers of these technologies perhaps could consitute a *sector 'D'* (micro-electronics/telecom and biotechnology/pharmaceutical). 'Media' in the sense of those operating on the projected 'information highway' in this perspective may be added to the micro-electronics/telecom group. For want of a better term, let us call the corresponding mode of accumulation *virtual*, because there is a particularly elusive, non-tangible quality about this form of capital accumulation due to miniaturisation and other economies of time and space characteristic of it. This is also reflected in the resurgence, indeed hypertrophy of the international circuit of money capital and the ephemerality of fictitious capital (derivatives, and so on).

Taken together, the analysis so far, while still centring on determinants at an intermediate level of abstraction, yet allows us to construct hypothetical collective orientations of the ruling class. We may speak here of certain 'generational perspectives' in the capitalist class, which, if specified for concrete fractions (financial groups and class and class-related organisations), persist up to the present day, reproduced in firm, financial group, party and broader social contexts. Let us now move on to a further, more comprehensive level of concretisation that can be distinguished in this procedure.

Profit distribution and the moment of control

Of course the really concrete level of analysis of class formation can only be a historical analysis of a given class in a given period and region. This is beyond the scope of this study, and we will confine ourselves to only an outline of such an analysis in chapter 4. However, a few general observations and some empirical reference points can be presented here. As Marx notes in volume III of *Capital*, the analysis has now reached the point where 'the embodiments of capital ... stepwise approximate the form in which they operate at the surface of society, in the action of the different capitals upon

Table 2.2 Profit rates per sector according to Andreff, progressive accumulation, 1959–69 (US), 1962–69 (France)

	Sector		
	A	B	C
US	7.4	5.3	8.6
France	12.2	6.7	17.7

Source: Andreff 1976: 188.

each other, competition; and in everyday consciousness of the agents of production' (*MEW* 25: 33). At this level of concreteness, the abstract value equations still used in volumes I and II have been left behind and competitive relations are now expressed in real prices (production prices) and profits. Hence, one measure of assessing the social prominence of capital fractions is the process of *profit distribution* between them.

It is our thesis that the capacity of fractions of capital to appropriate a share of the total mass of profits shapes the sense of identity of a particular segment of collective capital with the momentary functioning of the system, short-circuiting the general interest with the special one. 'In this form,' Marx writes (*MEW* 25: 205), 'capital develops a consciousness of itself as a social power, in which every capitalist participates in relation to his share of total capital.' As we will see, empirical profit distribution can help to determine the relative preponderance of certain fractions; hence, the relative prominence of a particular world-view (which is partly 'typical', partly historically contingent); and finally, the particular drift captured by the comprehensive concept of control.

Andreff shows that in the heyday of the progressive mode of accumulation, 'C' industries enjoyed the highest rate of profit, while 'B' industries were lagging in both the US and France (Table 2.2).

A snapshot comparison for 1992 would suggest that under virtual accumulation, the 'D' sector now enjoys the highest profitability, while there is a crisis of 'C' industries (Table 2.3).

Pharmaceuticals (also a 'D' industry) could not be included in this table, but fit entirely in the picture – British profit margins in this industry, for instance, were 20+ per cent for 1994, almost double the second industry, breweries ('A') (*FT*, 10 January 1995).

This shifting configuration is embedded in the broader flow of commodity, money, and productive capital. In turn, the flows of metamorphosed value in which separate firms compete for profit, combine into total capital imposing its discipline on society and nature. In addition to the distribution of world capital over different state sovereignties, this sums up the mediations through which the capitalist class continuously seeks to establish its unity in the face of obstacles, challenges, and resistance.

Table 2.3 Average sectoral profit rates, industrial sectors 1992; US, Japan, Britain (profits as a percentage of sales)

		Sector			
		A	B	C	D
US	rate	5.6	3.1	2.4	7.0
	(n)	(23)	(19)	(33)	(30)
Japan	rate	1.7	1.1	1.3	3.8
	(n)	(13)	(25)	(29)	(9)
Britain	rate	5.1	2.9	0.7	10.5
	(n)	(6)	(9)	(4)	(4)

Source: *Business Week*, 12 July 1993, 'The Global 1000'.

A: food & household products; textiles & apparel.
B: energy sources; building materials; steel.
C: chemicals; aerospace & military technology; electrical & electronics; automobiles.
D: electronic components & instruments; broadcasting & publishing; telecommunications.

The nationality of capital of course is problematic on account of capital interpenetration, but still may serve indicative purposes. Thus the mass of profit is also distributed over national economies. In a comparison of profits over the last six years, US firms (including foreign subsidiaries) netted 47.7 per cent of total profits, European firms 36.8 per cent, and Japanese firms 15.5 per cent (*FT*, 29/30 April 1995). But as the n lines of Table 2.3 suggest already, US profits are much more made in the rapid growth sectors even allowing for distortions caused by short-term profitability strategies prevalent in shareholder-regulated economies of the Anglo-Saxon type (see also Hampden-Turner and Trompenaars 1995: 319) (Table 2.4).

Now if the 'nationality' of capital already should be qualified, can we at all speak of commodity, money, and productive capital as separate moments of a contemporary accumulation process, structuring class formation? Has not socialisation of capital eroded the foundations of a separate banking bourgeoisie and a separate productive and commercial bourgeoisie, except for marginal groups of small business? This would be the thrust of any argument for finance capital (*Finanzkapital* in Hilferding's sense, or the *financial bourgeoisie* integrating long-term investment, productive, and distributive functions, see also Granou 1977).

Relative profit shares (of the total mass of profits *per country*) can be approximated from official statistics. The US financial sector in the period 1961–70 on average appropriated 10.4 per cent of the total mass of profits (*Economic Report* 1977: 279, Table B-79). In France, financial savings as a per centage of total corporate income averaged 4.6 per cent for the same period, West Germany's 24.6 per cent (*OECD* 1980, vol. 2, country tables). With due caution, this can be taken as an indication of the subordination of money capital to industrial accumulation. As indicated already, the crisis of profitability of progressive

Table 2.4 Profit shares per sector, US/Japan/Europe, 1989–94. (Percentages, selected industries)

	Sector	US	Japan	Europe
A	Food/household products	42.6	7.8	49.6
B	Steel	2.3	51.2	46.5
C	Automobiles	23.6	31.0	45.5
	Machinery/engineering	19.2	34.4	46.3
D	Electronic components/instruments	65.0	30.5	4.5
	Data processing/reproduction	65.1	20.7	24.2

Source: *FT*, 29/30 April 1995.

Table 2.5 Current receipts of financial corporations as a share of all corporations, 1972–95 (figures expressed as percentages)

	US	Japan	West Germany	France	UK
1972	44.8	38.9	25.6	42.4	31.7
1975	48.5	50.5	30.9	53.3	52.8
1980	54.3	51.8	35.6	58.5	48.5
1985	54.9	56.9	40.1	63.2	56.6
1990	58.1	62.0	36.0	57.4	74.7
1995	51.2	61.3	44.6*	56.3	66.3†

*1993; †1994

Sources: *OECD* 1986 and *OECD* 1997, 2 vols, country tables.

accumulation was met by allowing money capital a greater degree of freedom. The 1973 oil crisis led to a vast expansion of the pool of available loan capital in the London 'Euro' markets, and one aspect of the late 1970s and the 1980s was a resurgence of the international circuit of money capital. Thus the stock of international bank lending (324 billion dollars in 1980), rose to 7,500 billion in 1991. This was equivalent to 4 per cent of total OECD GDP in 1980, and 44 per cent of OECD GDP in 1991 (*Ec*, 19 September 1992). Parallel to this, income accruing to financial capital as a per centage of the total rose in all the major capitalist countries (although much less so in West Germany), as can be seen in Table 2.5.

But the 1979–80 monetarist intervention by the US Federal Reserve which triggered the global debt crisis also caused great pain to many banks, so that the suggestion of enhanced bankers' power through the 1980s is difficult to maintain. This again leads us to the notion of finance capital, the socialisation of financial, commercial, and industrial capital into interdependent webs. 'Under these circumstances,' Soref and Zeitlin write (1987: 60), 'the interlocking directorates tying together the major banks and top nonfinancial corporations take on a crucial political-economic role in integrating the simultaneous and potentially contradictory financial, industrial, and commercial

Table 2.6 Most centrally located firms in the international network of joint
directorates, 1970/1976/1992 (* = banks; sectors A/B/C/D)

	1970		1976		1992	
Rank						
1	J.P. Morgan	*/US	Chase Manhattan	*/US	Citicorp	*/US
2	Chemical Bank	*/US	Deutsche Bank	*/G	GM	C/US
3	Chase Manhattan	*/US	Canadian Imp.	*/Can	AT&T	D/US
4	Royal D./Shell	B/N–UK	Chemical Bank	*/US	IBM	C/US
5	Deutsche Bank	*/G	Dresdner Bank	*/G	CS Holding	*/Swi
6	Int. Nickel	B/Can	Ford	C/US	3M	D/US
7	AKZO	C/N	J.P. Morgan	*/US	Unilever	A/N–UK
8	Gen. Electric	C/US	Swiss Bank Corp	*/Swi	Hewlett P.	D/US
9			Volkswagen	C/G		
10			Royal D./Shell	B/N–UK		

Sources: for 1970, Fennema 1982: 117; for 1976, ibid.: 191; for 1992, compiled from Mattera
1992, company data. To make data comparable, 1970 and 1976 rankings (n = 176) are based
on number of firms linked to, and global centrality (mean distance to all firms) in order to
discount mere national prominence, possible if n is high. For 1992 (n=100) the ranking is only
by number of firms linked to. Categorising IBM as 'C' and Hewlett-Packard as 'D' is because
we rely here on the classification of *Business Week* (see Table 2.3).

interests of the wealthiest families, whose various investments span these osten-
sibly separate sectors.'

As Meindert Fennema demonstrates, such webs of interlocking directorates
can be observed to exist and evolve at the international level. Rival coalitions
of finance capital have increasingly assumed transnational dimensions cutting
across previously pre-eminent (and still persisting) national configurations
(Fennema 1982: 167ff.; see also Stokman *et al.* 1985). While the actual multiple
directors are only a relatively small contingent by themselves, they are over-
seeing the circulation of vast masses of capital. In Table 2.6, the centrality
structure of the international network is presented for three years (lists are of
different length for computing reasons). The trend, first towards a greater
centrality of banks in 1976, reflecting, perhaps, their functional pre-eminence
in a phase of restructuring of capital towards a new configuration; and,
secondly, the resurgence of American capital in the high-technology field in
1992, corroborates the idea of a restructuring from a Keynesian/'Fordist',
progressive mode of accumulation to a regime dominated by virtual accumulation within a broader hypertrophy of financial capital. To underline the
importance of 'D' sector industries, we have indicated to which sector industrial firms listed belong; banks are marked by an asterisk.

Firms with a high centrality in this network must be seen as the places
which interface with the greatest number of other places in the network and
hence, are central in terms of strategic information (see also Fennema 1982
for a discussion of problems associated with this type of analysis). The discussion of broader policy issues will have the widest resonance there, so that the
question which kind of firm is at the centre, becomes relevant.

The networks of information and influence converging on the most central corporations often overlap with the transnational planning groups we will discuss in chapter 4, but otherwise may belong to different financial groups. They will tend to register the shifts in profit distribution in the sense of adopting perspectives relating to its momentary drift. In what we will term *transnational political business cycles*, the overall requirements of class rule and capital accumulation will also fluctuate with profit shifts, as with worker/social resistance, degrees of international rivalry, etc. The apparent fusion of functional/historical fractions of capital notwithstanding, the ideal–typical perspectives synthesised in finance capital in fact retain their polar opposition – 'the contradictions between them are not eliminated, nor are the claims of [banking capital] to a share of the profits extracted by [industrial capital],' Soref and Zeitlin write (1987: 61).

In the process of synthesising a tentative class position, some 'fractional' positions are closer to the overall, 'systemic' requirements of the mode of production than others. They may accordingly gravitate to the foreground as leading ideas charting a direction for society at large (Gossweiler 1975: 56). Thus a money capital perspective may in a certain conjuncture (typically, a crisis of restructuring) get the upper hand over the productive capital perspective which becomes associated, on a plane of broader social perception, with inefficiency and default. One by one, fractional interests will assert and if necessary, redefine themselves to conform with this shift and support its articulation at the political level. This underlines that political pluralism is a necessary condition for a developed capitalist society. Only the 'simultaneous existence of different lines of imperialist policy', Gossweiler argues (1975: 57),

> lends it the elasticity that is necessary to adjust to new situations and to exchange a compromised and deadlocked policy for a "new" one. . . . At the same time only this plurality offers the opportunity to prepare a mass basis for such a policy at any time.

The bottom line in all fractional struggles remains the imposition of the discipline of capital and the overcoming of limits and resistance to it. There is no preordained outcome of fractional struggle, nor is there, obviously, to class struggles. There will be, however, a certain momentum following particular victories, bolstering the self-confidence of the adherents of a particular concept. Trends in profit distribution will provide a meaningful support to such confidence, but they also remind us that what would seem to be victorious strategy is often more of profiting from a tide. In Polanyi's words, 'such groups are pushing that which is falling and holding onto that which, under its own steam, is moving their way. It may then seem as if they had originated the process of social change, while actually they were merely its beneficiaries, and may be even perverting the trend to make it serve their own aims' (1957: 28).

In the final analysis, across the profound transformations of the capitalist class building on cumulative changes in accumulation from shifting geographical epicentres, four main concepts of control have so far emerged as the expressions of the capitalist general interest on a world scale (including national varieties and modifications). By way of conclusion, these four concepts – liberal internationalism, a state monopoly tendency, corporate liberalism, and neo-liberalism – are depicted in Figure 2.3. In the figure, we also recapitulate the patterns in capital accumulation and internationalisation, as well as class struggle we have distinguished and will elaborate below.

In the next chapter, we will proceed to situate these historical universes of total capital in the international political economy and state system.

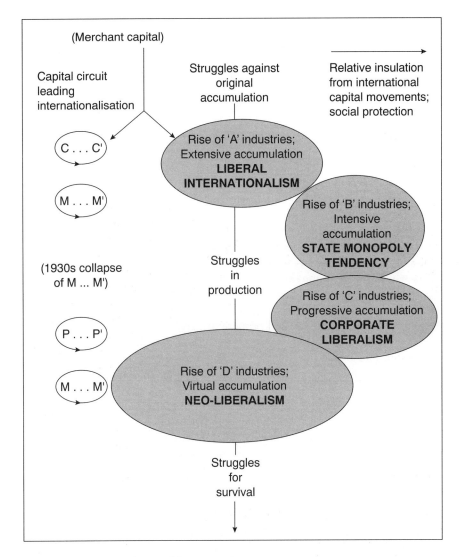

Figure 2.3 Concepts of control in perspective.

See also: Palloix 1974a, b; Andreff 1976.

3 The Lockean heartland in the international political economy

> The historical unity of the ruling classes is realised in the state, and their history is essentially the history of states and of groups of states.
>
> Antonio Gramsci

The historical formation of a capitalist class out of an aristocracy shifting to commercial land-ownership and a merchant community investing in domestic production took place in dialectical interplay with the crystallisation of a particular *state/society complex* on the British Isles. As Cox has argued (1986: 205), such complexes, rather than states *per se*, constitute the basic entities of international relations. Not only would the most important functions of the modern state, which can be summed up under the heading of sustaining total capital internally and externally, have no meaning without reference to the social substratum on which it is erected, but also, the transnational involvement of social classes cannot be assessed properly. In reality, all social action is simultaneously structured by the tendency towards global unification represented by capital, and by the fact that every concrete state/society complex is ultimately held together by a specific structure of power and authority mediating its relations with other such complexes.

In this chapter, we will analyse the growth of an organically unified group of states at the centre of the international political economy, of which the origins coincide with the primordial crystallisation of capital; as well as the successive appearance, on its horizon, of *contender states* challenging the pre-eminence of this original core, or as we call it, Lockean heartland.

The Lockean state/society complex

The Glorious Revolution of 1688 sealed the series of transformations by which the vestiges of royal absolutism and feudal forms of social protection in England had been torn down. Although it would take another century before the actual Industrial Revolution took place, the trend now was towards private enterprise employing wage labour. Parallel to it, overseas commercial and financial links were tendentially restructured into 'circuits of capital' connected to an industrial pivot. Britain soon was far ahead of other countries, and remained there for a full century. Still in 1860, the British Isles with two per cent of the world's population accounted for 40 to 45 per cent of world industrial production. As Senghaas (1982: 29) comments,

> when one considers international society in its entirety, there is no question that since the first industrial revolution in England, the major part of the world . . . was turned into a periphery and that only a small number of societies have succeeded in withstanding the pressure towards peripheralisation and achieve an autonomous, catch-up development.

The state/society complex sanctioned by the Glorious Revolution may be termed *Lockean* after the author of the *Two Treatises of Government* (although that book was only indirectly linked to the event; see Lasslet in Locke 1965: 60). The typical state/society complex of the countries resisting peripheralisation we will term *Hobbesian*, after the author of the *Leviathan*; a reference to the authoritarian prelude to Lockean liberalisation. Of course, a pure Lockean or Hobbesian state has never existed. Their authors were exploring possibilities for the ascendant social forces with which they sympathised and ended up with utopias on which these could set their sights (Kaviraj 1989: 170). Yet the models may serve as starting points for a concrete analysis.[1]

Merchant capital and commercially-minded land-owners have been active in many historical settings, but only in Western Europe did they encounter the particular balance between centralised state power and local self-regulation and initiative in which alone actual capital can come of age. A legal structure separating public from private law, defining *rights* not privileges, emerged only in Western Europe (Weber 1976: 394, 398). But as we can now reconstruct, if a 'civil society' (i.e. a society of property-owning individuals free to arrange their mutual relations legally and within certain limits, autonomously) is to emerge, the balance between the executive privilege of the state and the civil sphere has to be fine-tuned even further. The law itself has to be flexible and responsive to social development, following rather than leading it. Or, in Gramsci's words,

> the "juridical" continuity of the organised centre must be not of a Byzantine/Napoleonic type, i.e., according to a code conceived of as perpetual, but Roman/Anglo-Saxon – that is to say, a type whose essential characteristic consists in its method, which is realistic and always keeps close to concrete life in perpetual development (1971: 196).

The specifically British state/society complex, which turned out to combine the necessary preconditions to become the cradle of capital, has roots reaching back to the Middle Ages. The notion of a 'nightwatchman state' as often used to denote the nineteenth-century liberal British state is, as Barratt Brown (1988: 34) observes, a misleading term because it underestimates the highly centralised and effective state power established by the Norman invaders. The Plantagenets and Tudors further developed this state, but the original conditions under which it had been established, lingered on in the form of particular ideas about the *birthright* of Englishmen, and parallel institutions. The limits of the king's power in this respect were observed by the Lord Chancellor, 'Keeper of the king's conscience', who faced the 'Norman' king as an indigenous, 'Anglo-Saxon' confessor. When Henry VIII Tudor broke with the Church of Rome in 1534, Lord Chancellor Thomas More's failure to stop him and his subsequent execution have been interpreted as the ultimate source of the English revolution, determining its *political* character as a revolt against monarchical encroachment on the innate rights of Englishmen (Rosenstock-Huessy 1961: 293).

Birthright, 'English stock', was part of a long tradition of local autonomy, essentially self-rule of the aristocracy. As Justices of the Peace, their mandate laid down in parliamentary statutes, local lords administered justice with little formal reference (Trevelyan 1968: 197; Weber 1976: 471). The centralising state did impose royal authority at an early stage, but rather than seeking to crush local autonomies (churches, guilds, co-operatives, commons), it incorporated them into a national 'body politic', and feudal rights into a system of common law. In the sixteenth century, municipalities regained a degree of autonomy (Weber 1976: 435–6, 482). All this left a wide margin of local initiative and adaptation to specific circumstances.

The ascendant capitalist class, a commercial bourgeoisie as well as the aristocracy shifting to the commercial sources of income ('capitalisation of ground rent', in Poulantzas's words, 1971, 2: 179), in the seventeenth century aligned with the protestant sects against the king and the big company merchants who traded on account of royal privilege and who had become a conservative force resisting interlopers (Dobb 1963: 121–2). The newer bourgeoisie had a more specific need for state support – an aggressive foreign policy against commercial rivals for instance: Spain and later Holland (A. Callinicos in Gentles *et al.* 1994: 127).

Cromwell's Roundhead Commonwealth of 1649 served to break the 'private', patrimonial element in the state/society complex, synchronising social energies in order to advance English commercial interests along a broader front. The transition from privilege to generalised class ('national') interest was exemplified by the Navigation Act of 1651, which led to war with the Dutch Republic after an initial offer for a merger of the two protestant nations had been rejected by the Dutch (Geyl 1969: 82). But for an ascendant class like the English bourgeoisie, the tentacular, 'Hobbesian' state put in place by Cromwell soon became an obstacle again. The Restoration of 1660 restored aristocratic/bourgeois self-government and a market economy regulated by law – even more emphatically than it restored the monarchy as such (Trevelyan 1968: 285). As Christopher Hill has written:

Nobody, then, willed the English Revolution: it happened. But if we look at its outcome, when the idealists, the men of conscious will on either side had been defeated, what emerged was a state in which the administrative organs that most impeded capitalist development had been abolished ... in which the executive was subordinated to the men of property, deprived of control over the judiciary, and yet strengthened in external relations by a powerful navy and the Navigation Act (quoted in Gentles *et al.* 1994: 130).

The Glorious Revolution of 1688, again experienced as a *restoration* of rights (Rosenstock-Huessy 1961: 272), then sealed this 'Lockean' state/society complex against renewed encroachment by the monarchy and the church. From then on we can begin to speak of a *civil* society, a society from which the state has withdrawn after having imposed itself actively and constructively, shaping the institutions needed to permit the 'liberal' withdrawal from the sphere of wealth creation. This withdrawal leaves behind its traces in the form of the legal guarantee of private property and binding contract, as well as the infrastructure for their legal vindication without which 'civil' self-regulation would soon degenerate into violence again. Thus the property-owning classes obtain their autonomy from the state and the freedom to exploit whatever human or natural riches the world has to offer.

Transnationalisation of the Lockean pattern

The eventual Lockean state/society-complex rested on a transnational society well before the writing of the *Two Treatises of Government*. Overseas settlement, for religious as well as commercial reasons, predated the outbreak of Civil War in England. London private houses such as the Virginia Company and the Massachusetts Bay Company between 1630 and 1643 transferred tens of thousands of settlers to North America. With them went the pattern of local self-government which Tocqueville equates with democracy (1990, 1: 31–5). When the activist state set up by Cromwell began to directly interfere with colonisation as well, the undercurrent in state/society relations towards the Lockean pattern was already beyond its power to change (Trevelyan 1968: 245). In the New England colonies, ruling family dynasties were largely identical with local church authorities in the seventeenth century; while in the eighteenth, they owed their status to the hereditary privilege of representing a particular colony in its dealings with the mother country. 'But in all [American] colonies,' Heide Gerstenberger writes (1973: 85), 'the rise of the leading families was intimately connected with the realisation of *structures of effective self-government.*'

   The Glorious Revolution and the changes it codified were an expression of this transnational pattern of self-regulation as well. It 'not only realized the project of 1640–1641 of the parliamentary capitalist aristocracy,' Robert Brenner concludes. 'In so doing it also realized ... the project of 1649–1653 of its leading allies outside the landed classes, the American colonial and east-Indian interloping [merchants'] leadership' (quoted in Gentles *et al.* 1994: 108). Locke's writings actually had been inspired by his experiences in the American colonies, and according to the editor of his writings, his concept of self-regulation was even directly modelled on the relations within and between North American planters' families (Lasslet in Locke 1965: 277 note).

In the eighteenth and nineteenth centuries, emigration assumed epic proportions, spreading to Canada, Australia, New Zealand, and Southern Africa. Between 1812 and 1914, more than twenty million people emigrated from Britain (Gallagher and Robinson 1967: 237). Although by then, immigrants of non-British descent were numerically stronger in the United States, social and immigration restrictions served to sustain the dominant position of the white Anglo-Saxon protestants (Nederveen Pieterse 1990: 270). Tocqueville (1990, 1: 248) thought that by escaping the aristocratic spirit of society, the immigrants in the United States acquired an even greater respect for the law, which is the cornerstone of civil society, than Europeans. Self-regulation in turn led to prosperity. 'The prodigious commercial activity of the inhabitants [of the United States] ... is not created by the laws, but the people learn how to promote it by the experience derived from legislation' (ibid.: 251; see also Gramsci 1971: 20).

What held the English-speaking world together and facilitated the erection of the common arrangements and institutions to which we will turn presently, more basically was the notion of origin, blood tie, which was the spiritual novelty of the English revolution compared to earlier world-views defined in terms of religious authority, or the later republicanism of the French Revolution. As Rosenstock-Huessy (1961: 270) has argued, the English took this concept of 'English stock' with them to all areas of their overseas settlement; it was expressed both in the puritanism and the Old Testamentic allegories of a 'chosen people' (for a striking example of twentieth-century protestant fundamentalism's Anglo-American fantasies, see Armstrong 1980); and in the notion of birthright, going back to the Norman conquest and the Magna Carta. This latter aspect, to which we referred already, has turned each revolution and many political movements into a reassertion of self-regulation, a *restoration* of innate rights against the encroaching monarch or state.

When the American bourgeoisie liberated itself from the encroaching British state, the initial impulse was to draft the contours of a strong federal government. However, against the project of Hamilton and his fellow financiers and merchants, a planter bloc led by Jefferson and Madison promptly began campaigning for limiting its powers (Ferguson 1995: 52–3). Jefferson did differ from Locke – his concept of an innate right to work the soil ('the earth is given as a common stock for man to labor & live on') has democratic implications absent from Locke's natural right to property, and reflects the influence of Rousseau (Gerstenberger 1973: 163). But under capitalist conditions, this potential remained secondary to the Lockean emphasis on a self-regulating civil society. It is in this sense that, repeated incursions of interventionism notwithstanding, Jeffersonianism 'has unequivocally been victorious not only in the "Revolution of 1800", but also in later American history as the interpretive frame of the foundations and goals of American society' (ibid.: 145). Whenever a Hamiltonian countermovement occurred, as in the New Deal, it resulted from demands made on the state by society under a certain concept of control (state monopolism or corporate liberalism), never from the confiscation of the social sphere by the state which is typical of the Hobbesian configuration.

The centrifugal element which plagued the British Empire paradoxically allowed the real common bond to be asserted after each rupture (it was Jefferson's party which initially persisted in an anti-British attitude (Ferguson 1995: 53–4)). The common Lockean heritage not only fostered broadly congruent social arrangements, centring on what Gramsci calls 'the implacable play of free competition' by which the state is 'purged of its noxious elements through the free clash of bourgeois social forces' (1977: 46). It also consisted in comparable attitudes on how to deal with class conflict: ideally, challenges were to be met by deflecting popular aspirations into a synthetic, 'social–imperialist', moral internationalism, in which the export and overseas investment ambitions of capital imperceptibly merged with a missionary concept of democracy, human rights, and other 'universalist' aspects of Lockean doctrine (Nairn 1973: 68–76). As this perspective was necessarily inscribed in an expansionist process, it included the common identification of Hobbesian states as structural obstacles to internationalism.

There is no question that the Lockean state/society complex by itself would be superior to its Hobbesian counterpart – or even less so, that destiny or history 'chose' England or the US for anything. It merely constituted, on a historical trajectory in which chance elements and conditions not of a social origin (such as island location, etc.) played a large part, the terrain on which the capitalist mode of production finally crystallised in the eighteenth century. There was no inherent English advance position – indeed, often it was backwardness which created the favourable circumstances for capital accumulation. Thus Weber argues that contrary to the idea of progressive rationalisation, the English system of law with its many feudal elements and guild-like professional structures, in terms of its suitability for a capitalist system has proven superior to the continental, rational–institutionalised system of law, and has crowded out the latter wherever the two could compete directly, as in Canada (Weber 1976: 511).

What we have to retain is that with the Lockean pattern transmitted to the new areas of settlement, there emerged, on the foundations of industrial/commercial centrality and predominance, a *heartland* of the global political economy. As a transnational society it generated shared experiences and outlook, irrespective of whether or not its actual members were conscious of being part of it (Trevelyan 1968: 633; Hall 1971: 106).

Infrastructure of the heartland

The Lockean state was part of the complex of forces that shaped the liberal internationalist concept of control, and henceforth would remain a cornerstone of capital's collective arrangements. But this did not mean that it would dissolve itself into a *laissez-faire* void on the first occasion, on the contrary. The liberal state, Mayall notes, 'was limited, but within its proper sphere, strong,' and there even operated what he calls 'a concealed *etatism*' in the assumption that only the state could provide the framework of law and order to society and market economy. On that basis, world market competition could do its beneficial work, enriching the world community on balance but retaining the state as the sovereign party to international commercial exchanges and as repository of the 'comparative advantages' on which they flourished (Mayall 1990: 76). British tariffs during its industrial revolution and still in the first half of the nineteenth century ranged between 30 per cent and 50 per cent (Reuveny and Thompson 1997: 204–5).

As with many other instances of market economy, comparative advantages beyond agriculture did not arise spontaneously but had to be established by state intervention first. Thus the US in 1864 abandoned the liberal trade policy it had adhered to in the period of *rapprochement* with Britain after 1823, and the new high-tariff policy outlasted the Civil War emergency (Bagwell and Mingay 1987: 103). From that moment on began the American ascent to the position of an industrial rival, which fed on British money capital and people, reproduced the mother country's liberal internationalism, and partly *enlarged*, partly *replaced*, Britain's pre-eminence in the heartland and beyond.

Enlarged, because on the basis of kindred civil societies increasingly entwined by transnational circuits of capital, a process of socialisation was set in motion which spliced off certain tasks from the national states and recast them into quasi-state structures on the international level. The British Empire here paved the way for several institutional innovations which typically bore the Lockean imprint.

Replaced, because every separate state is also a structure of socialisation in which a historically concrete configuration of classes has become entrenched (see also Bettelheim 1972: 295). Therefore, as Cox notes (1987: 253), 'the tendency toward the internationalizing of the state is never complete, and the further it advances, the more it provokes countertendencies sustained by domestic social groups that have been disadvantaged or excluded in the new domestic realignments'. On top of the resilience of the single state as a cohesive social structure comes the magical sacrality of its authority, its power over life and death, which it partly derives from containing an imagined community.

The growth of a Lockean heartland accordingly involves, in addition to a transnationalisation of civil society, the restructuring of state power along two axes: one of international socialisation of state functions, the other of a struggle for primacy between the states between which these functions are to be shared.

Along either axis evolves an immanent 'world state' sustaining total capital on a global scale by upholding the Lockean state/society complex and the specific arrangements it defines – separation of politics from economics, a 'level playing field' in competition, individual freedom under the law, etc. In this sense Britain in the *Pax Britannica* enjoyed an unwritten superior right to intervention on behalf of private-property-owning humanity. The United States under the Monroe Doctrine assumed this task for the Western Hemisphere and later in the *Pax Americana,* and the notion of 'humanitarian intervention' has retained a distinct Anglo-Saxon resonance in the tradition of international law (Malanczuk 1993: 10). The two main elements of the state role for total capital, the monopoly of violence and functions with respect to money capital, can be seen to have evolved to the international level through a process in which conflictual and integrative moments alternated. Let us briefly review these moments.

Global money capital was initially anchored in the British state. Until the Glorious Revolution, the role of the world's banker had not been centralised in this sense. As Homer (1963: 122) writes, 'Only a little before 1700, when Dutch financial principles were brought to England by William III and his Whig supporters and were there greatly improved upon, did the history of modern banking and credit really start.' 'Within the first few decades of the century, England improved upon the Italian banking techniques and upon the Dutch principles of funded debt,' the same author continues, so that

> By the 1720s the English national credit could be effectively pledged behind the loans of the government in the manner of the mediaeval Italian republics, the provinces of seventeenth-century Holland, and modern democracies (ibid.: 149, see also 147).

The Lockean setting was crucial, because the fact that William of Orange was constitutional king implied that he borrowed in the name of the people rather than as a princely individual, which created a new type of security. The Bank of England was set up to express this pattern, and as industrial capital accumulation took off in the next century, would assume the quality of what we may term the central state/money capital nexus.

From the 1840s to World War I, the circuit of money capital and mass migration from the British Isles to the US combined the two economies into a single Atlantic one. Not only were 'long swings in the economic development of the United Kingdom and the United States . . . inverse to one another' (Thomas 1968: 47), but after 1870, Canada, Australia, and Argentina, too, became part of this vast swing mechanism connecting raw-material-producing, capital-importing countries into the circuit of money capital centred on London (Williamson 1968: 82). As to trade finance, British credit was the pivot on which world trade revolved. Especially once the Franco-Prussian War undermined the position of the Paris money market, the City became 'the one important free market for buying and selling gold'. Under the Gold Standard, foreign bankers after the 1870s began holding Treasury bills in London to have a ready potential to obtain gold in emergencies (Bagwell and Mingay 1987: 137). American foreign trade, too, until 1914 was mostly financed in sterling by London banks (Clarke 1967: 22).

Of the two functions of global money capital, loan capital invested for profit (M ... M') and money-dealing capital lubricating international trade (C ... M ...C), the former in 1914 lost its mooring in the City of London. The United States for the greater part of the nineteenth century had done without a central bank and its highly decentralised banking system worked with private notes, ungummed stamps, and counterfeit money on a vast scale (Bagwell and Mingay 1987: 138–9). But the suspension of gold payments by the belligerents in August 1914 was seized upon by a syndicate of Wall Street bankers with the help of the Secretary of the Treasury and the Federal Reserve Board, created only a year before, to turn New York into the world's banking centre 'almost overnight' (Faulkner 1968: 34). Although New York banks controlled only 18 per cent of US bank capital in 1912, their political connections made up for their economic weakness, and the war would turn around the Atlantic circuit of money capital as J.P. Morgan and other US banks financed the Entente and postwar reconstruction (Kolko 1976: 4; Ridgeway 1938: 68–9). As to commercial credit, Germany, by 1914, had practically succeeded in its fight for the introduction of mark acceptance in overseas trade alongside the universal sterling bill (Magdoff and Sweezy 1983: 5), but London could recover after the war, albeit increasingly as an 'offshore' centre divorced from the actual British economy.

In the meantime, the overarching political structure of the heartland had become much more integrated. Britain in 1887 began organising the Imperial Conferences to tie the self-governing Dominions more closely to its foreign policy again. At the 1911 Imperial Conference, the British Commonwealth was established and simultaneously, its foreign policy delegated to Britain (Hall 1971: 67). In the same year, the Arbitration Treaty between the US and Britain outlawed war between the two countries as a means of conflict resolution. Thus for the first time, with new contenders appearing on the horizon and a European conflagration imminent, the Lockean states drew together politically, placing themselves outside the Hobbesian universe of *Realpolitik* in their mutual relations.

In conjunction with capital flows providing the circulatory system for a transnational civil society, the Commonwealth model (of which the US was a silent partner) created a loose and highly flexible structure of sovereign states, 'a system of interlinked groups, organizations and societies within the greater community [which] was able to avoid in very large measure the growth of rigidities and compartmentalization in its political, economic and social structure' (Hall 1971: 106). Flexibility was achieved partly by transnational policy planning groups such as the Round Table which often charted the course that international bodies later were to follow, as in the case of the Commonwealth (Quigley 1981); or by recruiting groups of experts on particular issues, who likewise performed an 'intellectual' function. The inter-mediary between such private networks and the actual international quasi-state structure was a *secretariat* preparing meetings and deciding over the agenda. The British Committee on Imperial Defence pioneered this secretariat func-tion also for the League of Nations that was to carry on crucial aspects of the Commonwealth in its organisational pattern (Jordan 1971; see also Murphy 1994: ch. 2).

The Bolshevik revolution forced the elements of international socialisation which had already been developed, or which had been pioneered by pooling allied supply requirements during the war, to the surface (Haas 1964: 140–1). As part of the League of Nations system, they now served to control Germany and contain revolutionary socialism. 'During the war,' Gramsci observed in 1919, 'to meet the demands of the struggle against imperial Germany, the states making up the Entente formed a reactionary coalition with its economic functions powerfully centralized in London and its demagogy choreographed in Paris'. This apparatus had now become available to 'Anglo-Saxon world hegemony' (Gramsci 1977: 81). In fact, as Jean Monnet, the later architect of European integration, found out during his attempts to interest the US representative, Herbert Hoover, in participating in the joint administrative bodies set up to sustain this 'powerful centralisation', the Americans consid-ered them first of all as levers of British control of world raw material supplies (Monnet 1976: 85). Their retreat from Wilson's projection of a collective secu-rity system under the League made clear that the real social foundations, including the internationalisation of production, did not yet warrant the costs of prolonged US intervention in European affairs.

In 1921, the international conference on arms limitation convened in Washington. US Secretary of State Hughes in his invitation to the four great naval powers (Britain, France, Italy and Japan) expressly suggested a British delegation of six so that the Dominions would be able to take part. This change in atmosphere, Hall claims (1971: 461), 'was due in part to the Ameri-can discovery that Anglo–American relations now meant Commonwealth–American relations – a linking up of the English-speaking peoples'. The Washington Conference in this respect proceeded in a better spirit than Versailles, but this mainly resulted from the fact that 'the Commonwealth had surrendered the lead to the United States, partly out of its own weak-ness, and partly in the hope that this Conference could be the prelude to the fulfilment by the United States of the role of world leadership now open to it' (ibid.: 469). Such a US posture would not materialise for another twenty years though. Certain circles in the UK, Carr wrote at the time, during that period clung to 'the dream that British supremacy, instead of passing alto-gether away, would be transmuted into the higher and more effective form of an ascendancy of the English-speaking peoples'. From this perspective,

The *pax Britannica* will be put into commission and become a *pax Anglo-Saxonica*, under which the British Dominions, standing half-way between the mother country and the United States, will be cunningly woven into a fabric of Anglo-American co-operation (Carr 1964: 232).

But the bloc of interests supporting the interwar Republican Administrations, notably Hoover's, did not shrink from using German recovery in Europe, and Japan's ascendancy in Asia, as levers to quietly unhinge Britain's global pre-eminence in the context of friendship (Ziebura 1984: 32–4). Under the surface of co-operation (as with the Anglo-American monetary co-operation agreement of 1934, which made parity changes conditional on prior consultation – an agreement to which France acceded in 1936), the US carefully avoided shoring up the British position – in this case, sterling's (Palyi 1960: 29).

What characterised the period was not primarily the contingent 'Anglo-Saxon' bond, but the specific Lockean state/society complex which, at the national as well as the transnational level, secured the sovereignty of civil society over (quasi-)state structures by maximising the element of civil, *private* monitoring. Transnational extension of this state/society complex could only come about if the international quasi-state structures such as those of the League were in reality subordinated to private forces – and these for historical reasons were entwined with national complexes still struggling for pre-eminence. In the League period, the pattern of private and informal semi-public policy preparation and public decision-making that characterised the Commonwealth (i.e. Private planning group – Secretariat – Formal institution), can be seen to have worked for instance in the case of international business taxation. As Picciotto (1989) has shown, when the League's Fiscal Committee was stalled on this issue, only the informal coming together of experts from interested countries (including the US, not then a League member) with the assistance of the International Chamber of Commerce could eventually bring forth the desired model treaty. Some of the earlier international organisations such as the original International Labour Office, precursor of the ILO (International Labour Organization of 1919), and the International Railway Congress Association even were set up as private associations to avoid diplomatic complications, although their membership was predominantly made up of government institutions (Murphy 1994: 81). Every attempt to reach beyond the informal, 'functional' pattern of transnational co-operation was bound to fail on account of the fundamental incompatibility of formalised international state power with the Lockean context and requirements of transnational capital accumulation in the heartland states.

The postwar special relationship

Although the question of British versus US primacy still hung in the balance, the challenge mounted by the Axis powers projecting rival 'Grand Areas' (the German *Grossraumwirtschaft*, Japan's Co-Prosperity Sphere, and the *mare nostro* of Mussolini's Italy) had to be confronted together. Nevertheless, World

War II was a period of intense interallied manoeuvring for position (Kolko 1968). In the Cold War confrontation that emerged from it, Britain was locked into a 'special relationship'. This bond, which did not exclude moments of intense rivalry, constituted the core to which other states could accede in a manner often reminiscent of prior Anglo-American haggling. Just as the US had warded off British commercial penetration, and Britain resisted American pre-eminence after the war, so the contender states integrated into the postwar Western bloc put up resistance to it. But this, as much as the entire contender state phase leading up to it, did not signify resistance to integration *per se*. Such resistance rather signals an aspiration to *improve the conditions on which integration is to proceed, not a real wish to remain outside* (Clarke 1978: 62). Inter-state rivalry therefore not only preceded integration; it was absorbed into it, transformed but not eliminated. (Of course, as we shall see, the legacy of the Hobbesian state/society complex here also put up obstacles to integration of a more structural nature.)

Looking now at the main forms of integration in this light, the *United Nations* is the overarching structure of postwar internationalisation of the state. It was the result of Anglo-American consultations charting its overall orientation – from the Atlantic Charter of 1941, through the endorsement of the Charter's Wilsonian principles by European exile governments in London in January 1942, to the actual establishment of the UN and the symbolic setting up of headquarters in New York. At each step, Britain struggled to retain privileged imperial access against US Open Door pressures, but ultimately yielded to superior power. As with the League of Nations, the heartland states' ruling classes have always remained suspicious of universal international organisa-tion (see also Quigley 1966: 582). With the Soviet Union (but not the defeated Axis Powers) represented on the Security Council, and a growing majority of decolonised states voting in the General Assembly, the peoples' organisation was under constant suspicion of drifting out of its founders' control. More particularly, in the 1970s drive for a New International Economic Order (NIEO, Cox 1979), the basic Lockean framework became contested when the Third World countries, or the South, as Krasner puts it (1985: 124) '[was] able to take two legacies of the North – the organization of political units into sovereign states and the structure of existing international organizations – and use them to disrupt, if not replace market-oriented regimes over a wide range of issues'. Concerned over the 'Hobbesian' drift towards a state-moni-tored global political economy, the US and the UK and some lesser allies walked out of several UN functional organisations or stopped paying their dues. Private planning groups and consultative networks providing a parallel terrain of debate – reserved to the heartland's representatives and closed to public scrutiny – such as the Trilateral Commission set up in the same period (the TC incidentally is headquartered in the UN building in New York), advocated alternative structures of high-level consultation likewise confined to the metropolitan states and the EC, of which the G-7 is the most important (Gill 1991; Novak 1980).

A multilateral military arm of the UN necessarily remained a paper construction. *NATO* was formally constituted under article 51 of the UN Charter, the
article dealing with collective self-defence, but the organisation in fact was
another instance of US/Commonwealth collusion. As Wiebes and Zeeman
have shown (1983, 1993), secret negotiations between British, Canadian and
United States diplomats to link the US to the Brussels Treaty between the
UK, France and the Benelux countries, and openly deploy it against the Soviet
Union, already began in March 1948. It was to the structure created around
this Atlantic core that the other states were admitted, with the dividing lines
between the heartland and states committed to their own international sphere
of influence clearly transpiring though. France, challenging the US nuclear
monopoly, withdrew again from the military command structure in 1965.
West Germany could only be admitted in 1955 after France had obtained
the means to impose checks on German rearmament through a revamped
Western European Union (the Brussels Treaty organisation). With the demise
of the Soviet bloc, NATO has spectacularly moved to the forefront as the
military arm of the UN (in former Yugoslavia). This is still one step further
than the 'selection', in the war with Iraq, of the US, Britain, and France as
the UN forces, under American command (rather than under the Military
Staff Committee envisaged in article 46 of the UN Charter to assist the Security
Council in military action). Whether NATO's current expansionist posture in
Central and Eastern Europe will allow this role to be continued and developed, of course remains to be seen.

An aspect closely linked to military organisation (especially in light of
NATO's preoccupation with internal security), *intelligence*, likewise was built
around Anglo-American collusion. Under the UKUSA agreement of 1947,
wartime intelligence co-operation between the white English-speaking states
was formalised. The agreement concerned signal intelligence (SIGINT) and
was concluded between the US and Britain, Canada, Australia and New
Zealand (Richelson and Ball 1990: 5). This agreement was later expanded, both
functionally into other areas of intelligence and security, and in terms of third
parties: West Germany, Denmark, Norway, Japan and South Korea. The
organisation of a NATO infrastructure for clandestine violence, 'Gladio', originally envisaged as a 'stay-behind' guerrilla core but actually serving as an
armed wing of the Far Right in several countries, upon its disclosure proved
also present in apparently 'neutral' states such as Austria, Switzerland, and
Sweden (Müller 1991: 57–60). In all cases, these bodies were secret not only to
the population but often to host countries' governments as well. Intelligence co-
operation also linked such imperialist outposts as Israel and South Africa to the
heartland infrastructure. In 1979, co-operation in the signal intelligence field
was even extended to China (Richelson and Ball 1990: 171). But the core structure has remained under the founder states' control, and tensions, notably with
France and Japan, have flared up in the recent period (Schweizer 1993).

Turning to the international financial and monetary field, the conference
of Bretton Woods which created IMF and World Bank extended particular

functions of the US Federal Reserve to the multilateral plane. It too grew out of Anglo-American consultations in which a plan proposed by Harry Dexter White, acting for Treasury Secretary Morgenthau, faced one of British negotiator Keynes (Kolko 1968: 255–6). US conceptions carried the day, and Britain's strategy of entrenching in a sterling trade area even proved detrimental in the longer run – it accentuated its decline by cutting it off from industrial innovation along Fordist lines in continental Western Europe (Burnham 1990: 177). Meanwhile enhanced and expanded (with the body created by the Marshall Plan, today's OECD; as well as regional Development Banks up to the EBRD for post-Soviet Eastern Europe), the heartland infrastructure most directly pertaining to capital accumulation has reproduced the pattern set by the Commonwealth experience in that it remains highly secretive and dependent on informal policy preparation. Thus the officially 'open' structure of the IMF for instance is counterbalanced by a series of informal back channels. 'The group of 22 member states that guides IMF policy has been called "Interim Committee" since 1974,' Nitsch (1987: 39) writes.

> But it is no longer active on an interim basis, because the "Council" for which it would perform this task has never been established. Moreover, it is significant that the "Interim Committee" has no formal decision-making powers, but only an advisory role, so that even within the IMF the Staff, the "Board", which is superior, but only seldom meets, and the "Committee" can hide behind each other or behind "objective necessity".

This underscores Robert Cox's comment that while 'There is no explicit political or authority structure for the global economy, there is, nevertheless, something there that remains to be deciphered, something that could be described by the French word *nébuleuse* or by the notion of "governance without government"' (1996: 301). Especially now that the United States has become a capital-importing country, and its and Britain's pre-eminence in terms of foreign direct investment is eroding (from two-thirds of total FDI stock to 49 per cent in 1988 (Stopford and Strange 1991: 17), this *nébuleuse* has come to directly refer to a denationalised, total capital on a world scale.

The question how such a transnationally operating economy can still be *taxed* by states, also may be considered part of the terrain on which a Lockean international structure has been established (and incidentally has proved capable of defeating alternative proposals to impose taxes on business in the NIEO framework or related schemes, see also my 1993b). Building on pre-war negotiations in the League of Nations context referred to above, tax concepts typical of the Anglo-American notions about fairness and trust entered into the hegemonic canon around which the eventual postwar structure developed. In his study on international business taxation, Sol Picciotto writes that 'a turning-point in the development of international tax arrangements was the successful negotiation of a US–UK treaty in 1944–5. The agreement reached by these two powerful states, each with its own network of international relations, was the key to the development of the postwar system of tax treaties' (Picciotto 1992: 39).

Although none of the above international quasi-state structures are immune to mutation away from their Lockean foundations, or from control by the US or an English-speaking combine, so far they have been capable of largely absorbing and coopting the challenges mounted from the alternative, Hobbesian perspective. To this we now turn.

Contender states and the Hobbesian counterpoint

While in the English-speaking world, the rise of a bourgeoisie profited from the strong tradition of local self-government that could survive the Hobbesian interlude, in the countries resisting peripheralisation by the Lockean heartland, the strong state, once put in place, proved less easy to transcend. Forced by the overwhelming reality of a more powerful heartland as well as by a relatively backward degree of social cohesion, the state role here tends to become congealed in the moment of national unification, the moment, say, of the Navigation Act in Britain. At that point, the state, in Max Weber's words, is engaged in 'melting all other associations which have been sources of law into the one coercive institution of the state (*'staatliche Zwangsanstalt'*) which now claims to be the source of all "legitimate" law' (1976: 397).

In the process, the differentiation between state and society is suspended as the state gravitates to a position in which it becomes the subject of social development, too. 'Economics and politics are articulated in the bosom of the state; this state brings forth social relations which react on it, it is the producer and the product of these relations,' writes Lefebvre (1976: 36). Hence the difference, typical of the Lockean configuration, between a social *ruling class* and a *governing class* managing the state for it, is suspended as well. Here we must go back to the question, which kind of social force actually stood at the cradle of the modern state once aristocratic rule, including the patrimonial monarch's, was dislodged.

As suggested already, the bourgeois revolution was never the revolution of the bourgeoisie (which could be found on both sides in most cases). It was made by revolutionaries clearing the way for a bourgeois order, and the same goes for other 'national', or worker revolutions. Thus Gramsci writes of the Roundheads that they 'imposed themselves on the bourgeoisie, leading it into a far more advanced position than the originally strongest bourgeois nuclei would have spontaneously wished to take up' (1971: 77). The followers of Cromwell acted as a vanguard holding the state in trust for the ascendant social class. So did, still according to Gramsci, the Jacobins, and we might add, the Bolsheviks, who assumed a comparable task for the proletariat; Castro's guerrilla army, etc. But not every *équipe* seizing power for a class appearing on the horizon, and forcing the social formation into its progressive configuration, can subsequently be dislodged by the main social force for which it clears the way. In Britain, the bourgeoisie came on the heels of its vanguard, ready to take its place. This ensured that the situation remained fluid; political structures were not allowed to harden in the mould of the moment. But in the contender states, the vanguard is not likewise dislodged as soon as the ascendant class is 'in place' socially; as the process of class formation proceeds more slowly and the distance between vanguard and main force (if any) is greater, temporary structures get a chance to crystallise and become encrusted in institutions. Under such conditions, state power becomes subject to bureaucratisation, society is con- fiscated by the state and state power turned against anyone resisting it. The resulting state/society complex we call Hobbesian.

The main external factor congealing the Hobbesian configuration is of course the existence of a more advanced state/society complex, which by its transnational expansion has already occupied the international terrain commercially and culturally, whereas the contender state still is struggling to forge national/state unity and demarcate its territory. Therefore the bureau- cratised vanguard cannot and will not relinquish state power; the Glorious Revolution by which the ascendant class confirms its primacy and the relative autonomy of society *vis-à-vis* the state, is postponed. We will term the bureaucratised vanguard (which also may have its origins in the armed forces, or even in the old regime assuming a 'revolutionary' posture) a *state class* because its power primarily resides in its hold of the state apparatus rather than in a self-reproducing social base (see Cox 1987: 366–7; Fernández Jilberto 1988: 55; Elsenhans 1991: 44).

The Hobbesian state/society complex

France is the prototype of the Hobbesian contender state. 'French society of the seventeenth and eighteenth centuries,' Barrington Moore observes (1981: 58), 'presents us with an illuminating mixture of competing traits that scholars sometimes regard as characteristically Western and characteristically Oriental.' Here the kings ruled by dispatching governors and royal officials to the provinces, and 'the impulse toward establishing the bases of a modern society, i.e., a unified state and even some of the habits of precision and obedience, came much more from the royal bureaucracy than from the bourgeoisie' (ibid.: 57). The tendency of the latter to cling to state power in the above sense of a state class (lured for instance by the sale of bureaucratic positions) was mani- fest well before the revolution of 1789.

France's effort to mobilise social energies in a state-led development effort follows what Tocqueville (1990, 1: 86–7) calls the method of *centralised admin- istration* (in distinction from, and coming on top of, centralised *government*). Tocqueville already concluded that such a state strategy in the long run exhausted a country's creative energies, even if it could profit from the total mobilisation of resources in the short run. In the case of France, a contem- porary critic (Cohen-Tanugi 1987: 6) has observed that the drain exerted by the tentacular state is still today a brake on society's capacity to engage in transnational competition.

Meant originally to accompany the development of civil society, state tutelage often ends up constituting an obstacle to that development. Even disregarding authoritarian regimes, a tentacular state most often represents a weak society, if only for the "crowding out" effect operative between the one and the other. In the case of France, it is clear that the channelling of élites through the system of the prestigious schools, the economic-financial drainage of resources realised by fiscal and para-fiscal means, as well as the statisation of society, permanently effectuate a gigantic transfer of human and material resources and responsibilities from society to the state, which, enriching the latter to the point of saturation, necessarily impoverishes the former.

What, then, is the nature of the relations of production by which contender states beginning with France have attempted to confront, and catch up with, the Lockean heartland? Looking at late industrialisation as such in the sense of Gerschenkron and others (for an overview, see Schwartz 1994: ch. 4), cannot answer this question entirely. One might say that by aiming to catch up with the leading social system of production in the world economy, every contender state has by definition been 'capitalist' already before it 'turned capitalist' in those cases where an explicit turn-about was necessary in light of previous self-identifications – as in the case of contemporary Russia. This has always been the implication of Frank's (1975) and Wallerstein's (1979, 1984) thesis of a capitalist world economy. And even beyond this categoric statement, the actual cases of late industrialisation are replete with references to merchants, banks, foreign capital, etc. (see also Schwartz 1994).

Yet the specificity of the Hobbesian configuration resides (to varying degrees of course) in the paramountcy of the state as the institution driving forward the social formation and pre-emptively shaping, by action, sometimes *revolution* from above, the social institutions which have evolved 'organically', if not necessarily autonomously, in the heartland. Therefore, even capitalist firms (in their capacity of 'particular capitals') in the domestic context relate, not to the self-regulating market ('total capital') as the comprehensive social structure, but to the state first. The socialisation of labour here is primarily if not entirely shaped by the territorial confines of the single state. The sovereign state, rather than capital, ultimately determines the status of social actors and constrains for instance their capacity to articulate their interests in the transnational space dominated by the Anglo-Saxon ruling class, the flexibility that goes with such informal consultation, and integration.

Therefore, we might employ Henri Lefebvre's (1977) notion of a *state mode of production* to denote the type of relations of production in which economic development of the Hobbesian state/society complex proceeds. The relative backwardness and social heterogeneity of the social substratum, the coincidence of several historical stages of social development within a single sovereign jurisdiction, sometimes further confounded by national/ethnic and religious divisions, all require the permanent presence and priority of the state as the

Figure 3.1 Challenging the more developed world with pride, toil and muscle:
left-hand panel, *Friendship of the People* (1924, detail), Soviet painting,
© Novosti Press Agency, USSR; right-hand panel, *The Three Sowings*
(*c.* 1940, detail), Italian Fascist painting by Arnaldo Carpanetti
(1898–1969), © Moro, Rome.

driving force of economic development (Houweling 1996: 144). Social forces
are shaped pre-emptively, often violently, from above, rather than formed
organically on the ground of social development and production; accordingly,
they remain dependent on the state for their existence – their 'class' organisations, parties, employer and even trade unions, are in effect state institutions.
Hence the designation 'state class', but also the corporatist organisation of
economic interests and the sometimes enlightened authoritarianism of the
Hobbesian state. As Gramsci writes (1971: 262), the interventionist state 'is
connected on the one hand with tendencies supporting protection and economic nationalism, and on the other with the attempt to force a particular
state personnel . . . to take on the "protection" of the working classes against
the excesses of capitalism'. Hence the 'humanistic' idealisation of the worker
and his dependants, vulnerable and yet capable of taking on the more powerful
and developed world with their bare hands (Figure 3.1).

This idealisation of the human substratum on which the contender state
mounts its challenge to the heartland is of course functional and aesthetical
rather than the expression of real popular democracy. The people, however
praised and celebrated, are not supposed to act in any way other than
contributing their energy to the collective effort. Indeed, the capacity of the
Hobbesian state to digest social tensions in a flexible way is severely constrained

by its confiscation of the social sphere, benevolent or not. This is one more criterion by which it is distinct from the Lockean counterpart. The circulation of different concepts of control, one of which becomes comprehensive by its greater adequacy to a material constellation of forces, can only be a feature of the Lockean setting. This includes its permeability to the outside world, from the outside in and vice versa; without, though, suspending the integrity of the single state. Indeed, as Holman argues (1997: 14), 'the state forms the political framework within which internationally operating concepts of control can be synthesized with particular national political cultures, attitudes, constitutional arrangements, etc., or, conversely, the very medium through which national, hegemonic concepts of control can transcend national frontiers'.

A Hobbesian state, on the other hand, ideally is closed off from these transnational processes. All political energies are contained within the state, and conflicts have to be solved there. Accordingly, a compromised and deadlocked policy endangers the state class and the order it represents directly; the state class cannot, at least not to the same degree, hide behind a governing class as the ruling class in the heartland can. This explains also why in metropolitan capitalist countries with a strong Hobbesian legacy like France or Japan, the alternation of government may entail constitutional crises and occasionally, the demise of an entire party system.

This does not mean that the political process is stifled as a terrain of struggle. The state classes of various function and orientation have to reckon with domestic social forces developing surreptitiously, 'molecularly' in the direction of the pattern prevailing in the heartland; if only as a consequence of the very transformations that are being wrought by the revolutions from above. This process is captured by Gramsci (1971: 114) in his concept of *passive revolution*. At some point (and here, the political orientation of the state class and the stringency of state control are of course crucial determinants) this social stratum is bound to surface and constitute itself as a class. Capital links, integration into transnational élite networks, and eventually, a class struggle with the state class of the type that dislodged the Roundheads in seventeenth-century England, will eventually accompany the belated repeat performance of the Glorious Revolution. This struggle also may involve an opportunistic change of colour, just as part of the Roundhead élite survived as Whig lords under the new order. To this aspect we will return in the next chapter.

In Table 3.1, the main characteristics of the Lockean and Hobbesian state/society complexes have been summed up.

To the concrete picture that can be constructed on the basis of this classification, we have to add a third, residual ideal type, the *proto-state*. By this concept, Cox (1987: 230) broadly refers to the situation in which the differentiation between state and society is still to come and authority is still part of a community framework, or imposed from abroad. Houweling (1996: 162) writes in this connection that 'most "Third World" states are able to penetrate society to a certain extent by means of violence, but find it difficult to regulate behaviour by administrative means' – which is why often, pre-state

Table 3.1 The Lockean and Hobbesian state/society complexes

	Lockean	*Hobbesian*
Privileged terrain of social action	Civil society	State
Framework for interest articulation	Transcendent comprehensive concept of control	Explicit doctrine of national interest
Ruling class	Bourgeoisie (with governing class)	State class
Mode of regulation	Self-regulating market (civil law)	Centralised administration
Mode of expansion	Transnational	International

institutions and authority survive in the context of an effectively malfunctioning state.

Structural aspects of world politics

Beginning with the Anglo-French confrontation, we may reinterpret the structure of the international political economy evolving from the time of the Glorious Revolution as a process of uneven expansion of the Lockean heartland, challenged by successive generations of Hobbesian contender states. Against all the challenges and in the wars which brought them to a head, the heartland was able to hold its own and expand, often absorbing one or more contenders following their defeat; sometimes, though, reproducing the previous antagonism out of impotence and/or prohibitive incompatibilities in terms of state/society complexes. Through these political conflicts, the internationalisation/transnationalisation of capital under the impetus of a particular circuit (C . . .C′, etc.) proceeded to the present-day level in which few if any states remain outside its reach, but with the different legacies (Lockean/Hobbesian) persisting under the surface of a unified, 'globalised' capitalist political economy also within the expanded heartland itself (Albert 1992; Hampden-Turner and Trompenaars 1994). Therefore, any semblance of our argument with Fukuyama's 'end of history' thesis (1989, 1992) is only superficial: not only do conflicts on account of structural antecedents continue, but class struggles have been liberated from the Cold War mortgage and actually have entered a new phase on a global scale.

The internationalisation of capital, then, historically does not evolve as an economic process in a fixed landscape of sovereign states. It is an aspect of a process of expansion of the state/society complex in which capital crystallised under what proved to be the most favourable conditions. However, social self-regulation, the key factor here, makes it appear *as if* we are dealing with a self-sustained economic process, so that the contenders by default appear as the states breaking into the inherently peaceful, legal/economic realm which the Lockean states merely seek to uphold (Lasswell 1965: 18). From this perspective, the 'development' effort inevitably assumes elements of a confrontation in which war is the ultimate test between rival state/society complexes and their modes of production. The political aspect of such confrontations cannot be reduced to military or geopolitical factors. 'The real competition and selection,' Houweling and Siccama write (1993: 405), 'may not be materialised in terms of sea powers versus land powers as challengers, but in terms of different institutions able to mobilize human productivity.' But while the heartland has expanded by transnational penetration and integration, the Hobbesian contenders have necessarily operated on their own, fighting each other (mobilised by the balance-of-power policies of Britain and/or the United States) as often as they fought the united heartland.

As indicated already, capitalist structures can be part of a Hobbesian constellation, but, as Gramsci points out, the only way a backward country can catch up 'in competition with the more advanced industrial formations of countries which monopolise raw materials and have accumulated massive capital sums,' is to modify economic organisation in the corporative sense, 'in order to accentuate the "plan of production" element' (Gramsci 1971: 120). If capital's need to expand is part of the driving forces of a contender state's foreign policy, it too is subordinated to this plan, adding the dimension of competition for world market shares to the confrontation. Specific circumstances have even produced a particular form of salvaging transnational linkages by cloaking foreign assets, as in the case of German capital in the Nazi era (Aalders and Wiebes 1990). Capitalist exploitation exacerbates social conflict in any state, but the rigidities inherent in the Hobbesian confiscation of society and its sharp demarcation from the heartland, fostering economic and cultural autarky, lend it a particularly explosive quality. The mobilisation of social energies but the simultaneous impossibility of allowing their release in a wider setting – say, by emigration – has tended to charge the Hobbesian states with energies they could not contain, and the more developed the capitalist sector in them, the more they have pursued expansionist designs.

Let us now proceed to a more concrete level of abstraction by introducing the *forms of state* distinguished by Robert Cox (1987). Cox's forms of state can be considered, with one significant exception, as concretisations of our Lockean/Hobbesian dichotomy. This is shown in Table 3.2. Although Cox does not always place these forms of state in a straight chronological order, and this tabular presentation schematises his often conditional and more nuanced descriptions, we may for our purposes fill in this table with states exemplifying particular state forms. Some are of course rather obvious, such as the liberal state (Britain). The US until the New Deal was an instrumental liberal state at the hands of rival social interests. France is the obvious Bonapartist state. The welfare nationalist state, like the coincident state monopoly concept (see also Figure 2.3, p. 63), covers both the heartland and the most developed contender states: especially Prussia/Germany and Austria–Hungary. France by this time was in the process of being incorporated into the heartland – without as we saw, entirely shedding its Hobbesian antecedents.

Table 3.2 State/society complexes and forms of state, 1800–1990

Era	Lockean heartland	Hobbesian contenders
Eighteenth and nineteenth centuries	Liberal state (Britain) Instrumental liberal state (US)	Bonapartist state (France)
Late nineteenth to early twentieth century	Welfare nationalist state (Britain)	Welfare nationalist state (Prussia/Germany) Fascist–corporative state (Axis Powers)
Mid-twentieth century	Corporate liberal state* (US/North Atlantic Bloc)	Redistributive party-commanded state (Soviet Bloc) Cartel state (South European/American dictatorships) Neo-mercantilist develop-mentalist state (late
Late twentieth century	Hyperliberal state (Thatcher/Reagan model)	industrialising Third World states)

*Cox (1987) uses 'neoliberal state' which more often is employed to denote what he terms the 'hyperliberal' state.

The crisis of the 1930s created a sharp rupture between the capitalist contenders, which became the Axis powers, and the Soviet Union. In the heartland, however, a progressive synthesis between liberal internationalism and state monopolism was achieved (first in the New Deal, and subsequently extrapolated to Western Europe and Japan) that produced the corporate liberal state. These newly incorporated states (including the defeated Axis powers), like France before them, retained particular characteristics that on occasion proved pertinent in world politics.

Michael Löwy's (1981) typology of transformations resulting in Hobbesian (not always 'contender') states, may help us to expand on Cox's understanding of the cartel state (by which he means authoritarian–populist states close to fascism – Franco Spain or corporatist Portugal). In Latin America, North Africa and Asia, revolutions of a populist nature but without the reactionary component that is implied in the cartel state concept, produced states with significant common traits. Thus Löwy distinguishes, under the heading of 'unfinished bourgeois revolutions', between states shaped by 'interrupted popular revolutions' (Mexico, Bolivia, and Algeria); and states shaped by 'semi-revolutions from above'. These include Turkey, Brazil, Mexico (second phase), Argentina, India, Guatemala, Egypt, and Indonesia. Often, the 'cartel' experience laid the foundations for the actual emergence as a contender state in the neo-mercantilist category: thus Mexico and Brazil could build their credit-financed industrialisation drive of the late 1960s, early 1970s on the infrastructure and experience dating from the earlier import-substitution experiments (Frank 1981: 4–6; for an analysis of Brazil as a Hobbesian state, see Lamounier 1989). Algeria and India, too, can be analysed in this perspective.

The hyperliberal state ushered in by Thatcher and Reagan under a neoliberal concept of control, which has spread to the greater part of the world in the meantime, today is challenged by states following a 'state–capitalist path' juxtaposed to it. Cox uses this category to sum up the state-driven catch-up category as a whole, in light of its contemporary confrontation with the heartland – mentioning France and Japan in light of their historical antecedents, and Brazil and South Korea as today's examples (Cox 1987: 292). This, then, is apparently a category broadly equivalent to our Hobbesian state/society complex comprising more specific forms.

Having defined specific states making up the heartland and a series of contenders by using these labels, we may now proceed to draw the outlines of the historic confrontations on the heartland/contender state dimension.

War and the balance of power

As indicated above, war is the ultimate test of whether a contender state has successfully advanced to a position where it can pose a real challenge which it for reasons of structural incompatibility with the heartland, cannot further pursue by economic competition. This goes for all contenders in which a capitalist element was part of the social substratum being mobilised by the state; after World War II, and in particular in the case of the USSR, a different situation obtained as a consequence of the limits placed by atomic weapons on total war. However, all contender states not only had to confront the strongest core states directly, but the prime contenders often had to fight off weaker Hobbesian rivals, too (see also Schwartz 1994: 106). These in several cases were enlisted, as part of a balance of power policy, by the Lockean states.

Hence we might expect that major wars in the era that begins with the Glorious Revolution of 1688 and ends with the collapse of the USSR, a three-century cycle, had a definite structure as far as the combatants' state/society complex was concerned. This structure would look like the following: the heartland state(s) pursuing, in a 'balancer' role, a balance of power policy; Hobbesian contenders being played off against each other; and a periphery of pre-Hobbesian formations serving as a 'prize area', additional resource base etc., for the combatants, usually with privileged access for the heartland. Here we should qualify the image of the lone contender state, though. Certainly, one crucial weakness of the Hobbesian configuration in challenging the heartland consisted of its failure to develop the socialisation of labour and integration beyond the national confines. But although bloc formation sponsored by a challenger therefore always was of an additive, occupation/'limited sovereignty' type with only marginal benefits, the resource base of the primary challenger was never literally confined to the single state. Of these blocs, we may mention Napoleon's continental system; the Nazi *Grossraum* and Japanese co-prosperity sphere; the Warsaw Pact/COMECON; and, a final instance of multilateral/state (instead of transnational/social) bloc formation, the NIEO drive of the 1970s, which coincided, mainly on account of rising oil prices, with expanding East–West trade and *détente*, and with crisis in the heartland.

Figure 3.2, then, depicts the hypothetical structure of war. In order to fill in this structure, we may look at the 'global wars' as defined by William Thompson (1988: 50, Table 3.4), that fall into the 1688–1991 period. These are: (a) the French wars of 1688 to 1713 in which England and the Netherlands faced France as a 'Primary Challenger'; (b) the French wars of 1792 to 1815 in which Britain was aided by Russia and Prussia against France; and (c) the 'German wars' of 1914 to 1945, in which the US and Britain, aided by Russia/ USSR, warded off the challenge of Germany. In Thompson's table, the USSR is already identified as the next primary challenger, but the outcome of the contest was not yet decided when his study was published. Today it can be argued, however, that the acceleration of the arms race by the NATO states beginning in 1978–79, with China as an ally in the balance, served to bring down the Soviet bloc including the USSR itself in 1989–91 (the arms race was interpreted in this perspective already by Halliday 1986; a view mean- while confirmed by e.g. Schweizer 1994). Parallel to it, this exacerbation of the international situation served, as argued by Gerbier (1987), to destabilise the NIEO coalition of Mexico, India, and other challengers. The more radical survivors of the Hobbesian NIEO coalition, such as Cuba, Iran, Libya, and Iraq, in the 1980s decade were isolated, played off against each other, and actually attacked in the case of the Gulf War.

In Figure 3.3, the heartland coalitions including a weaker Hobbesian state enlisted in the struggle against the primary challenger(s), are defined by state form in Cox's nomenclature. Of course, Holland was a pre-Hobbesian forma- tion, a proto-state still lacking an effective centralised state apparatus; while France in its first confrontation with liberal Britain, should perhaps be labelled a 'continental power state', like Russia in the Napoleonic period. The term is borrowed by Cox from Ludwig Dehio to label the pre-modern form of state in absolutist France in its confrontation with the 'insular state' that was Britain (Cox 1987: 116).

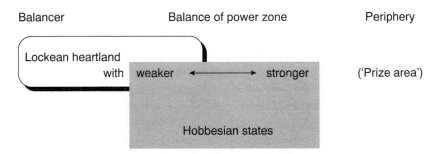

Figure 3.2 Hypothetical structure of war in the 1688–1991 cycle.

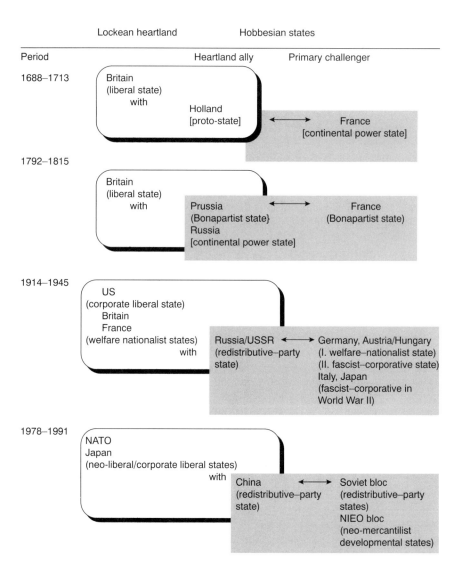

Lockean heartland   Hobbesian states

Period	Heartland ally	Primary challenger

1688–1713   Britain (liberal state) with Holland [proto-state] ←→ France [continental power state]

1792–1815   Britain (liberal state) with Prussia (Bonapartist state} Russia [continental power state] ←→ France (Bonapartist state)

1914–1945   US (corporate liberal state) Britain France (welfare nationalist states) with Russia/USSR (redistributive–party state) ←→ Germany, Austria/Hungary (I. welfare–nationalist state) (II. fascist–corporative state) Italy, Japan (fascist–corporative in World War II)

1978–1991   NATO Japan (neo-liberal/corporate liberal states) with China (redistributive–party state) ←→ Soviet bloc (redistributive–party states) NIEO bloc (neo-mercantilist developmental states)

Figure 3.3 Coalitions in global wars and the terminal East–West arms race, 1688–1991.

Note: square brackets indicate the type of state prior to the Lockean/Hobbesian divide.

See also: Thompson 1988; Cox 1987.

Our thesis is simple and obvious, namely, that the Lockean heartland ultimately weathered all the storms and expanded through them. Its superior position resides, we argue, in its capacity to provide the setting to the most advanced and profitable forms of capital accumulation. This refers to both industrial development, the growth of productive capital; and the widening of its circulation, that is, being a pivot on which international circuits of capital revolve. Eventually, this has resulted not in the end of history, but in a dual crisis. One of the Hobbesian states, which have by and large collapsed as state/society complexes capable of sustaining their challenge to the heartland; the other a crisis of the heartland itself, which is being exhausted, like the rest of the planet, by a mode of production which rules supreme over the world economy.

Let it be clear that we do not postulate a transhistorical mechanism which governs the course of events in the idealist sense. We only claim that in the struggles with Hobbesian contender states, the Lockean states have so far been victorious, because (and as long as) they collectively represent, and are home to, the capitalist mode of production. Marx's statement that 'no social formation disappears as long as the productive forces which have developed within it still find room for further forward movement' (quoted in Gramsci 1971: 106), here is acted out on the world stage. Given the initial priority of England as an advanced state/society complex which then allows capitalist development (which in turn really *begins* with the industrial revolution, because only then the elements of agricultural revolution, market economy, merchant capital, and international finance, come together in the exploitation of wage labour and real capital accumulation can take off) and its centrality as the pivot of international capital circuits, the first defeat of the main challenger was perhaps already sufficient to make subsequent victories possible. After all, British control of the 'prize area' allowed its expansion as a transnational society on which the heartland is based, thus solidifying its lead and simultaneously planting new centres of future leadership within the same civilisation. Therefore, one might also say that once capital had found a centre in England (largely on historically contingent grounds), and this country defeated its primary challenger, the future triumphs of capital and the heartland were cumulative expressions of this initial advantage. In this sense there is a circular element in 'explaining' the victories of the heartland.

Some illustrative evidence

The Pax Britannica

The first element of our argument is that at no point in time was the Lockean heartland ever seriously in danger of being surpassed in terms of economic performance by any challenger. On the other hand, the contribution of the contender states to capital's capacity to rejuvenate itself by developing new modes of accumulation (at higher levels of socialisation) should not be discounted either. The need for alliances with certain Hobbesian states in a balance-of-power context derives primarily from manpower and related requirements, crudely put, the 'cannonfodder factor'. Let us first review the period between the first and second global war episodes, in which Britain's lead was established.

The Glorious Revolution stands at the outset of Britain's advantage. The wars with France were not yet a contest between the capitalist and the state mode of production, because these would mature only later. Global wars, William Thompson points out (1988: 7), 'are wars fought to decide who will provide systemic leadership, whose rules will govern, whose policies will shape systemic allocation processes, and whose sense or vision of order will prevail'. The establishment of a Lockean state/society complex and the liberal inter-nationalist concept of control which underlay the Whig project were what the 1688–1713 contest was about. France was a continental power state congealed in a Hobbesian configuration, a society mobilised by the state: that is, by the Cardinals, Louis XIV claiming to personify it, and his mer-cantilist minister, Colbert. England's agricultural revolution (crop yields already were higher before the Restoration than anywhere in Europe except for the Low Countries (Hill 1975: 150, 154n)) could further develop under a liberal regime, while France's stagnated. The average harvest-to-seed ratio in England rose from 8:0 in the seventeenth to 10:1 in the eighteenth century and up to 11:1 in 1820; in France (as in Spain and Italy), it remained at between 6:2 to 6:7 until 1820 (Schwartz 1994: 50, Table 2.1). Let it be noted in passing that all the lands of English settlement reproduced the orig-inal agricultural advantage at a later stage, underscoring the heartland connection in this area, too (Senghaas 1982: 68; see also Schwartz 1994: 51, Table 2.2).

The Netherlands was linked to this development by its own agricultural revolution, shared elements of religion, the dynastic bond established in the events of 1688, and of course the flow of funds which followed William of Orange to England (Boxer 1965: 110). By the same token, however, the *rentier* view prevailing in the outlook of the Dutch bourgeoisie reinforced its partic-ularism and resistance to state centralisation, which is why we may speak of a pre-Hobbesian proto-state. Still, the Dutch were necessary allies to provide the arms and ships for the ultimate victory over France. Notably, against France's 120 warships, England with 100 probably could not do without Holland's 66 (data for 1689/90 in Kennedy 1987: 99, Tables 4 and 5). The War of Spanish Succession which ended with France's defeat in 1713, as well as the subsequent eighteenth-century wars in which France was beaten, led to the loss of the bulk of French colonies in North America and facilitated Britain's imperial expansion. As we have shown elsewhere (see my 1996a: 62–3), the balance-of-power policy and theory was a product of this episode – associated with the names of Bolingbroke and Hume – and was motivated by the priority awarded to commercial expansion and overseas settlement – the 'prize area'.

The mode of accumulation developed in the industrial revolution is Andreff's extensive mode. It is embodied in sector 'A' industries, first of all the cotton textile industry, which in this period emerged as 'leading sector' in the world economy (Thompson 1988: 136, Table 6.3). Modelski defines a 'lead economy' by reference to the presence of such sectors and a qualitative (i.e. in the leading sector) and quantitative trade pre-eminence (see also Thompson 1988: 123). In the half-century between 1750 and 1800, Britain's share of world manufacturing output, in which textiles held pride of place, rose from half that of France to par; in 1830, it further rose to almost twice the French share (Kennedy 1987: 149, Table 6). The qualitative jump of British foreign trade, now turned into a circuit of capital (C ... C′; 55 per cent of British exports were textiles in 1800) also took place between 1780 and 1800 – from 12 per cent of world trade to 33 per cent (Thompson 1988: 120, Table 6.1; Palloix 1971: 53, Table 2). Against this pace of ascent, the *ancien régime* lacked the capacity for mobilisation to sustain the challenge. When a free trade treaty was concluded with Britain in 1786, large parts of French manufacturing were thrown into crisis. This contributed, in conjunction with the social strains produced by the French catch-up effort and its intercontinental military implications, to the revolution three years later (Schama 1990: 190, 233, 62) – which in turn provoked the global war considered here.

Britain's allies in this global war were no longer required to provide it with extra naval power, because Britain's own war fleet of 195 ships in 1789 (214 in 1812–15) could handle France's (81 in 1789; 80 in 1812–15) without difficulty. To fight the land war, however, in which France eventually mobilised an army of 600,000 men (1812–15; from 180,000 in 1789), Britain's army in spite of its expansion from 40,000 to 250,000 was not enough. The three-quarter million men of its allies (to which eventually, Austria–Hungary's 250,000 men should of course be added as well) were indispensable to defeat the French (figures from Kennedy 1987: 99, Tables 4 and 5).

Now it can be argued that on the economic plane, the challenge posed by France only took shape after Napoleon's defeat. Thus Thompson's ten-year figures for leading sector shares indicating states' qualitative economic leads, show that France fell back during the revolutionary and Napoleonic wars. By 1820, though, the industrial economies driven by capital accumulation (Britain's, and at a distance, France's) take off, leaving behind those economies such as Russia's which purely quantitatively still had an equal share until well into the nineteenth century (Thompson 1988: 140, Table 6.6; see also Kennedy 1987: 149, Table 6). In textiles, France could not follow Britain's development. Only during the American Civil War, when the US cotton textiles sector contracted, did it relatively improve its cotton spindlage capacity again (Landes 1972: 215, Table 5). But capital accumulation by now had begun to shift to other fields of investment such as iron production and railroads. And although Britain's lead was undisputed here, too, France stood at second place in iron production (against Britain's 3.8 million tons in 1860, it produced 0.9 million tons).

The German states (Prussia, Bavaria, etc.) by 1840 had left France behind in railroad mileage. The vast expansion of railroad construction which then set in, in 1860 saw Britain with 14.6 thousand kilometres of track only slightly ahead of the German states with 11 thousand and France in third place with 9.2 thousand (Schwartz 1994: 97, Table 4.2). The war launched by Napoleon III against Prussia, which sought to channel domestic tensions into foreign aggression (the label 'Bonapartist' strictly speaking refers to the second Napoleon), ushered in Germany, united in victory, as the primary challenger. Britain in fact had been a silent partner (or, as Marx put it at the time, functioned as an insurance company) in France's state-driven expansion plans ever since the Cobden–Chevalier free trade treaty of 1860 (*MEW* 15: 17; Schwartz 1994: 183). Henceforth, France continued to expand in crucial areas such as imperialist colonisation and the emerging international circuit of money capital. As a per centage of Britain's fast-rising foreign investment, French money capital invested abroad stood at 37 per cent in 1851–54 and rose to 78 in 1881–82 – after which it declined again to half the size of British holdings in 1914 (calculated from Kenwood and Lougheed 1971: 43, Table 3; 45, Table 5; British figure for 1882 from Hobson 1968: 62). But its capacity to sustain the challenge to British supremacy had been critically undermined and the rapid rise of Germany drove it into the British imperial camp.

Heartland pre-eminence through the twentieth century

The twentieth century would prove to be the real testing ground for the Lockean heartland. First, because in this century, the transition of leadership from the British Empire and Commonwealth to the United States took place, which resulted in imbalances and unstable situations in which contender states could advance. Thus decolonisation critically exposed the prize area. Secondly, because on the threshold of the century a new mode of accumulation had come to maturity, Andreff's intensive one, which coincided, in terms of the paradigmatic scale of operation we discussed earlier, with the national state which in this period developed its socially protective dimension to accommodate the ascendant labour movements – Cox's Welfare Nationalist State. The trend affected the traditionally cosmopolitan Lockean states in the sense that they, too, had to tie their fate more closely to the ascendant industries, thus reciprocating the carving up of the global political economy by imperialist rivalry. Third, and finally, the 'plan of production' element which Gramsci (1971: 120) as we saw considers the hallmark of the contender state, and the broader state mode of production, in this century were perfected, posing a challenge that was all the more formidable.

Of course, here we can only draw the broadest contours of the balance of forces put to the test in the 1914–45 global war. The heartland now had assumed a more durable shape by the structural innovations of 1911 (Commonwealth and Arbitration Treaty) so that we may add up US and

British economic indicators. As to the 'A' industries, Germany and Austria–Hungary were hardly a challenge – in 1913, their cotton spindlage capacity was 18.2 per cent of heartland capacity. In trade, using the latest time series (Reuveny and Thompson 1997: 207, Appendix Table 2), Germany alone stood at 47 per cent of the combined Anglo-American world trade share. The growth of mark acceptance in international trade on the eve of World War I to a critical level was mentioned already, but as a source of loan capital, Germany in 1914 only accounted for 13 per cent against Britain's 43 per cent (the US stood at 7 per cent, France at 20 per cent of total foreign money capital outlays; Kenwood and Lougheed 1971: 41, Diagram 1). But then, in the state–monopolistic thinking that was prevalent among the German ruling classes (and among many of their counterparts in other countries), this was a struggle between *schaffendes* as against *raffendes Kapital* – creative against parasitic capital. Therefore, we must turn to the 'B' industries to assess the dimension of the challenge posed by Germany. If we put British, American, and French combined steel production at 100, Germany's production rose from 23.6 per cent in 1880 to 38.2 per cent in 1900 and remained there until the war (Hexner 1943: 324–5, Appendix VI). From Thompson's 'Leading Sector' index (1988: 140, Table 6.6), we learn that in terms of qualitative development, Germany in 1910 had bypassed Britain, but given the ascendant and highly innovative US economy, Germany's relative position was only 24.5 per cent of the combined US/UK/French leading sector share. In energy consumption, Germany and Austria–Hungary combined stood at 30 per cent of the US/UK/French level in 1900, which slightly eroded to 29.6 per cent in 1913 (Kennedy 1987: 201, Table 16). In all cases, however, the US contribution was decisive – in steel production, Germany had already bypassed Britain in 1900 and enjoyed a 4:3 advantage over Britain and France combined in 1910; while Germany and Austria–Hungary together practically equalled these two in energy consumption in 1913.

As before, the rationale for a heartland ally (which we again pose abstractly as if there were a choice and no concrete interests building up to such coalitions) resided in manpower. Although Russia had by now embarked on its own revolution from above to spur economic development (see Schwartz 1994: 100–1; Berend and Ránki 1982: 67–70), its energy consumption was roughly equal to Austria–Hungary's, and in steel, to France's on the eve of the war. Its 1.3 million military personnel, however, was a crucial factor to decide the contest between the central powers' 1.1 million and the heartland's (UK/US/France) 1.5 million (figures for 1910, Kennedy 1987: 203, Table 19).

If one compares the military power projected by the contender states with their relative economic resources, Tocqueville's comment (1990, I: 87), that a Hobbesian contender state can profit from its capacity for mobilisation in the short run but in time will exhaust the country's energies, comes to mind again. Indeed, in 1937, on the eve of World War II, the major contender states (Nazi Germany, Japan, the USSR), spent between a quarter to one-third of National Income on defence, while the British Empire spent only 5.7 per cent and France 9.1 per cent (the US even less, but this was before mobilisation – Kennedy 1987: 332, Table 31). This time, though, the German challenge was more formidable. In steel production, Germany alone in 1938 stood at 51.8 per cent of the heartland (US/UK/France). However, the USSR, although with 39.6 per cent still behind Germany, had become a major producer as well and under the Molotov–Ribbentrop non-aggression pact, the two countries outproduced the heartland by a small margin (Hexner 1943: 324–5, Appendix VI). Therefore, its role as a heartland ally in 1941–45 was no longer merely one of a supplier of manpower although this of course was a major factor. By 1957, the Soviet Union had again reached a level of steel production of slightly more than one-third of the US/UK/France figure (ECE 1959: 22, Tables 16, 17).

At this point, we should remember that intensive accumulation coexists with extensive accumulation, and the progressive mode with 'C' industries had meanwhile risen to prominence. But Japan's meteoric rise, for a considerable period, rested on sector 'A' industries, notably textiles (see also Maddison 1971: 60). Therefore, one-industry indicators become problematic as the composite, multiple-sector economy develops. This development takes place on a world level and is controlled by the heartland as far as the integration of circuits of capital and actual sectoral production are concerned. From the 1960s onwards, this involved a gradual dismantling of sector 'B' industries in the heartland, and the consequent integration of contender states often concentrating on this sector. As Andreff shows, the new contenders after World War II (primarily the USSR, but also the newly decolonised or otherwise emancipated, formerly dependent formations, such as China, India, Brazil and Algeria) concentrated their development effort precisely in sector 'B' industries, and in the run-up to the formation of the NIEO coalition, increasingly so. The weight of sector 'B' industries in the USSR grew from 52 per cent to 56 per cent between 1959 and 1972; in Algeria, sector 'B' accounted for 46 per cent in 1973. Only in Brazil, a substantial sector 'C' could be noted in that same year (Andreff 1982: 113, Table 1). The Soviet Union's sector 'C', although growing at a rapid pace, remained marginal; in Andreff's system, 'C' rose from 1 per cent to 6 per cent between 1959 and 1972. Therefore, progressive accumulation dominated the world economy after World War II, but not necessarily those of national economies and certainly not those of the contender states.

One way of establishing the pre-eminence of the heartland in terms of the progressive mode of accumulation is by looking at the GNP per capita, which sums up the consumptive capacity of the economy central to progressive accumulation but which also transcends single-sector comparisons. By setting average GNP per capita for North America, Western Europe, and Australia and New Zealand at 100, Giovanni Arrighi provides a measure against which contender performance can be set (Arrighi 1991). Thus Japan increased its relative GNP/c from one-quarter in 1960 to half in 1970 to three-quarters in 1980 and 117.9 per cent in 1988. In its tracks, South Korea advanced from 7.2 per cent in 1970 to 12.7 per cent in 1980 and 20.2 per cent in 1988. These countries sided with the heartland in the final contest with the Soviet bloc and the NIEO countries. Figures for the USSR are not given by Arrighi, but using Italy as a key, they can be calculated for 1971 as 43.3 per cent of the heartland average and for 1980 as 50.5 per cent (*Statistical Abstract* 1984: 865, Table 1509). This fits into the relative improvement of contender states in the crisis-ridden 1970s – thus NIEO countries such as Brazil and other Latin American states improved their relative position from 12.7 per cent to 17.5 per cent in that decade (Brazil) and 17.3 per cent to 21.1 per cent (other Latin America). The Middle East and North Africa, too, improved their relative position from 8.1 per cent to 11.1 per cent (Arrighi 1991: 45, Table II, 49, Table III).

It was against this development and the political shifts accompanying it (including the advance of the working class in the heartland) that the neo-liberal offensive was launched in the late 1970s. The complexities of this offensive deserve a separate treatment that falls outside the scope of the present study. However, we may briefly indicate how this historic onslaught in some respects conformed, in others differed from the real wars of the past. First, in the confrontation with the Soviet bloc, China was enlisted by the heartland as an ally. Again, the only rationale for this recruitment was manpower in case of a real conflict, because in advanced weapons sectors, the Warsaw Pact never equalled NATO (see also Kennedy 1987: 503, Table 47; 511, Table 48) and neither did Chinese economic power (2.5 per cent of the heartland average GNP per capita in 1980) play a role. The qualitative superiority of the West was even enhanced, especially by shifting the arms race to high-technology areas such as AirLand Battle and SDI ('Star Wars') (Hesse 1984).

Second, there was an element of disciplining the NATO allies, especially West Germany, but also Italy and France, and mobilising them into head-on confrontation with the Soviet bloc. This should be understood also in light of different structural heritages in state/society patterns.

Third, within the context of the final struggle, Soviet support, in fact neutrality, was secured to allow a US/UK/French coalition under UN flag to attack Iraq after this country, exhausted by eight years of war with neighbouring Iran, had annexed Kuwait. At this point, the Soviet Union was already sliding towards economic collapse, its bloc disintegrating, so that it could conceive itself to be at the mercy of Western 'aid'. Indeed, for 1988, PlanEcon and CIA estimates[2] of Soviet GNP/c, (if we use Yugoslavia as a key in the Arrighi model) range between 15.9 per cent and 23.8 per cent of heartland average, down from 50.5 per cent in 1980. NIEO countries such as Brazil fell back from 17.5 per cent in 1980 to 12.1 per cent in 1988; other Latin America from 21.1 per cent to 9.7 per cent; Middle East and North Africa from 11.1 per cent to 7.1 per cent; Indonesia and the Philippines from 4.6 per cent to 2.3 per cent, etc. The efforts of the contender states, mounted along two axes (the East–West and the South–North), had come to naught in the face of the determined and often reckless counteroffensive by the heartland states. As Arrighi, from whom we have taken the preceding figures, concludes, 'The contraction of the 1980s ... has been a reflection of the general collapse of these efforts and marks their abandonment in the face of mounting challenges from above and below' (1991: 51).

Finally, the position of the original heartland countries showed an important transformation relating to the changing configuration of capital. Both the US and UK lost ground in the circuit of productive capital, P ... P', which has developed along with the progressive mode of accumulation under the corporate liberal concept of control. Thus, foreign direct investment (stock) of the US and Britain combined, as we saw declined from two-thirds of the world total in 1960–70 to 56 per cent in 1980 and 49 per cent in 1988 (Stopford and Strange 1991: 17). But although the position of these countries, especially the US, in the global debt economy that has come to characterise the latest phase of capitalist development, looks much more gloomy, they apparently have been able to use the newly prominent circuit of money capital to their advantage in building a strong position in what we have called the 'D' industries of virtual accumulation (see Thompson 1988: 140, Table 6.6; Table 2.4, this volume). Between 1985 and 1993, the US net overseas asset position as a per centage of GDP became negative (a net debtor position, 1 per cent to minus 10.4 per cent); Britain's declined from 21.7 per cent to 3.5 per cent; France's from –2.2 per cent to –6.0 per cent; while Japan increased its net asset position from 9.6 per cent to 14.4 per cent; Germany from 7.7 per cent to 11.6 per cent (*FT*, 9 March 1995). However, the Americans in particular succeeded in overcoming European resistance to their policy of confrontation, which they conducted both against the USSR (Schweizer 1994) and against the radical Middle East countries (Bichler and Nitzan 1996: 636–50). Ultimately, they and the British were even fully compensated by the countries with a positive net asset balance (and Kuwait and Saudi Arabia) to wage war on Iraq.

The collapse of the Soviet bloc and the NIEO project, and the placing of the successor states (as well as corporate liberal states in the heartland) under tutelage of international capital markets and the IMF has inaugurated a *global crisis of the Hobbesian state/society complex* (a 'second Glorious Revolution') with this time, appalling consequences for the world. This crisis has relegated the social formations hitherto mobilised behind a state-monitored catch-up effort into the category of the straight periphery by removing the critical element in their capacity to resist peripheralisation. It should be emphasised that the suggestion of a historical evolution from Hobbesian to Lockean is intended: the drama of today's new periphery is that its demise was also internally generated, a sign of the exhaustion of the confiscated social sphere on which the attempt to catch up and challenge was feeding. However, whether we are actually witnessing the emancipation of a *civil* society in the Lockean sense is a matter of debate. Resonating well into the heartland itself, the breakdown of the Hobbesian state has removed the protective shield from the lives of hundreds of millions of people, but existing legal structures are clearly insufficient to allow self-regulation of the Anglo-Saxon type – which as we saw has not prevented the exhaustion of the social substratum in the heartland itself.

4 Transnational class formation and historical hegemonies

> The unforeseen will happen – shocks, crises, turning-points in cycles, shifts in trends – and when it happens we are not to be defeated by it or just ride with it but to manage it, and manage it masterfully. That word implies technical competence, but it also implies a sense of direction.
>
> Sir Jeremy Morse, Chairman, Lloyds Bank

Although elements of a cosmopolitan business culture have existed, like markets, throughout recorded history, it was only with the growth of capital and the Lockean state that they were subsumed by a process of transnational class formation. This process coincided with the successive stages of internationalisation of capital. Thus, the internationalisation of the circuit of commodity capital was premised on 'the growth and global spread of trade diasporas or merchant communities who were linked across wide geographical spaces by complex social networks' (Helleiner 1997: 97). The subsequent internationalisation of money capital saw the emergence of an internationally interlocked *haute finance* of central bankers and investment bankers; while after World War II, a transnational managerial class emerged with the comprehensive internationalisation of production by the multinational corporation (ibid.).

In this chapter, we will discuss, first, the initial formation of a transnational bourgeoisie by applying Benedict Anderson's concept of 'imagined communities' to the cosmopolitan brotherhood that was Freemasonry. Second, we will argue that in the late nineteenth century, élite private planning groups branched off from these transnational networks. Such planning groups served as meeting grounds for developing common strategies and adjusting the hegemonic concept of control in response to resistance and other challenges. Finally we turn to the role private planning groups have played in integrating the ascendant bourgeoisie from the contender states into the expanding heartland. Through these stages and social forms (and all along, through crises and wars), the comprehensive capital relation can be argued to have become global in the three-century era between 1688 and the present.

Freemasonry as imagined community

The first of the imagined communities in which we may discern the formation of a transnational bourgeoisie is Freemasonry. The rise of masonry has
been traced to the aftermath of the Glorious Revolution which consecrated
the Lockean state/society complex. In the late seventeenth century, 'one thing
united a majority of politically conscious people . . . the need to preserve the
gain of the Civil War of 1642–51 – the limitation of the power of the King,'
Stephen Knight writes in his study on the subject (1985: 21–2). 'The "accepted"
Masons [i.e., lodge members who were not actually craftsmen] of the last
quarter of the seventeenth century would appear to have been largely drawn
from the type of people most anxious to preserve and to increase the steadily
growing influence in society and government of men of quite moderate wealth
and standing.'

By championing the separation of church and state and religious toler-
ance generally, Freemasonry also transcended the Protestantism and counter-
reformation of the previous century, which had emphasised the moment
of national unification. But it transformed the humanistic universalism of the
Renaissance, too. Masonry was part of the complex of forces which in the
eighteenth century subtly transformed the universal doctrines of natural law
into the more narrowly circumscribed citizens' rights doctrines of cosmopolitan
law, thus putting in place the class dimension of the 'Rights of Man' (Archibugi
1995: 441). Its agnostic, paganised Christian ritual allowed the inclusion of
various denominations including Jews into a brotherhood which offered an
element of guild loyalty and exclusive 'social insurance' in an increasingly
competitive environment. As status was becoming fluid and the element of
personal acquaintance eroded, masonry served to provide a passport of gestures
and signs of recognition that allowed otherwise anonymous members of the
upper and middle classes to gain the confidence and credit of their counterparts
abroad (Waite 1994, 1: 101; see also Rich 1988: 186).

As Rosenstock-Huessy has argued (1961: 364), the cosmopolitan bourgeoisie
in the eighteenth century came to adopt a perspective on its own society as
if it were a foreign one, a target for 'colonial' exploitation. Freemasonry
provided a cover for developing the new identity on which the exploitation
of members of one's own community is premised. By entering the masonic
lodges, merchants and those otherwise involved in the long-distance money
economy such as lawyers and accountants, realised the primordial alienation
from the community which is the precondition for market relations, exploitation of wage labour, and abstract citizenship. In addition, masonry rehabilitated
earlier transnational links by its references to the medieval guilds and myths
about Templar origins and other knightly orders (Waite 1994, 1: 434); but,
as Trevor Burnard notes, unlike aristocratic, guild-like associations, networks
such as Freemasonry were not 'fortresses designed to hold a hostile world at
bay'. Rather, they were 'sprawling and spatially discontinuous domains open
to, interspersed with, and elaborately enmeshed in their environment' (quoted

in Rich and de los Reyes 1997: 15n). Only thus could Freemasonry become a vehicle of transnational class formation, relaying the Lockean mind-set to ascendant bourgeois elements abroad.

Spread across the heartland

Freemasonry was grafted on medieval English stonemasons' guilds. After a period of disintegration, these revived in the early seventeenth century by admitting people from other professions, often the gentry, who were attracted by the practice of mutual assistance as well as by the atmosphere of conviviality and brotherhood – which is also why they often met in taverns instead of the previous guild halls (Lennhoff and Posner 1932: 422). Once a united Grand Lodge had been formed in 1717, the 'upper classes moved in on the small gentry just as the small gentry had moved in on "operative" artisans a century earlier' (Knight 1985: 25; eventually membership reached into successive royal families beginning with the Hanoverians). The class compromise between the commercially-minded aristocracy and ascendant bourgeoisie thus was sealed in the masonic lodges.

Public processions with banners through the streets of London were part of the early activities. But in light of street disturbances and suspicion as to their true motives, the Freemasons gradually withdrew from public view. The original Whig radicalism, too, was restrained as more of the higher nobility entered the lodges (Waite 1994, 1: 26). A schism between the original, orthodox Freemasons ('Antients'), and later 'Moderns' was only resolved when after the French Revolution, in which it had been so prominent, masonry was threatened with an Act of Parliament which made private societies taking oaths illegal. In 1799, a joint intervention of the two Grand Lodges obtained an exception for Freemasonry, which resulted in the United Grand Lodge of England in 1813 (Lennhoff and Posner 1932: 430).

By being expressly non-manual, divorced from actual labour, British masonry reproduced the aristocratic preference for arms-length control over direct entrepreneurial involvement. The English gentleman preferred 'to sit above the commercial fray, pulling levers, dangling rewards and applying sanctions' (Hampden-Turner and Trompenaars 1994: 321). In England itself, industrial entrepreneurs did not in fact need masonry to be able to exploit their fellow men, because they often were 'strangers' already – Quakers, Jews, and immigrants, especially from central Europe (Overbeek 1990: 45). Masons, therefore, would mostly be found among the 'not directly productive middle and professional classes' (Knight 1985: 370). Masonry also was congenial to the pattern of informal, behind-the-scenes policy preparation which, as we saw, characterised the organisation of the British Commonwealth and subsequent international organisations modelled after it. Its third Grand Master in Britain, Desaguliers (a French Huguenot by origin), who was the architect of the transnational spread of masonry, upon leaving his post in 1721 became 'the prototype of the long line of powerful masonic figures who preferred the shade to the limelight, the reality of power to mere appearances' (Knight 1985: 26; see also Waite 1994, 1: 278).

From the early eighteenth century onwards, masonry expanded abroad, both to the English-speaking settler lands and to Europe. The first lodge in North America was set up in 1733 in Boston (Waite 1994, 1: xxxiv). In New England and Virginia, Freemasonry rallied the free-thinking élite among the settlers, and it soon became part of the clash between the more independent-minded American bourgeoisie and British colonial interests. Although there were 'Moderns' among Tory elements, the North American 'Antients' were overwhelmingly in favour of independence (Lennhoff and Posner 1932: 1125).

The lodges' secrecy and their transnational connections also provided a cover for revolutionary conspiracy, in British North America and elsewhere. The Boston Tea Party occurred during an adjourned meeting of the St. John's lodge in Boston, and at least eight signatories to the Declaration of Independence, but possibly thirty-two, belonged to the 'Craft' (Waite 1994, 1: xxxiv; Knight 1985: 34). George Washington was initiated as a Freemason already in 1752. He took the oath as President from the chancellor of the Grand Lodge of New York and wore a masonic apron embroidered for him by the wife of the Marquis de Lafayette when he laid the foundation stone for the Capitol (Lennhoff and Posner 1932: 1126; Schama 1990: 29; masonic symbols such as the triangle and the all-seeing eye still today adorn the US dollar note). Benjamin Franklin became provincial Grand Master of Pennsylvania in 1749 and during his stay in Paris as American plenipotentiary was a member of the famous lodge of the Nine Muses along with Desmoulins, Condorcet, Helvetius, and Danton (Waite 1994, 1: 70–1; 2: 59). The presidents of the early nineteenth-century Jeffersonian party – Jefferson, Madison, and Monroe, were masons, but then, Alexander Hamilton, the champion of centralisation, was a mason as well (Lennhoff and Posner 1932: 1126). So was Andrew Jackson, who challenged the creeping reinforcement of centralised state power by reasserting the Jeffersonian principles in 1829 (Knight 1985: 34; Beard 1957: 186–9). The Lockean bloc unified by Jackson, which remained hegemonic until the Civil War, 'tended to oppose a strong federal role on everything except [territorial] expansion' (Ferguson 1995: 58).

After the American secession and the French Revolution, British Freemasonry became a bulwark of conservatism, but its expansion abroad continued. 'Undaunted by the loss of the first empire and with it direct control over American Masonry, the British took Masonry with the flag as they created their second empire' (Knight 1985: 34; see also Sampson 1965: 54–5 on the parallel role of clubs). Public schools, the training grounds for empire, had their own lodges so that a world-embracing, interlocking network of public schools and masonic lodges served to knit together the English-speaking bourgeoisie into a quasi-tribal unity. It provided its members with a potent élitism 'compounding the mystique which was a necessity in the imperial administrator's portfolio of tricks' (Rich 1988: 177, 175). As R. Hyam writes,

> The role of Freemasonry in building up the empire, and of its doctrines of brotherhood in sustaining the world-wide activities of traders and empire-builders, is not easy to document. Its role in spreading British cultural influences has thus been seriously underrated (quoted in Rich 1988: 187n).

This applied first of all to the remaining settler colonies. Canadian lodges had been set up from the mid-eighteenth century onwards; the first lodge in Australia dated from 1803. As in the US, Freemasonry also played a role in their striving for autonomy. Thus the Canadians in 1855 established their own Grand Lodge divorced from England (Waite 1994, 1: 198). In India, the British Raj was underpinned by a relatively tight web of masonic nodes under provincial Grand Lodges for Bengal (established around 1755, with seventy-nine lodges in the early twentieth century); Bombay (1764), forty-six; and Madras (1767), thirty-one (Waite 1994, 2: 198). Only later were non-whites admitted into the colonial lodges. In India for instance this began with recruiting – around 1860 – commercially-minded Parsees, later also other Indians. While the colour line was thus transgressed (which would also facilitate the future transfer of power under decolonisation, Knight 1985: 34), the class line never was.

The British ruling class and middle classes perhaps were numerically weak in the face of a vast proletariat (compared to countries such as France; see Rosenstock-Huessy 1961: 403). But their internal nervous system was far better developed. By 1872, there were about four million Freemasons in the British Empire compared to half a million trade unionists and 400,000 members of the co-operative movement (Rich 1988: 176). Already in that period, one of the strongholds of masonry was the police (Knight 1985: Part 2), and as we will see later, the privacy and secrecy of masonry have all along provided a cover for intelligence operations as well. Since the same applies to the subsequent private planning groups, this may remind us of the fact that class power is always backed up by coercion – and not only at the formal state level.

Locally, masonic connections were and remain entwined with comparable affiliations such as Rotary, Lions Clubs, or Chambers of Commerce (Knight 1985: 131), although the former two networks, both American in origin, like the Chambers are more closely attuned to the world of productive capital and international business. Rotary, a non-religious and non-secret fraternity serving as a transnational class network, was set up in Chicago as a businessmen's luncheon club by the lawyer, Paul Harris, in 1905 (*Chambers' Biog. Dict.*: 'Harris'). It expanded to the wider English-speaking world with clubs in Winnipeg, Dublin, and London, in 1912 became an international association, and finally, in 1922, 'Rotary International'. Rotary's aim is to establish 'international understanding through a world fellowship of business and professional men' (*Encycl. Brit.*: 'Rotary Club'). Lions Clubs, too, originated in Chicago. Its founder, Melvin Jones, a businessman, in 1917, launched his network of local business clubs to 'expand their horizons from purely professional concerns to the betterment of their communities and the world at large'. The Association of Lions Clubs branched out to Canada in 1920 and henceforth to the rest of the world; on the way, it helped set up the Non-Governmental Organizations section of the UN in 1945 (*Lions Clubs*, n.d.).

In these and comparable networks, the idea of a brotherhood providing some balance to a harshly competitive life otherwise, remains operative – relatively open and businesslike in the US (where multiple memberships are not uncommon and masonry is voluntarily revealed), more secretive and élitist in Britain and elsewhere (see also various national entries in *Who's Who in the World 1982–1983*; Knight 1985). As channels of communication centred on the heartland, they continue to provide the ground level to transnational class formation in addition to the more restricted élite networks created by internationally operating capital.

Enlightenment and revolution

In the eighteenth century, masonic lodges were set up throughout continental Europe – often, paradoxically in light of the liberal antecedents of masonry, by Jacobite English aristocrats in exile. The cosmopolitan moment in the eighteenth century prevailed over any attempt to carve out rival centres of power confronting Britain's – as the French monarchy had still tried in the period culminating in the 1688–1713 'global war'. The process of bourgeois class formation in the period preceding 1789 was a truly transnational process. Several enlightened, continental European monarchs had embraced the free-thinking deism of Freemasonry with a view to modernising their societies from above, however, seeking to pre-empt the revolution from below. Frederick the Great of Prussia, who invited Voltaire (himself a Mason) to Berlin in the second half of the eighteenth century, was of course the most famous example of a royal Freemason, while Catherine II of Russia and emperor Joseph II of Austria were tolerant of masonry for the same reasons (Waite 1994, 1: 173, 59; 2: 19; Lennhoff and Posner 1932: 43). 'The Enlightenment,' Gramsci wrote, 'was a magnificent revolution in itself . . . it gave all Europe a bourgeois spiritual International in the form of a unified consciousness. . . . In Italy, France and Germany, the same topics, the same institutions and same principles were being discussed' (1977: 12). Masonry was one vehicle of this cosmopolitan enthusiasm, inspiring composers such as Haydn and Mozart as well as political activists, traders, and confidence tricksters (Archibugi 1995: 451).

In France, the lodges became hotbeds of revolutionary conspiracy, as they had been in America. In 1771, the dissident Duke of Orléans, Philippe 'Egalité', became Grand Master of the National Grand Lodge of France which two years later was transformed into the Grand Orient (Waite 1994, 1: 292). 'The Masonic Lodges,' writes Georges Lefebvre (1967: 49), '. . . included not only bourgeois but priests, nobles and even the brothers of Louis XVI as members . . . They had the same ideal: civil equality, religious toleration, liberation of the human personality from all institutions which kept it immature.' The Lodge of the Nine Muses has already been mentioned. The 'Templar Tribunal', which organised the storming of the Bastille, included Mirabeau, Robespierre, Danton, and Philippe Egalité (Waite 1994, 1: 88).

Still, the lodges should not be seen as a central committee of the revolution as a whole, because, as Lefebvre notes (1967: 53), the aristocratic members, especially in the Grand Orient, would not have followed instructions to side with the Third Estate without protests and schisms. In fact, there were masonic elements in different currents within the revolutionary movement. The Jacobin party, vanguard of the revolution, in 1789 combined the radical egalitarianism of masonry with a Lockean emphasis on civil society, 'the subordination of state to citizen' (Schama 1990: 479); while a rival tendency around Mirabeau, Sieyès, and Talleyrand rather cultivated the élitist secrecy of the masonic tradition. When in 1793, the bourgeoisie of Lyon, Bordeaux, and Marseilles rose against the Jacobin terror, the lodges were part of the broader bourgeois movement seeking to normalise the situation (ibid.: 527–8, 726–7). They became a relay of state-driven modernisation under Napoleon and spread with French influence across Europe, now as a network of the power-ful, notably in the army (all the famous marshals), the police (minister Fouché) and the civil service, the precursors of today's *énarques* (Markov 1989: 114–5; 106). Several of Napoleon's brothers, the Kings of Naples, Spain, Holland, and Westphalia, were Masons; while one of the Marshals–Masons, Bernadotte, became King of Sweden and Grand Master of that country's Grand Lodge in 1811 (Waite 1994, 2: 26, 15).

In the Latin American revolutions inspired by the French Revolution, Freemasonry likewise provided the nodal points for transnationally connected bourgeois emancipation. While lodges in Spain and Portugal had been set up under English jurisdiction in the second quarter of the eighteenth century, Latin American lodges were set up in the early nineteenth under French and American obediences. As in North America and France, most Latin American revolutionary leaders were masons – Hidalgo, Bolívar, Martí, and many others (ibid.: 2: 9–11; 1: xxxv). Summed up by Nederveen Pieterse (1990: 135, quoting I. Nicolson):

> In Spanish America, the masonic lodges *(Lautaros)* founded by [Francisco de] Miranda spread all over the continent. "These masonic lodges were the binding force between Creoles in all parts of Spanish America, and through them they were able to achieve remarkable cohesion in spite of local jealousies and the extreme difficulties of communication . . . They explain the resilience of the movement . . .". In certain respects, then, the liberation movement in Spanish America formed part of the same intercontinental political constellation that nibbled at ancien régimes on both sides of the Atlantic.

Passive revolution and Masonry in the contender states

In Europe, counter-revolution not only restored the power of the Roman Catholic church which had all along combated Freemasonry, but also undermined the cosmopolitanism which had allowed its spread abroad. The French Revolution created a strong, centralised state resuming the attempt to catch up with Britain and 'nationalising' the bourgeoisie into a state class. But in so doing, it destroyed the original universalist pretensions of the revolution and provoked, not simply *counter-revolution*, but also *passive* revolution in Italy, Central Europe, and beyond. Denoting the impact of an original revolution on a different society resisting it on the political level, passive revolution (Gramsci 1971: 114) in this connection combines two elements:

(a) a 'revolution from above' without mass participation (Gramsci speaks of 'successive small waves of reform' and 'interventions from above of the enlightened monarchy type' – the example of Frederick the Great and some of his contemporaries was already briefly touched upon), and

(b) a creeping, 'molecular' social transformation, in which the progressive class finds itself compelled to advance in a more or less surreptitious, 'compromised' fashion. Hence, as Gramsci notes elsewhere, 'Restoration becomes the first policy whereby social struggles find sufficiently elastic frameworks to allow the bourgeoisie to gain power without dramatic upheavals, without the French machinery of terror' (ibid.: 115). In other words, by a strategy summed up in the notion of a protracted 'war of position' rather than a lightning 'war of manoeuvre'.

The instrument of the transformation summed up in the concept of passive revolution is the *state* – a state confiscating its social foundations in a 'Hobbesian' manner. To quote Gramsci again, 'what was involved was not a social group which "led" the other groups, but a state which, even though it had limitations as a power, "led" the group which should have been "leading" and was able to put at the latter's disposal an army and a politico-diplomatic strength' (ibid.: 105). The ascendant bourgeoisie under these conditions merely moves into the spaces opened up to it, in fact as a (fraction of the) state class; until at some point it will be able to advance as a class for itself.

Initially, the French Revolution forced continental Freemasonry underground. In 1792, the Austrian lodges closed of their own accord to avoid being subject to persecution, while in Russia, tsar Paul I outlawed them (Waite 1994, 1:59; 2:72–3). But following the Restoration, masonry became part of the contradictory development towards a bourgeois state – that is, a state committed to modernisation in a passive revolution mode, which seeks to preserve, as much as possible, the prevailing structure of political power; while allowing, unintentionally, the 'molecular' advance of the bourgeoisie. Henceforth, masonry would be present in both the enlightened monarchy and the democratic camps.

In France, Louis-Philippe, the son of Philippe Egalité, was installed in 1830 to lead a bourgeois monarchy. But Louis Blanc, the organiser of the *ateliers* and a leader of the 1848 revolution, represented the radical egalitarian tradition with which he equated masonry at large (Waite 1994, 1: 69). Garibaldi, who came back a mason from South America to lead the campaign for Italian unification, in 1873 established masonry in Italy as a political institution which had 'little communion with England' (Waite 1994, 2: 9; *Chambers' Biog. Dict.*: 'Garibaldi').

Imperialist rivalry and revolution further tore apart the once unified transnational brotherhood of Freemasonry, leaving only the heartland unaffected. Between France and the English-speaking world, masonic links were cut when the Grand Orient, reacting to clerical revanchism after the Paris Commune, declared itself atheist in 1877 (Waite 1994, 1: 297). Relations between British and German Freemasonry remained friendly, but the war of 1870–71 had destroyed whatever intimate bonds had existed between masonic France and Prussia–Germany. Towards World War I, there were attempts by French and British masons to seek conciliation with their German brethren; it was only with the sinking of the *Lusitania* in 1915 that a real rupture between British and German masonry came about (Lennhoff and Posner 1932: 432–3). Therefore, it is of some significance for our argument concerning France's integration into the heartland that masonic bonds were re-established along these lines as well. World War I, the *Encyclopaedia of Freemasonry* notes,

> welded fresh bonds of union between America, France and Belgium, which in their turn have raised, and in a spirit favourable thereto, the question whether a *rapprochement* is possible between Freemasonry in Latin countries and that of the English-speaking race at large (Waite 1994, 2: 4).

However, by this time, the transnational webs established in the heartland by masonry, Rotary etc., had been enlarged by more purposeful, and less cosmopolitan forms of transnational class formation.

Class planning in the era of high finance

Towards the close of the nineteenth century, along with the eclipse of liberal internationalism centred on Britain, new forms of class organisation and direction emerged. The 'undeniable harmony between British interests and the interests of the world' which had existed in the heyday of the *Pax Britannica* (Carr 1964: 81) and on which the cosmopolitanism of Freemasonry had been grafted, evaporated with the advent of a new mode of accumulation in powerful contender states such as Germany, unified in the wake of its victory over Napoleon III. Also, the rise of what Friedrich Engels called the 'Sixth Great Power' of Europe, the socialist labour movement (*MEW* 10: 8), required a more activist posture on the part of the ruling class. The combined effect of this changing configuration of forces was to shift the emphasis in bourgeois class formation from the cosmopolitan to the national level, shaping a state monopoly tendency in the bourgeoisie (tendency, because a full state monopoly would be incompatible with capitalist relations of production).[1]

To deal with these challenges, the by now most powerful segment of the capitalist class, the international investment bankers, or *haute finance*, had to find new ways of shaping their common interests in agreement with the emerging state monopolism. The merchant bankers had evolved from more modest positions as traders themselves. Until the Glorious Revolution, the commanding positions in English foreign trade had been the preserve of the nobility (see also the succession of heads of the Hudson's Bay Company: Prince Rupert; the Duke of York, the future James II; and Marlborough – Trevelyan 1968: 306). In the course of the eighteenth century, however, successful traders with a bourgeois background, often from Germany, settled in London as 'merchant bankers'. 'Money earned in merchanting gave them the ability to back others ... [and] soon developed into banking and the transition from commodity trading, through foreign exchange and accepting bills of exchange to issuing business' (Clarke 1967: 27). The first of these were Barings, a Bremen wool merchant family which set up their banking business in 1762 and under various aristocratic titles (Cromer, Northbrook, etc.) became one of the most powerful dynasties in the British ruling class and empire (Sampson 1965: 408–12; see also on its collapse in 1995, *Nw*, 13 March 1995).

Barings's pre-eminence by the turn of the nineteenth century was challenged by the Rothschilds, who combined a web of European family connections with masonic brotherhood (Knight 1985: 222n). Originally money-changers in Frankfurt's Jewish quarter, the Rothschilds from their cotton trade office in Manchester moved to set up a bank in London in 1804 (Morton 1963: 44–7). There were Rothschild bank houses in Paris, Frankfurt, Vienna, and Naples; other merchant banks, such as Schröder's, which began in wheat and coffee before becoming a merchant bank in the City (also in 1804), and later in the century, Lazards (1877), commanded comparable transnational networks (Schröder/Schroeder's in Hamburg and New York, Lazards in Paris and New York).

Although banking, and the City in particular, were and remain a stronghold of Freemasonry (Knight 1985: 135; ch. 24), the latter's sprawling, often disjointed networks could not be expected to respond adequately to the immense challenges facing the established order as the nineteenth century drew towards a close. Freemasonry as such did perform what Gramsci calls an 'intellectual' function, that of a planning institution on the international level (1971: 182n). 'A religion, Freemasonry, Rotary, Jews, etc., can be subsumed into the social category of "intellectuals", whose function, on an international scale, is that of mediating the extremes, of "socialising" the technical discoveries which provide the impetus for all activities of leadership, of devising compromises between, and ways out of, extreme solutions,' he wrote in the *Prison Notebooks*.

> [They] propose political solutions of diverse historical origin, and assist their victory in particular countries – functioning as international political parties which operate within each nation with the full concentration of the international forces.

Now that the *Pax Britannica* was coming apart, this function was redefined, anchored more firmly in the heartland, and lifted to a higher level of sophistication. The model for later bodies of this kind was pioneered by Cecil Rhodes, the British financier and South African empire-builder. Working closely with the most prominent of the City merchant bankers mentioned, Rhodes founded a quasi-Masonic secret society to which he left his fabulous fortune.

The Rhodes–Milner group model

Organised policy planning behind the scenes is a form of the socialisation of the conduct of class struggle on the part of the bourgeoisie. The trade union, the political party, and certainly the Leninist vanguard party, in fact were its counterparts on the working class side. In the concrete circumstances of the late nineteenth century, the rise of these working class organisations threatened to withdraw policy-making from control by the traditional ruling class. Of course the ruling class formed its own mass organisations, but as Norman Angell, the Nobel Prize winning pacifist writer and protégé of Lord Esher (one of Rhodes's intimates) put it, democratic politics easily falls prey to emotions and it is 'the business of those outside politics to prepare the ground for the wiser politician' (quoted in de Wilde 1991: 88).

Rhodes's 'Society of the Elect' and its 'Association of Helpers', were meant to provide the element of preparation and direction in the new context. The 'Elect' included Rhodes himself; Nathan Rothschild, grandson of the founder of the City Rothschilds's bank; William T. Stead, the journalist; Reginald Baliol Brett, the above-mentioned Lord Esher, confidant of Queen Victoria, King Edward VII (who was also Grand Master of British Freemasonry in his days), and King George V; Alfred Milner, British High Commissioner during the Boer War, and others (a full list is in Quigley 1981: Appendix). Milner's think tank of young Oxford graduates in South Africa, the 'Kindergarten', served as a breeding ground for future Commonwealth and Atlantic ruling class planners and it was after him that the Rhodes network has been named in its further development. The Rhodes–Milner Group overlapped with the *Round Table* groups set up in 1909 to provide a forum for discussing Commonwealth affairs; and with the 'Cliveden Set', after the country estate of the Anglo-American Astors which in the 1920s became a meeting point for the group and its foreign contacts. According to Quigley (1981: 5), the Union of South Africa, the British Commonwealth, as well as the League of Nations, were largely shaped by the planning work of the Milner group, operating behind the scenes at crucial junctures and in the places that mattered.

As a structure of socialisation through which a momentary ruling class consensus is shaped, transmitted and transformed into policy, the Rhodes–Milner Group became the model for all subsequent policy planning groups. In the context of the early twentieth century, it was able to find an imperialist way out of national class conflict.

State monopolism implies that the state prominently assists in the task of imposing the discipline of capital on the vastly enlarged industrial working class, employed in new types of industry. The welfare–nationalist state as defined by Cox can be understood in this light. 'The merger of nationalism and welfare was in the first instance an initiative from above, a pre-emptive stroke by state managers aware of the disruptive potential of the social forces generated by urbanization and industrialism' (Cox 1987: 157). To the ideologues of the British Empire rallied by Rhodes, this configuration of forces was to be geared to imperial expansion. The working classes should be educated into conceiving the British Empire as a historic structure of civilisation, the realisation of a moral idea of freedom – an idea which Rhodes took from Oxford art historian John Ruskin and from historian Alfred Toynbee (uncle of Arnold Toynbee of *Study of History* fame, one of the 'Association of Helpers'). The benevolent attitude towards the workers was primarily aesthetical, aimed at displacing scenes of bloodshed to beyond the horizon. As Lenin quotes Rhodes in a famous passage of his tract on imperialism (*Coll. Works* 22: 257), 'If you want to avoid civil war, you must become imperialists.'

A civilisational mission of this magnitude dovetailed with the projections for foreign ventures conceived by the City financiers, but finance alone could not realise it and neither could its execution be planned by an insufficiently coherent network such as Freemasonry. Although a mason himself (Rich 1988: 188n; Milner, too, was a mason – Lennhoff and Posner 1932: 41), to Rhodes the model for his secret society were the Jesuits. His society was to be, in the words of an American secretary to the Rhodes Trust, 'a church for the extension of the British empire', and W.T. Stead claimed afterwards that 'Mr. Rhodes . . . aspired to be the creator of one of those vast semi-religious, quasi-political associations which, like the Society of Jesus, have played so large a part in the history of the world' (quoted in Quigley 1981: 34, 36). The 'reclaiming' of the United States was a crucial ambition in the Rhodes project, but effectively, it was a British Empire/Commonwealth network.

Carroll Quigley has documented the role of the Rhodes–Milner Group in amazing detail. His *Anglo-American Establishment* (1981, originally of 1949 – which, incidentally, hardly deals with any Americans) and the subsequent *Tragedy and Hope* (of 1966, in which the same information is embedded in a larger history of civilisation) are almost unreadable for their wealth of factual information on personal life histories, webs of intermarriage, financial group and industry links, and Milner group actions leading to political decisions of great importance. Gramsci's notion of the role of planning groups and think-tanks as 'collective intellectuals' of/for the ruling class transpires clearly from

Quigley's work. Thus as long as Britain's power was undisputed, the real rulers of country and empire were drawn from the loose network of families called, after the family name of Lord Salisbury, the Cecil bloc. It was only after the disintegration of this bloc after the turn of the century (i.e. when Balfour, a nephew of Lord Salisbury's, took over its reins and the pattern of rule they held on to lost its effectiveness) that the Milner group moved to centre stage. In Quigley's words (1981: 29):

> Milner shifted the emphasis from family connection to ideological agreement. The former had become less useful with the rise of a class society based on economic conflicts and with the extension of democracy. Salisbury was fundamentally a conservative, while Milner was not. Where Salisbury sought to build up a bloc of friends and relatives to exercise the game of politics and to maintain the Old England they all loved, Milner was not really a conservative at all. Milner had an idea – the idea that he obtained from Toynbee and that he found also in Rhodes and in all the members of his Group. This idea had two parts: that the extension and integration of the Empire and the development of social welfare was essential to the continued existence of the British way of life; and that this British way of life was an instrument which unfolded all the best and the highest capabilities of mankind.

Oxford colleges served as the main training and recruiting ground for the leaders in this movement, in particular All Souls, Balliol, and New College (Quigley 1981: 20–2, 97–9; see also Sampson on these same colleges, 1965: 226, 246–7, 260). The group's influence also extended, less exclusively, to other universities and particular chairs, both in Britain and e.g. in Canada (University of Toronto and Upper Canada College), and radiated through various international academic co-operation networks set up by Alfred Zimmern in the League period (Quigley 1981: 259; Zimmern later became a driving force behind UNESCO, see also my 1996a: 93). Other networks spawned from the Rhodes–Milner group are the Rhodes Trust which to this day recruits promising English-speaking students (see for example the Rhodes trustees including the President himself in the Clinton administration, *Nw*; 4 May and 26 October 1992); the Royal Institute of International Affairs (RIIA) and its publications; the Carnegie foundations in the US; and key newspapers such as *The Times* of London. Thus a body like the Milner Group could bring cohesion to the outlook of the class it was serving, but in fact, was also leading.

A central concern of the Milner group, and as we saw, of Rhodes, was to draw a privileged segment of the workers into alliance with the ruling class by rallying them behind a chauvinist imperialism. Lionel Curtis, one of Milner's 'Kindergarten' in South Africa, and later to ascend into the 'Society of the Elect', in 1900 outlined the nature of the class compromise underlying corporate liberalism when he wrote that whites were turned indolent and incompetent by the presence of large numbers of blacks. In his view, 'It would be a blessed thing for us if the negro like the Red Indian tended to die out before us, for he acts like decay among teeth. The tendency of Trade Unions to exclude coloured labour should be fostered by all patriotic men in Australia and America' (quoted in Sampson 1987: 69).

The willingness to involve the metropolitan working class in imperialism illustrates that neither empire, nor the particular mode by which the discipline of capital was to be imposed, were ever formulated dogmatically, disregarding the shifting grounds of class relations. To acknowledge this is where a class analysis parts ways with élitism or a conspiracy theory. For after reading Quigley's work and running through the lists of 'members' of the Milner group in its various editions, one realises that only the function of providing ideological cohesion is a constant. Otherwise, *all* the points of disagreement between fractions of the ruling class emerge *within* the Milner group itself. The momentous shift from liberal internationalism to a state monopoly tendency for instance took place within the same group of power-brokers. On a question like appeasement with Germany or supporting the League of Nations, the dividing lines ran straight through the Milner group (Quigley 1966: 581–2); both International Relations 'idealists' like Zimmern, and their fiercest critic within the circle of legitimate academic discourse, E.H. Carr, are listed among the membership (1981: Appendix). This highlights the flexibility and capacity for adjustment and initiative of a directive centre such as the Rhodes–Milner group. Indeed as Tom Nairn points out (1973: 33), 'The task of an effective ruling-class ideologist is not merely to "reflect" existing fields of force in a static sense … but to "sound out", to prospect a plausible future and synthesize some decent new clothes for a reality still emergent, naked, and not quite conscious of itself.' (See also the Morse quotation at the head of this chapter.) This 'plausible future' may be radically incongruent with the present and yet, from a ruling class view, retain its key structural characteristics.

What remains, then, is the notion of class power operating through a shifting structure of processes of capital accumulation and imperial expansion, but seeking to hold its own through the changes. As to the critical passage from liberal internationalism to state monopolism, Quigley's analysis reveals how the ruling class was able to adjust to changed circumstances by regrouping behind hitherto marginal notions and allowing their representatives a more prominent place. The Rhodes–Milner group had been supported financially by the banking bourgeoisie financing Britain's imperial push – Rhodes himself set up De Beers Consolidated Mines, the South African diamond monopoly in 1888, as well as Consolidated Gold Fields, with support from the London Rothschilds who still today control world gold trade (Morton 1963: 125, 183); Alfred Beit and his German associates, who later brought Rhodes into their gold mining company, Central Mining, worked with money from the German and French Rothschilds (Sampson 1987: 62); several of the other merchant banks (Barings, Hambros, and Lazards), as well as Barclays, Lloyds Bank, and

Midland Bank, were linked to the Milner group by one or more of their directors (Quigley 1981: 190). But the group's role was not one of a bank pressure group. For if high finance in this era 'functioned as the main link between the political and the economic organization of the world' (Polanyi 1957: 10), capital accumulation had come to depend increasingly on the new heavy industries and the overseas infrastructural projects on which they thrived. Their requirements for political support eventually overturned the entire constellation of nineteenth-century capital.

> After the banking crisis of 1931, the whole structure of international finance with which the Group has been so closely associated disappeared and, after a brief period of doubt, was replaced by a rapid growth of monopolistic national capitalism. This was accepted by the Milner Group with hardly a break in stride. [W.L.] Hichens [chairman of Cammell Laird] had been deeply involved in monopolistic heavy industry for a quarter of a century in 1932. Milner had advocated a system of "national capitalism" with "industrial self-regulation" [i.e., cartels] behind tariff walls even earlier. . . . As a result, in the period 1931–1933, the Milner Group willingly liquidated reparations, war debts, and the whole structure of international capitalism, and embraced protection and cartels instead (Quigley 1981: 248).

Anglo–American ruling class rivalry

The Rhodes project aimed at integrating the heartland including the United States. Its 'Anglo-Saxon' mythology was reciprocated from the other side of the Atlantic even if ultimately, the ambitions of the American bourgeoisie could not be accommodated in the *Pax Britannica*. In spite of many of the same forms of entrenched class privilege (such as family listings in the Social Register, etc.), the vast spaces open to enterprise in America tended to evade the fixed hierarchies and strictures of the British class structure. 'What emerges after the first four decades of modern capitalism is a significantly higher economic mobility into the elite, but in a manner which in no way alters the economic and social structure of capitalism or the distribution of income and wealth,' Kolko concludes (1976: 254).[2]

Rhodes's concern to integrate the working classes into an imperialist alliance, too, obtained an American counterpoint. But in the US context, pragmatism prevailed over secret society romanticism – even if the missionary twist to class compromise could not do without idealism. The corporate liberal concept, for which Fordism would eventually provide a solid foundation, was already elaborated in the context of the National Civic Federation (NCF) in the period leading up to World War I. Prominent in its articulation were Secretary of State Elihu Root and George Perkins, a J.P. Morgan partner. President Taft, Andrew Carnegie, and the future President, F.D. Roosevelt, were also involved in the NCF (Weinstein 1970: 104–8).

J.P. Morgan was the American counterpart to a City magnate and the towering force in the Atlantic economy around the turn of the century. Morgan reorganised the Carnegie interests into US Steel, and set up a series of other investment trusts attracting British portfolio capital (General Electric, AT&T, and others). The US Steel venture left Carnegie, a fervent supporter of the English-speaking idea, with a vast fortune which he devoted to furthering English-speaking civilisation, education, and world peace through the philanthropies referred to already. Elihu Root became the first president of the Carnegie Endowment for International Peace (see my 1996a: 131–2).

By their press and political connections, the American investment bankers also ensured that the conditions for sustained class power and privilege remained in place. In a sense, an investment bank empire such as Morgan in this period functioned not unlike a planning group – albeit with economic management much more in the foreground, unadorned by the imperial ideals of the type entertained by Rhodes. As Lundberg has shown in his 1937 classic, *America's 60 Families* (to which he adds a supporting layer of another ninety), the investment banks and their economic strongholds explore opportunities and oversee ongoing operations for the families they serve. 'All these families . . . own more wealth than the individuals they deputize to watch over their interests. In general, they leave most of the supervision of fiscal affairs to [the likes of] J.P. Morgan and Company, or act upon Morgan advice, knowing it to be in their own interest' (Lundberg 1937: 36).

In 1901, Morgan sought to link up to the Rhodes–Milner group directly by soliciting Milner to become his partner in the City. When Milner declined the offer, E. C. Grenfell instead lent his name to the merchant bank Morgan, Grenfell (Quigley 1966: 950–1; see also Sampson 1965: 437). Morgan partner Thomas Lamont was a member, along with Walter Lippmann and others, of the American Round Table group, a branch of the British Round Table (see my 1984: 53). Many other connections can be mentioned, because 'the Milner Group has always had very close relationships with the associates of J.P. Morgan and with the various branches of the Carnegie Trust' (Quigley 1981: 183). But the US also included a Mid-West and other regional centres in which, across the different classes, the self-evidence of associating with Britain was much less obvious or even actively contested (Hofstadter 1955: 78–9; 278).

Lippmann in the course of the World War I assumed the role of an intellectual courier between the British and American ruling classes, developing his ideas of collective Anglo-American control along the way. Indeed in two world wars, Lippmann championed the notion of an 'Atlantic community' at moments when this was far from self-evident, i.e. in 1916 and 1943, respectively (see my 1984: 53–5; 134–5). Dispatched to explain Wilson's Fourteen Points to the British government, he urged the President to intervene and save bourgeois Europe from collapse. In Wilson's body of advisers at Versailles, nicknamed *The Inquiry* (which also functioned as an intelligence unit (O'Toole 1991: ch. 26)), Lippmann again was the animating spirit. Otherwise, it 'was manned almost completely by persons from institutions (including universities) dominated by J.P. Morgan and Co.' (Quigley 1981: 183).

At this point, along with the transfer of the City's international creditor role to Wall Street in the course of World War I, the scales between the Morgan network and the Rhodes–Milner group were turned as well. In the Dawes Plan and Young Plan episodes of 1924 and 1929, the Morgan bank was the chief player and it was the only private partner alongside six European central banks in the Bank for International Settlements in Basle, put in place by the Young Plan (Rochester 1936: 280). In South Africa, the Milner group's backyard, Morgan supported Ernest Oppenheimer and his Anglo-American Corporation, Anglo-American, eventually engulfed De Beers, Rhodes's company, and became the biggest financial group in South Africa (Sampson 1987: 72–5).

The attempt to launch a single transatlantic planning body by building on the activities of the Inquiry and the Rhodes–Milner Group, did not succeed – on the one hand, because of the shift in the US domestic mood away from European involvement; on the other, because of underlying frictions with the British ruling class. The envisaged Anglo-American Institute of International Affairs remained still-born. The RIIA, founded by Lionel Curtis, and the American Council on Foreign Relations (CFR) dominated by Morgan men, went their own ways (Shoup and Minter 1977: ch. 1). At various junctures, especially when the larger heartland structure needed an overhaul in the light of new challenges, the CFR served as a testing ground for alternative policy recommendations, interlocking with the transnational planning groups we will discuss in the next section. Thus in late 1940, the CFR made an inventory of 'the political, military, territorial and economic requirements of the United States in its potential leadership of the non-German world area including the United Kingdom itself as well as the Western Hemisphere and Far East' (ibid.: 128). Many more examples of CFR policy planning, including the '1980s Project' which explored a world under collective western management, are detailed in Shoup and Minter's study. All along, the central concern of these projects was to disrupt the crystallisation of a closed, rival bloc in a contender posture based on a Hobbesian state/society configuration (such as a German-dominated Europe in the 1930s and 1940s, the Soviet bloc, and the NIEO coalition later) and to raise the level of integration of the heartland (see also Silk and Silk 1981: ch. 6).

Transnational faultlines in the contender states

High finance in the contender states from the start faced the reality of an already established, hegemonic heartland in control of the commanding heights of the world economy. This on the one hand tended to produce a faultline in the capitalist class between a fraction seeking to expand by concentric circles and with state aid, and one willing to ride the coat-tails of Anglo-American capital. The capacity to establish directive centres such as the Rhodes–Milner group in the British Empire, or the Morgan orbit in the US around the turn of the century, hence was critically undermined to the extent that such an 'off-shore' fraction existed. On the other hand, the transnationally fractured condition of capital in the contender states in turn reinforced the state role as the necessary means to provide cohesion and thus sustain the catch-up effort.

In France, for instance, rivalry between the Rothschilds who emerged as a transnational network (including a masonic one) linked to British hegemony, and Fould, who supported Napoleon III and the strong state, worked against a unified stance. Fould, backers of the famous Crédit Mobilier bank of the Péreire brothers (Morton 1963: 112), were also among the founders of the Paribas investment bank in the late nineteenth century, which built its financial group and sphere of influence in North Africa and Russia with close state support. The Entente Cordiale with Britain on the eve of World War I in no small way was prepared by compromises 'between the interests of the Banque de Paris et des Pays-Bas [its full name] and the interests of British banks' (Claude 1969: 23). After the war and still after World War II, the Paribas group became linked by several connections to the Chase group of the Rockefellers (via Lazard Frères, also through FIAT – Pastré 1979: 105, 162–3; see also my 1984: 80–1), but always with a strong emphasis on retaining its autonomy. This applied also to the prominent nationalised sector, which was closest to the Paribas pole in French finance.

The opposing pole, that of 'off-shore' capital oriented towards its own economy as if it descended on it from the outside, in the twentieth century crystallised around the Suez Canal company, part-owned by British interests, and the financial group configured around its successor bank. After the nationalisation of the Canal in 1956, the Suez bank aligned with the Schneider and Indochine groups with which the Giscard family had a privileged relationship (see my 1984: 170–1). The French Rothschilds, retaining intimate links with the London branch, later gravitated into this alliance as well (Morin 1974: 169). But its political connections (the French Rothschilds split into two rival financial centres) were more diverse, to Gaullism for instance (see also Claude 1972).

While in France itself, the state has remained a necessary and indispensable arbitrator between these different orientations, the élite planning bodies in which French capitalists participated typically were the transnational ones we will discuss in the next section and which among other things served to integrate the bourgeoisie from the former contender states into the emerging global ruling class.

If we look next at Germany, we may observe a comparable pattern of a strong national, state constraint and a paradoxically fractured ruling class. Because the purgatory effects of the French Revolution remained limited, the German class structure long retained certain pre-Hobbesian, quasi-feudal aspects. The banking aristocracy occupied a position which in this respect resembles the British configuration – a characteristic Germany shares with its 'generation' of contender states – Italy, Austria–Hungary and Japan.

Nineteenth-century merchant bankers settled in different urban centres (Bleichröder in Berlin, Schröders in Hamburg, Steins, Schnitzlers, and Oppenheims in Cologne (Coston 1963: 37–8)) and won aristocratic titles for their financial services. But much more than their British counterparts, the German banking barons remained a closed caste. Quoting Robert Michels, himself a Schnitzler descendant, Pritzkoleit (1959: 210) shows that inter-marriage 'hermetically closed off this stratum "from below", in a material and of course also in an ideological sense'. As a consequence, the very class which on account of its wealth was entitled to lead the process of industrialisation, 'remained too small and too weak to achieve it' (ibid.: 187). The ennobled merchant bank families retained a power to act as the guardians of the general class interest, but in practice, this general interest was refracted through the prism of a broader, Atlantic one. Thus Baron Kurt von Schröder, a partner of the Stein bank since 1921 and a member of the pro-Nazi Keppler Circle, secured business support for Hitler at a moment when this also worked as an insurance for accumulated Anglo-American capital in Germany (Gossweiler 1975: 344; Stegmann 1976: 47f).

Back in the nineteenth century, the ascendant new industries seeking an investment banking connection, however, had to help themselves. Here too, the availability of a heartland connection as a potential competitive advantage worked to split off an 'off-shore' fraction from the banking bourgeoisie. The Deutsche Bank was set up by Georg von Siemens in 1870. It henceforth remained closely linked to the Siemens electrical engineering concern, as well as to Mannesmann, Daimler-Benz, and other powerful industrial corporations typically of an independent, often innovative orientation (*OMGUS* 1985: 19–25; Gossweiler 1975: 329). Against its 'European' orientation, comparable to that of Paribas in France (with which it co-operated at the EEC's foundation in 1957, see also Coston 1963: 24), a rival constellation, configured around Dresdner Bank, Krupp, and AEG, after World War I fell back to a dependent position relative to Anglo-American capital. Thus the business agreement between the Dresdner Bank and J.P. Morgan in 1905, after the war, turned the former into a junior partner, and US investment henceforth would typically flow through this bank and the Danat bank in the same coalition (see also Figure 2.2, p. 54; Gossweiler 1975: 42–3; *OMGUS* 1986: 34–5).

In Japan, the subordination of capital to the state, sustained also by the distance in time and space from the heartland, has long worked against 'off-shore' alliances of capital. A liberal orientation existed around the Mitsui group, and certain aspects of a straight world market strategy later emerged in the case of e.g. Sony (Ruigrok and van Tulder 1995: 158). But the revolution from above, by which the Hobbesian configuration came about, incorporated a strong feudal element. 'Already before the [Meiji] Restoration,' Norman writes (1940: 61), 'one notes a blurring and breaking down of the old class lines, the uneven fusion of one wing of the feudal ruling class . . . with the more powerful merchants.' Through the successive phases of the country's 'passive' adaptation to outside-imposed reforms (van den Berg

1995), the clan-like structure of the Japanese ruling class has remained largely intact. The big financial groups built their empires by purchasing, at bargain prices, state-launched strategic industries and most have remained in the managerial state embrace (Norman 1940: 131; Alletzhauser 1990: 64–5). Hence, whereas French and Germans and other European capitalists were already involved in transnational planning groups centred on the heartland in the 1930s and 1940s, the inclusion of a Japanese contingent in such bodies had to wait until the 1970s. Let us now turn to these transnational élite planning groups and the role they have played in integrating the bourgeoisie from the contender states.

Hegemonic integration of the state classes

Often building on the 'off-shore' integration into international circuits of capital discussed above, the aspiring bourgeoisie in France, Prussia/Germany, and all subsequent challengers to heartland pre-eminence, were simultaneously being integrated into informal networks and private planning groups which from the interwar years onwards served as meeting grounds with the heartland bourgeoisie. All along, through confrontation and even war, processes of transnational class formation cut across apparently fixed inter-national dividing lines. The 'elastic frameworks' created by passive revolution in the Hobbesian states themselves thus were enhanced and complemented by transnational channels preparing hegemonic integration. In the process, the impulses passed on to the interior of these states (increasingly on the rhythm of transnational political business cycles) worked to dissolve the dependency of all social classes on the state and turn the various state class fractions (e.g. those designated by Granou 1977 – 'state banking bourgeoisie', 'state industrial bourgeoisie' etc.) into a bourgeoisie increasingly active in the global political economy on its own account, as part of an immanent world capital facing the working classes. This of course was not a straight evolutionary process, but one characterised by highly unequal development, interruptions and shock-like accelerations – always in unique combinations. All along, moreover, 'hegemony' as the dominant mode of integration was accompanied by coercion and occasionally, actual violence backing up the imposition of capitalist discipline on an expanded scale and in novel forms.

Our general proposition (which must remain a hypothesis here) is that in the transnational political business cycle, enhanced internationalisation of capital and heartland hegemony will tend to activate the 'off-shore' element in the contender states, both in the fraction sense and as a prevailing mood across the board. This can be argued to have happened in the second half of the 1920s, the late 1940s, the early 1960s, the second half of the 1970s and again after 1985 (see my 1984 and 1989a). Contraction of the internationalisation process, on the other hand, will tend to leave the terrain to the contender element – as in the 1930s, 1950s, and through the crisis conjunctures of 1966–74 and 1979–85. Since policy planning is typically a product of crisis conditions, when a current concept of control unravels in the face of challenges it cannot satisfactorily deal with, one would expect the creation of new planning bodies to have been concentrated in the contraction periods, when the challenge of the contender states became acute and rivalry generally mounted. At such junctures, the constellation of financial groups and planning bodies by which ruling class power has been reproduced so far, inevitably loses ground to new claimants for a directive/intellectual role. Also, as the spatial and structural coordinates of the discipline of capital are being redefined, planning, too (which, as we saw, is a moment of socialisation ultimately driven by capital accumulation itself), requires being recast at a higher level of sophistication and determination.

A final observation here is that in many cases, new planning groups have been the initiative of *mediators* between the heartland and the main contender bourgeoisies. These mediators tended to come from smaller countries situated in between the major blocs confronting each other along the lines drawn in chapter 3. Sometimes, the mediating function rested on the structural position of such a country's corporations in between major groupings (as with Dutch corporations connecting 'the Anglo-Saxon network with the West German network', Fennema 1982: 113). Occasionally, the mediating position also resulted from a state's remaining outside a major confrontation while providing a 'neutral' safe-haven for capital links which had to be cloaked to survive the emergency, such as Sweden in World War II (Aalders and Wiebes 1990). But there was perhaps also the element of perceiving the broader, transnational class interest more clearly from a country with no possible great power ambitions. At any rate, the Belgians, the Dutch, the Polish, the Swiss and, in Asia, the South Koreans, have performed this mediating function, acting as initiators/convenors of crucial fora in which the main antagonists were to meet.

The coming of corporate liberalism and Atlantic unity

State monopolism in the early twentieth century militated against transnational integration, but World War I investment bankers attempted to resurrect liberal internationalism in the changed conditions. The central forum for transnational consultations available to the capitalist class from the heartland and the contender states was the International Chamber of Commerce (ICC) in Paris, the successor body to the pre-1914 International Congress of Chambers of Commerce.[3] A petition to reduce German and Austrian reparations was started by British and American bankers jointly with neutral Dutch and Swedish colleagues (Ridgeway 1938: 39–45; see also my 1984: 63). After the Dawes Plan of 1924, a German contingent was admitted into the ICC. It included Kurt von Schröder, E. Poensgen of the German steel trust Vestag, and others (Ridgeway 1938: 21).

Parallel to this *rapprochement*, the Rhodes–Milner Group prevailed on Gustav Stresemann to pursue the 'fulfilment policy' of paying wartime reparations.

This paved the way for the 1925 Locarno Treaty fixating Germany's western borders (Quigley 1981: 244–5). The International Steel Cartel, set up in 1926 and on a revamped basis again in 1933 (Hexner 1943), also should be understood as a meeting ground of Anglo-Saxon and continental European capitalist interests. Private co-operation agreements between German and American capital (e.g. IG Farben and Rockefeller's Standard Oil, N.J.), direct investments (General Motors in Opel, General Electric in AEG (Allgemeine Elektrizitaets Gesellschaft)) in the late 1920s created many additional links (Aalders and Wiebes 1990: 27).

Appeasement with Hitler built on these connections and also prefigured postwar European integration. In the Anglo-German Fellowship, a key role was played by the Dutchman, Paul Rijkens, of Unilever, and his fellow director D'Arcy Cooper, in addition to British economic statesmen with links to German capital such as the Chamberlain family and Oliver Lyttelton (Overbeek 1990: 69; Rijkens 1965: 76). But the 'off-shore' fraction in Nazi Germany, grouped around Carl Goerdeler (the internationalist mayor of Leipzig, adviser of the Robert Bosch electrical concern, and main organiser of the July 1944 *coup* attempt) was weak and divided – as was, in this case, the Milner Group (Quigley 1981: 146–7; Aalders and Wiebes 1990: 52).

In the meantime, the restructuring of American capital in the New Deal had created a new configuration of forces. In the effort to contain the groundswell of working class revolt and agrarian protest, the American productive and class structure was recast around the progressive mode of accumulation (Fordism). By several steps, the initial state-monopolistic orientation of the New Deal was deflected towards a corporate liberal concept which rehabilitated internationalisation of capital as an escape route out of domestic class compromise (Ferguson 1984; see also my 1984: 93–4). One aspect of this restructuring was that (also due to New Deal bank legislation) Morgan's influence was eclipsed by the Rockefeller financial group and its allies, configured around the Chase National Bank, also in the Council on Foreign Relations (Shoup and Minter 1977: ch. 3; see also Menshikov 1973: 273). But the very idea of a single power centre is no longer valid for the postwar situation, although as we shall see, David Rockefeller would play an important role both at the level of planning group formation and in guiding US presidential decisions directly.

The corporate liberal concept as it crystallised in the course of the New Deal's evolution was articulated in such settings as the Committee on Economic Development (CED) and the Ford Foundation. Its full implications perhaps became apparent only with the New Deal's extrapolation to Western Europe in the Marshall Plan and after, because then the aspect of internationalisation allowed the broadening of the class alliance to include the pre-war liberal internationalists. It also removed concern about the implications of the compromise with the organised working class in a sealed-off domestic context. The backbone to corporate liberalism however were the ascendant 'C' industries in which progressive accumulation had matured, first of all the automotive complex and 'Fordism' (Rupert 1995; Andreff 1976). Hence the key role of Studebaker executive Paul Hoffman in the CED, the Marshall Plan, and the Ford Foundation (Silk and Silk 1981: chs 4 and 7).

The envisaged projection of American power under a new concept of control was made the basis for a renewal of transnational consultations in wartime London. Significantly, the secretary to General Sikorsky of Poland and intelligence agent, Joseph Retinger, emerged as the animator of various discussion groups bringing together European leaders-in-exile. Its most important outcome, the European (originally Independent) League for Economic Co-operation (ELEC), aimed at organising the European bourgeoisie away from state monopolism. Its members 'represented the élite of modern liberalism in Europe,' Rebattet writes (1962: 4–5): '[ELEC] was in fact an association for promoting free trade, sharing the laissez-faire spirit of the International Chamber of Commerce with which it had many personal links.' Paul Rijkens and the Dutch Prince-Consort, Bernhard, were active on the same circuit, and the first and second chairmen of ELEC were a Belgian, Paul van Zeeland, future Foreign Minister and linked to the Solvay chemical concern, and a Dutchman, Kerstens, Minister of Economic Affairs in London. The mediating role of these small countries' representatives then helped to bring the economic statesmen from the main powers together in the aftermath of war. E. Giscard d'Estaing, father of the future French president (see also my 1984: 170) and representing French Indochina interests, became president of the French branch; from West Germany, the head of the Deutsche Bank group, H. J. Abs, the Bavarian fiefholder, F.J. Strauss, as well as the Atlanticist liberal, Erhard (the spokesman of the export and foreign-owned industries deployed around the Dresdner Bank), were members of ELEC (names in Rebattet 1962).

Although for the British ruling class, the remoteness of the domestic political scene which the groups exiled in London could use to their advantage, did not exist, the Labour election victory catalysed a shift away from the imperialist bloc around the Rhodes–Milner group. But the City *haute finance* and masonry (to which even Attlee owed his rise in the party, see also Knight 1985: 207–8) remained strong. Yet in spite of the stunted growth of Fordism in Britain (Overbeek 1990), Lord Nuffield (William Morris), the nearest British equivalent of Henry Ford, did establish new intellectual centres attuned to corporate liberalism which the strongholds of the Rhodes–Milner group could not match. To give but one example, All Souls in Oxford was marginalised by Nuffield College, founded in 1937. Topics here no longer were theology and Latin, but sociology and International Relations (Sampson 1965: 247; *Chambers' Biog. Dict.*: 'Nuffield'). Quigley's 1949 claim that Nuffield College (and the powerful Nuffield philanthropies) were controlled by the Milner Group (1981: 100) is questionable, although it took until the Suez débâcle before ELEC member Harold Macmillan and fellow corporate liberals could take over the Conservative Party.

By this time, centrifugal tendencies surfacing in the wake of the Marshall Plan were reactivating the forces which in the 1930s and 1940s had sought to integrate the German bourgeoisie. Jean Monnet's considerations in launching the Coal and Steel Community included not only playing off German and French workers against each other (Kolko and Kolko 1972: 468), but also, as he notes in his memoirs, fears that overproduction of steel would lead to a return of protectionism and cartels, 'and perhaps a reorientation of German expansion to the east, prelude to political agreements' (Monnet 1976: 346; on Monnet's network of acquaintances from his pre-war investment banking days, see my 1984: 65, 225–6). The most important outcome of this episode in terms of transnational planning groups however were the Bilderberg Conferences for which discussions began in 1952 (a first conference was held in 1954 in the Netherlands). Again, Retinger, Rijkens and Prince Bernhard were primarily involved.

Bilderberg was the first truly North Atlantic planning body. It assembled, in the spirit of corporate liberalism, representatives of Right and Left, capital and organised labour, thus side-stepping the élitist connotations of earlier experiences with private policy-planning (Rijkens 1965: 138). With help from the CIA and Unilever, and an American support committee including David Rockefeller, Dean Rusk, head of the Rockefeller Foundation; and Joseph Johnson, head of the Carnegie Endowment, Bilderberg served to involve West German (again, Abs, Strauss, etc.) as well as other continental European economic statesmen into the 'long-term planning [on] an international order which would look beyond the present-day crisis', as the minutes of its first conference put it (quoted in Eringer 1980: 22; see also Thompson 1980). According to Rijkens, the Americans in particular came to value Bilderberg as the only platform for confidential discussions with European counterparts on often sensitive issues (1965: 145–6).

The question which actual 'decisions' have been taken at Bilderberg meetings meanwhile would be a wrong one, because as we saw, planning groups are fora for exploring new ground, overcoming disagreements, and building confidence. But several participants credited the relaunch of European integration after the Defence Community débâcle to the 1955 Bilderberg meeting in Garmisch, West Germany. The consensus at that conference was such that those present were encouraged, according to the minutes, to 'pass these views on to public opinion in their own spheres of influence, without disclosing their source' (quoted in Eringer 1980: 30, see also 26). At the Fredensborg, Denmark, meeting a year later, attention shifted to NATO unity in the face of the changing posture of the USSR and to the threat of a declining Western hold on the expanding UN (ibid.: 30–1). The actual establishment of the EEC and Euratom in 1957 was accompanied by private agreements, such as the setting up of the European Society for Industrial Development by the Deutsche Bank and its French counterpart in terms of 'European' allegiance, Paribas (Coston 1963: 24).

A vehicle of transnational class formation parallel to Bilderberg in paving the way for hegemonic integration in this period was the Fondation Euro-péenne de la Culture, launched again by Rijkens, Retinger, and Prince

Bernhard. It more particularly was designed to foster a 'European identity', defined around the 'freedom of the soul' and against communism. Among its members were such scions of European culture as Abs, Gustav Stein, and steel magnate H. Reusch next to corporate statesmen from other countries (Rijkens 1965: 149–50; for parallel cultural networks, see Lasch 1967). Further Atlantic bodies emerging in the early 1960s were the Atlantic Council, the Ditchley Foundation, and the Atlantic Institute (see Gill 1991: 132).

A true mass movement never got off the ground, although the attempts to launch one were often meaningful. The European Movement, the postwar umbrella organisation for ELEC and various Federalist movements remained an élite body subsidised by the CIA, industrial and banking interests and connected mainly to political parties (Rebattet 1962; see also my 1978: 102–8). More directly linked to Fordism was Rev. Frank Buchman's Moral Re-Armament movement (MRA), which dated from the interwar years. Seeking to provide a code of behaviour that combined anti-communist militancy with the social standardisation required for early mass consumption, the MRA was actually endorsed by Henry Ford. It already reached out to the Nazis before resurfacing in Western Europe in the 1950s (Nederveen Pieterse 1992: 5–6; see also on Fordist standardisation, Gramsci 1971: 303). But the religious twist which the MRA sought to provide to the Cold War was already accounted for by developments in the main churches. While the Catholic church was most outspoken in its anti-communism all along (van Wesel 1992), the World Council of Churches (WCC), in which John Foster Dulles during the 1940s held a key position, already during the war prepared plans to reintegrate Germany and Central European countries such as Poland and Czechoslovakia into an expanded free world centred on the United States. The need to modernise religious life in line with the changing realities of a mass consumption society and the WCC's commitment to European integration had induced the Rockefellers to start subsidising the ecumenical movement and the World Council during the war. At that time its Secretary-General, Visser 't Hooft, resided in Switzerland where he stood in contact with the later head of the CIA, Allen Dulles – like his brother, a director of the J. Henry Schroeder bank in New York and trustee of German interests abroad (Visser 't Hooft 1971; see also my 1978: 170–1).

These forces, too, should be taken into account when assessing the capacity of a planning group such as Bilderberg to actually mobilise a broader class alliance and influence the course of events. After all, Bilderberg's role in synthesising conflicting forces and viewpoints was amplified by them and by links to other planning bodies or private associations, diplomatic links at the state as well as inter-state level (IMF, OEEC/OECD, etc.), and through intelligence services. Neither should we forget that such older networks as Freemasonry continued to function. To give but one example, when the headquarters of the Italian Grand Lodge, confiscated by Mussolini, were returned to it in 1960, James Zellerbach, US ambassador in Rome, and CIA agent Frank Gigliotti, who had assisted in the preceding negotiations with the Italian government, were both guests of honour. Zellerbach, chairman of the board of paper company Crown-Zellerbach, was also a rapporteur at the first Bilderberg Conference and a prominent member henceforth. In light of the later role of the *Propaganda Due* (P2) lodge in Italy and the profusion of masonic lodges at NATO bases in Italy, an event like this should be part of our understanding of how state (including intelligence) and private forces combine to form a complex web of Atlantic class links, with a potential operational capacity at that (Willan 1991: 58; Eringer 1980: 49; *Who's Who in America 1964–1965*: 'Zellerbach, J.D.' – see also also 'Zellerbach, H.L.').

Another example of how apparently unrelated forms of organisation assist in the process of transnational class formation (and in this case, also very definitely in integrating a Hobbesian state class) is provided by the 'opening' towards Europe of the Francoist Spanish economy in the late 1950s. This development, as Otto Holman has shown, occurred under the auspices of technocrats of Opus Dei who had entered the government in 1957. Their aim was to adjust class relations in Spain to the pattern of the newly established EEC but simultaneously, to guarantee continuity with the authoritarian Spanish political order (Holman 1996: 57). In this classic example of a passive revolution, Opus Dei, a catholic lay organisation committed to modernisation in a rigidly conservative socio-political framework, acted as part of a transnational network extending across Europe to Latin America and including a number of major banks (van Wesel 1992: 263–7). Ultimately, the opening of Spain to the world market entailed the unforeseen consequence, upon Franco's death, of a transformation of the state form itself to a corporate liberal one coinciding with Southern Europe's tentative integration into the heartland under Social Democratic auspices (Holman 1987–88).

The crisis of corporate liberalism and the trilateral interregnum

In the late 1960s, mounting working class militancy, a youth movement marking the rise to adulthood of the first postwar generation, the black emancipation drive in the United States, and world-wide protest against that country's war in Vietnam, combined to unravel the corporate liberal concept of control which had become hegemonic on the promise of material fulfilment. But now that its promises were about to be fulfilled, it seemed not only that material demands related to mass consumption had become secondary to ethical and cultural aspirations, but heartland pre-eminence was crumbling in the face of a profit squeeze and the rise of a bloc of Hobbesian states committed to demands of equal treatment and a reordering of the global political economy towards what later became the project for a New International Economic Order (Cox 1979; Krasner 1985).

The Club of Rome, set up between 1968 and 1970 with money from European philanthropists linked to the automotive industry such as the Agnelli and Volkswagen foundations, in this context was an attempt to provide a framework for accommodating and integrating the forces of change. Launched by OECD planner Alexander King and Olivetti manager A. Peccei, the Club was a meeting place of the professional–managerial 'cadres' we will discuss in our next chapter (Braillard 1982). Hence perhaps we can explain the fact that it remained committed to class compromise rather than exploring the possibilities of an authoritarian and/or market solution beyond it, as would the other planning bodies emerging in this crisis. The 1971 MIT report to the Club of Rome, 'The Limits to Growth', on the basis of linear extrapolations into the future made clear however that continuing the Fordist/corporate liberal pattern of capital accumulation would exhaust the natural substratum of the mode of production (Roobeek 1987: 137; Meadows *et al.* 1972). Matching a concern for protecting the biosphere with stressing the need to find compromise solutions, the Club of Rome increasingly drifted to a position emphasising the dysfunctionality of capitalist discipline. This was an instance of the autonomisation of the cadres that will concern us in chapter 5. The contender state membership integrated into the Club also did not embody its ascendant capitalist element, but rather the cadre element in the state classes of Brazil (four members in 1979), Poland, Romania, and Egypt (each with two). Practically all of the remaining contender state representatives were state planners, researchers, and comparable functionaries (Braillard 1982: Annexe 2). As a result of its commitment to democratic and equitable solutions, the Club of Rome therefore increasingly became part of the challenges to be met, rather than a framework for devising a response to them.

The Trilateral Commission (TC) was established in the same period, but as a consultative ruling class forum stood in the tradition of the Rhodes–Milner group and Bilderberg. David Rockefeller at Bilderberg meetings in the early 1970s raised the idea of an expanded planning group covering the original heartland including Western Europe, and incorporating a Japanese membership on a equal footing. In this body, the alarm over Nixon's unilateralist attempt at solving the deteriorating trade and financial position of the United States and Japanese irritation over the President's surprise opening to China was to be assuaged and common ground regained. Although Bilderberg would continue separately, it slipped into a crisis when, following the Church Committee hearings in the US, Bilderberg chairman Prince Bernhard and luminaries such as Franz-Josef Strauss were implicated in the Lockheed airplane bribery, for which Lockheed and the Prince had used the World Wildlife Fund as a cover (Sampson 1978: 271f).

Unlike Bilderberg, the TC sought to develop a profile with greater transparency, public activities and sophisticated publications, responding to the greater sensitivity towards public relations. Otherwise, it retained the membership structure of Bilderberg by including Social Democratic politicians, union leaders, and journalists into what remained, basically, a consultative body of owner–managers and officers of transnational corporations. Of the 100 biggest global companies, about two-thirds were affiliated to the TC by directors' membership in the mid-1980s (Gill 1991: 157–8).

North American chairmen of the TC have been: Gerard Smith, a US diplomat married into the Rockefeller family; David Rockefeller; and Paul Volcker, former Chase Manhattan banker and past Chairman of the Federal Reserve, and currently a director of the investment bank of World Bank head James Wolfensohn. In fact, fourteen personalities among the first decade TC membership were linked to Chase Manhattan as directors or members of its International Advisory Council. European chairmen were men with a European Movement background (Max Kohnstamm, private secretary to Prince Bernhard and later Principal of the European University Institute in Florence; and G. Berthoin, former private secretary to Monnet). In 1994, Count Lambsdorff, former investment banker at Trinkaus in Düsseldorf, a director in several major companies including Volkswagen, was European chair (in the tradition of aristocratic investment bankers intervening at crucial junctures in German history, Lambsdorff as Minister of Economic Affairs in 1982 terminated Helmut Schmidt's Chancellorship by crossing the floor to Helmut Kohl). Japanese chairmen, finally, have been T. Watanabe, former IMF/IBRD director linked to the Bank of Tokyo, Japan's 'quintessential international bank' recently absorbed by Mitsubishi Bank (*NW*, 12 May 1986; *FT*, 29 March 1995); top Civil Servant N. Ushiba; former Mitsui manager Yamashita; and former Prime Minister Miyazawa (Gill 1991: 151; Sklar and Everdell 1980; TC membership list, November 1994).

Another index of the business connections of the TC can be gained by looking at Executive Committee members of the TC. In Table 4.1, we have listed corporations linked to the ExCom by more than one director; and, to illustrate the element of overlap with the most central corporations in the international network of interlocks (as in Table 2.6, p. 61), those firms on that list which were also on the TC ExCom in an adjacent year. However, except for Chase Manhattan, which was on its way to becoming the most central corporation in the interlock network when it also became the nodal point for the TC, there is no particular correspondence between the two sets of firms. Actual ExCom connections are much more extensive than presented here: thus there were thirty-two ExCom members in 1973 of whom fifteen held thirty-six directorates/advisory functions, and so on.

Although there are interesting overlaps with other networks and corporations – say, the Schroeder Bank which through its 1970s director Harold Brown (Carter's Secretary of Defense) was linked to the TC, but through director Paul Nitze to the alarmist US Cold Warrior pressure group set up in the mid-1970s, the *Committee on the Present Danger* – the names of firms merely illustrate which information channels were available to the TC apart from the commission as such. There is no question of a corporate/TC 'world government' being implied here, as corporations listed often belonged to rival financial groups, and bodies such as the TC have been consciously created to allow different perspectives to be articulated and accommodated.

The TC's preoccupation was with containing centrifugal forces threatening to disrupt 'Western' unity (Novak 1980: 190; see Gill 1991: 217–22 on regional

Table 4.1 Multiple corporate links of Trilateral Commission ExCom members (1973, 1979, 1994)

1973	1979	1994
Chase Manhattan (5)	Chase Manhattan (4)	Chase Manhattan (3)
IBM (3)	IBM (3)	Soc. Générale (Belg.) (2)
Bank of Tokyo (2)	Bank of Tokyo (2)	FIAT/Iveco (2)*
Schroder Bank (2)	Honeywell (2)	*Also on 1992 centrality list:*
Also on 1971/1976	INA/Blyth-Eastman	Citicorp
centrality lists:	Dillon (2)*	IBM
Royal Dutch/Shell		Unilever
Int. Nickel		

*Addition on account of ownership of second corporation by first-named one.

Sources: Sklar and Everdell 1980; Mattera 1992; http:www.bundestag.de/mdb/htm (Lambsdorff); *Insurance Company of North America Corporation* Annual Report 1977.

differences in this respect). It sought to reaffirm the integration of the outward-looking ruling classes of the metropolitan areas rather than integrating the contender state classes coming to the fore in the 1970s. Thus, an envisaged meeting with the Soviet leadership was cancelled in 1979–80, in light of the 'Second Cold War' then setting in. In May 1981, there was a TC/Chinese meeting in Beijing, the new heartland ally, at which the Chinese were advised on a suitable economic reform course; while David Rockefeller, who also had featured prominently in the Beijing meeting, at the 1986 TC plenary in Madrid reported on discussions in Baku with Soviet 'businessmen' emerging in the perestroika context and showing a new willingness to engage in joint ventures (Gill 1991: 185, 187–8; see also 156).

More fundamentally, the forces guiding the Commission's deliberations sought to develop, as one TC report put it, 'a global system where the communist philosophy withers and has no new converts' (quoted in ibid.: 202). The quest for a new concept of control with which to contain and confront challenges at home and abroad included, first, a formula for restoring the discipline of capital. Its influential 1975 report, *The Crisis of Democracy*, recommended constraining democracy and enhancing the authority of 'expertise', notably in the economic field (Crozier *et al.* 1975; Fernández Jilberto 1985: 187).

Second, the authoritarian turn should be made part of a global moral order. In the attempt to shape the contours of a 'global domestic policy', Trilateralism inspired the Carter presidency's universalist foreign policy (US TC members held practically all the key posts in the Carter cabinet – Burch 1980, 3: 321). Boldly reclaiming the moral high ground one year after having withdrawn from a devastated Indo-China, the United States, working in tandem with its allies on several concrete issues such as energy and economic policy, raised the issue of human rights as the touchstone for a state's legitimate existence. Human rights universalism replaced the rigid anti-communism of the previous era, which had become discredited in the Vietnam War and as we saw, un-ravelled along with the arms trade networks in which prominent Bilderberg members had been involved. It emphasised the reduced status of national sovereignty (on which the contender state role had been premised, both in the Soviet bloc posture and in the NIEO experience – Krasner 1985: 124); while projecting, on a global scale, the Lockean constitution of the individual, bourgeois subject as the universal norm and limit on state jurisdiction (Greiner 1980: 192–5).

This long-term, world-historical perspective, of which David Rockefeller's right-hand man in the TC and Carter's National Security Adviser, Zbigniew Brzezinski, was a key exponent, had the disadvantage that it could be rendered irrelevant by sudden political crises. Moreover, a commitment to the equilibrium of compromises enshrined in corporate liberalism persisted and commissioners privately and in government tended to be wary of a radical deflationary strategy to cut the working class and credit-financed contender states down to size. Still, as Gill notes, the *Crisis of Democracy* report had expressed the opinion that an economic recession would make short shrift of these forces of resistance (1991: 227). Only when unforeseen emergencies (Iran and Nicaragua) threw the hegemonic compromise approach into disarray, however, could more radical options be applied. Such options had been under consideration by planning bodies such as the Pinay Circle.[4]

The Pinay Circle, launched in 1969 in response to the May revolt and alternatively named Cercle Violet after the former French Prime Minister's lawyer, included continental statesmen such as Strauss and G. Andreotti (who also were members, like Pinay, of Bilderberg); in addition to an array of intel-ligence chiefs. It was supported by Carlo Pesenti, of Italcementi and closely involved in Vatican finances, and had links both with the world of intelli-gence services (notably in France and West Germany) and with groups like Opus Dei and Catholic organisations for Christian European unity (Teacher 1993; Pallenberg 1973: 123–4). One of these groups, the Knights of Malta, dates back to the crusades and in the modern era brings together both European dynasts such as Otto von Habsburg, and Americans such as the Grace and Buckley families, as well as successive CIA directors (who have often been Irish-American Catholics, see also van Wesel 1992: 269–70; *BW*, 1 May 1995). The Pinay Circle not only was connected to the terrorist Right in Italy which later became operative also in Latin America, it also inter-faced with the New Right orbit in the United States, which included the Heritage Foundation. This foundation was set up in 1973 by Paul Weyrich with funds from a group of revanchist US millionaires (beer magnate Coors, Richard Mellon Scaife) and subsequently gained the support of firms like Chase Manhattan and Mobil Oil (*NRC*, 19 October 1985). Heritage was only the most visible of a broader array of new 'free market' and Cold War think-tanks emerging in this period, such as the Smith Richardson and Olin foundations (Ferguson and Rogers 1986: 86–8) and the already mentioned Committee on the Present Danger (CPD, Scheer 1982).

The Reagan 'Revolution', for which the Heritage Foundation (as acknowledged in the President's own address at its tenth anniversary) had written the blueprint, drew heavily on policy planning by these reactionary networks. The CPD, which upon the departure of several Trilateral directors into the Carter cabinet, also had taken over the CFR, was the single most important network in Reagan's government (thirty-two members including the President, Secretary Shultz, CIA director Casey, etc. (Brownstein and Easton 1983: 533–4; Silk and Silk 1981: 220)). But not only in the new Cold War, also in the strategy of rolling back socialist-inspired forces in the Third World, Reagan took his cue from, in this case, Lewis Lehrman, Heritage director and Knight of Malta. Lehrman in 1985 organised a much-publicised 'tri-continental' meeting of pro-Western counter-revolutionary leaders such as Savimbi of Angola, that was to be endorsed by the Reagan doctrine a year later (*MD*, October 1986: 6).

The Reagan policy of confrontation was also supported by the South Korean, Rev. Sun Myung Moon. Moon's Unification Church was built with the aid of his Tongil financial group (Gifford 1988: 73–7; *Niw*, 23 December 1991). It worked to link Japanese and Taiwanese Far Right elements to the groups supporting the Reagan revolution in the US. In 1974, Moon was introduced into Washington by right-wing Congressmen John Sparkman and Barber Conable, later head of the World Bank. In 1982, the Korean launched a US newspaper supporting the Reagan revolution, the *Washington Times*, as a counterweight to the establishment press judged to be in the Trilateral fold (*MD*, May 1987: 20). Through the establishment of CAUSA ('the cause') in 1980, an organisation committed to combating Third World communism, the Moon church joined forces with General Pinochet and his intelligence network abroad. It also was closely linked to the World Anti-Communist League (WACL) launched by the government of Taiwan in 1967 (rebaptised World League for Freedom and Democracy in 1990). This body, like others of its kind such as Western Goals, often functioned as a cover for terrorist acts against progressives (Western Goals e.g. was officially implicated in the assassination of ANC leader Chris Hani in South Africa, *Vk*, 15 October 1993).

But already in the second half of the 1970s, political violence must be considered to have been at least partly orchestrated from these quarters (rather than discounted as a random phenomenon). In fact, one aspect of the tri-lateral interregnum covering the period between the fall of Nixon and the Reagan–Bush era may have been that in the absence of a really effective, hegemonic concept of control, violence was resorted to in order to enforce a consensus of fear. Although this must remain a hypothesis to be worked out later, the succession of high-level assassinations and engineered removals of top politicians (Willy Brandt in 1974, Gough Whitlam in 1975, Harold Wilson in 1976, Aldo Moro and Pope John Paul I in 1978, and Olof Palme in 1986, to name but the most spectacular cases) can probably only be understood if seen in the context of a single process (Scott 1986; see also Leigh 1989; Dorril and Ramsay 1992; Willan 1991; Yallop 1984). The presence of the architect of the Gladio undercover network in Europe, former CIA director Colby, at a two-day Washington conference of the Pinay Circle in 1979 along with Heritage president Feulner, Paul Volcker (the TC commissioner who, at the suggestion of David Rockefeller, was appointed to the chair of the Federal Reserve by President Carter to restore the discipline of capital on the world economy (Burch 1980, 3: 356n)), EU (and TC) commissioners Narjes and Pandolfi, and other exponents of the emerging neo-liberal consensus, is only one illustration of how the worlds of clandestine violence and economic rationality are entwined. Also, the envisaged use of provocative terrorism as part of a Pinay Circle campaign to bring Strauss to power in Germany (exposed by his old enemy, *Der Spiegel* magazine, in 1982 – excerpts in *Lobster* 17, 1988: 14–5) reveals how violence was part of restoring class unity and discipline in the absence of hegemony.

Hegemonic integration under neo-liberalism

The core of the new concept of control which expressed the restored discipline of capital, neo-liberalism, resides in raising micro-economic rationality to the validating criterion for all aspects of social life. Much more than corporate liberalism which incorporated state-monopolistic and welfare-corporatist elements often copied from the contender states, neo-liberalism was a product of heartland history and Lockean political culture – its eventual triumph a 'Second Glorious Revolution' (see my 1995). Among the broad array of planning groups which contributed, in one way or another, to the defeat of corporate liberalism and the world order in which it existed, one has not yet been mentioned – the Mont Pèlerin Society (MPS). Building on pre-war criticisms of the New Deal by men like Walter Lippmann (see his 1936: 203, 214), a group of Austrian *émigré* economists and philosophers such as Friedrich von Hayek and Karl Popper in 1947 were encouraged by Swiss bankers and businessmen organised by A. Hunold, as well as City financiers led by Alfred Suenson-Taylor (Lord Grantchester), to set up the MPS as a permanent forum (Cockett 1995: 9–12, 102–7).

Unlike the Rhodes–Milner group and later bodies such as Bilderberg and the TC, the MPS did not offer a forum for the articulation of a still nascent concept of control, but 'knew "the truth"' (ibid.: 139). This, among other things, condemned it to a marginal existence for two decades. Only when the corporate liberal concept and the class configuration supporting it unravelled, did the MPS emerge as a crucial source of neo-liberal propaganda and policy advice in various countries, from Pinochet's Chile to Britain under Margaret Thatcher (Overbeek 1990: 28, 162–4; Desai 1994). Even as late as 1971, Hayek's and Milton Friedman's ideas of organising society solely around the market had been rejected by right-wing ideologues (see Kristol 1971). But the MPS had all along worked to create a network of affiliates (eventually organised in a single cupola, Atlas) of which the best-known is the Institute of Economic Affairs (IEA) established in 1955 in the UK by a group of new rich eccentrics around poultry millionaire Anthony Fisher and subsequently subsidised by Shell and other corporations (Cockett 1995: 129–43). Also, many links existed with other New Right groups – thus Heritage president Ed Feulner was Treasurer of the MPS in the early 1980s (*Who's Who in the World 1982–1983*: 'Feulner').

Again in contrast with the emergence of previous planning groups, the MPS depended on the mass dissemination of a largely preconceived gospel, which also implied a more militant intellectual function than an adaptive/directive role in the background. Although the crisis of corporate liberalism in which it intervened, was real (in the sense that the economic equations and class compromises on which metropolitan Fordism had been based, were breaking down (Lipietz 1982)), the neo-liberal intervention was of a much more 'willed' than organically hegemonic nature. Providing a rigid doctrine to what was essentially an owners' revolt against the class and international compromises of corporate liberalism, neo-liberalism lent a politically reactionary quality to the technologically highly innovative round of capital accumulation which made the reimposition of capitalist discipline possible in the first place.

The process of integrating aspiring bourgeois elements from the contender states was only resumed (this time on a world scale) when the crisis of corporate liberalism was overcome by neo-liberalism in the early 1980s (although on the margins of the earlier experience, a man like Ludwig Erhard had been made an MPS member at its second meeting (Cockett 1995: 108)). In the 1980s, however, the society actively engaged in recruiting like-minded elements in the former NIEO and Soviet blocs. Thus a Chilean magazine reported the participation of Chilean bankers and Argentinian economists at an MPS meeting in Viña del Mar in 1981 (*Hoy*, 25 November 1981). In Eastern Europe, the most prominent MPS member is the Czech prime minister, Vaclav Klaus (Klaus 1993). Most prominent in actually penetrating the former Soviet bloc in this spirit is George Soros, the Hungarian *émigré* financier. Inspired by the theses of Hayek and Popper since he studied at the LSE after the war and before settling in the US, his Open Society Fund and the Soros Foundation disbursed a total of $30 million between their establishment in 1984 and the fall of the Berlin Wall in scholarships and support to opposition groups such as Charta 77 in Czechoslovakia. With the break-up of the Soviet bloc, Soros subsidies have been raised to $300 million a year. The Central European University in Budapest and Warsaw, the Open Media Research Institute in Prague, and incidental gifts to other projects have created a vast network of neo-liberal intellectuals and managers with some Soros connection throughout Eastern Europe, including several alumni of Soros's own training institutes (e.g. in the Ukraine government of President Kuchma, *Vk*, 24 June 1995; *BW*, 23 August 1993).

The element of prior emigration before adopting the role of a capitalist entrepreneur is also visible in the economic sphere itself. Thus in the Czech Republic, *émigrés* returning to their former home country with economic expertise acquired in the West have made the headlines as the advance guard of the new bourgeoisie. This applies to investment banks such as Harvard Capital and Patria, whose owners have used their experience to appropriate large chunks of privatised assets (see *Nw*, 7 July 1995 and *BW*, 6 March 1995, respectively). Emigration often is a form of establishing the 'off-shore' role conducive to class integration which we noted earlier. Overseas Chinese are of course well known as an example (see also Kolko 1997), but in a country like India, too, an 'off-shore' fraction has been operative in trying to accelerate the transformation of the Hobbesian state/society complex. Now that capital is establishing itself outside the paternalistic structures of Congress state capitalism with its supporting strongholds in the Tata and Birla financial groups, what seems to emerge as the real vanguard of a neo-liberal bourgeoisie not only is closely linked with foreign capital, but actually operated from outside India for at least a considerable time in the past. The Reliance group of the Ambani brothers, the Chhabria and Mallya families, the Ispat group, and the house of Hinduja all are examples of this trend (Roy 1994: 23).

Of course, such processes of class formation in the case of the former Soviet bloc had to be postponed to the actual collapse of state power. But as soon as circumstances allowed, the Free Congress Foundation (FCF), founded in 1974 by Paul Weyrich with Coors money, and part of the Heritage network, linked up with the Yeltsin forces in the tottering Soviet Union, supplying them with funds, equipment, and training from 1989 on (Bellant and Wolf 1990; *MD*, October 1986: 6).

The Moon Church in fact began sending missionaries into the Soviet Union already in 1983. In 1990 the position of the Unification Church and its front organisations had advanced to the point that Gorbachev received Moon in the Kremlin. Under the free scholarships in the US, offered by the Korean on that occasion, 3,500 Soviet students and teachers went to the US in the second half of 1990 alone (*NRC*, 4 December 1993). Of course, the role of the Roman Catholic church under its Polish pope in penetrating and integrating the Polish, the Lithuanians, and the Croats, and other East European catholic countries should not remain unmentioned in this connection (Krims 1985; Schweizer 1994; see also C. Bernstein in *Time*, 24 February 1992).

The element of adopting a changed identity in line with a new universe of values and economic system, which we saw was among the functions of Freemasonry at the outset of capitalist development, played a part in several of these processes – emigration and return, inner emigration with the help of a religion, or conversion to a new faith. Thus the protestant fundamentalist drive into the former contender states, of which the Moon church is one example, has provided a mass counterpart to what was often an élite process involving only a privileged segment of the ascendant bourgeoisie in other forms of hegemonic integration. Protestant fundamentalism of course is more radical and aggressive (as when it is called in to support repression and torture). But 'the neo-Puritan ethics of many evangelicals represent a "this-worldly ascetism",' Nederveen Pieterse writes (1992: 19):

In combination with the ethos of individual achievement and entrepre-
neurialism, this resembles the profile of an "accumulation religion", along
the lines of the Protestant ethic, that is, a religion conducive to savings
and investment.

This was taken very literally by Rev. Billy Graham, who on a visit to China,
and with the prior blessing of the Chinese leadership, exhorted mass rallies
to 'work hard and don't complain' (*Nw*, 2 May 1988). China and the Soviet
Union indeed seem to be the areas of expansion for protestant fundamentalism and sects in general. Whereas in the early 1980s, their activities were
still concentrated in Latin America, the Philippines, South Korea and Southern Africa, the former Soviet Union is clearly on the rise as a target area.
In Russia, evangelical protestants are estimated to have converted 3 million
people to membership (*Nw*, 2 August, 1993). But then, as Paul Gifford notes
(1988: 26), US-sponsored protestant fundamentalism thrives on 'massive
cultural dislocation and serious social and political crises' – the anomie accompanying original accumulation combined with, in this case, the collapse of the
tentacular state.

Planning and the limits of capitalist discipline

As we argued in chapter 2, the neo-liberal concept enshrines a stage of penetration of capital into its social and natural substratum which in the current
period has led to exhaustion and to new forms of resistance. As the limits of
the mode of production are becoming manifest, the capitalist class has once
again mobilised its most trusted instrument for developing a class perspective,
the planning group.

Thus the environmental theme upon the marginalisation of the Club of
Rome by neo-liberalism was reappropriated by a strictly capitalist body, the
Business Council for Sustainable Development (BCSD). The BCSD was set
up in 1991 by Stephan Schmidheiny, a scion of one of the foremost Swiss
business dynasties (see also Mattera 1992; Holliger 1974). It worked closely
with TC member Maurice Strong in preparing the UNCED environmental
conference in Rio in 1992 and practically wrote its conclusions in advance
(Nelson 1993). If the non-metropolitan Club of Rome members still had been
exclusively cadre/state class, the BCSD includes only businessmen, often from
the same areas (three from Brazil, three other Latin Americans, three Africans,
and one each from India and Thailand (BCSD membership 1992)).

The most comprehensive transnational planning body operative today, the
World Economic Forum (WEF), also was a Swiss initiative. It was launched
in 1971 by Klaus Schwab and is best known for the annual symposia at
Davos, where world leaders from business and politics mingle (as its glossy
bimonthly, *World Link*, puts it in the July/August issue of 1994, 'the best way
to achieve progress is through interaction among those who really carry the
reponsibility'). Let us conclude this chapter by briefly reviewing how a truly

global network such as the WEF registers, and is beginning to deal with, the second form of exhaustion by capital, that of the social substratum.

The WEF's component bodies all are acknowledged *class* organisations, in the sense of being 'subject to strict conditions of admission in order to preserve their peer character' (*World Link* July/August 1994). These components are (according to the same source):

- Foundation Members – the world's 1,000 foremost global enterprises
- Global Growth Companies – a club for the world's leading entrepreneurial companies with a global orientation
- Industry governors – more than 300 chief executives from the most influential companies and organisations in eleven different industry sectors
- Global Leaders for Tomorrow – 300 individuals born in the second half of [the twentieth] century who will shape the future
- World Economic Leaders – regular discussion with partners from governments and international organisations
- World Media Leaders – editors-in-chief and commentators from over 100 influential media groups
- Forum Fellows – academics and experts from political, economic, scientific, social and technological fields
- NERO – heads of the world's foremost national economic research organisations
- World Cultural Leaders – 100 distinguished figures from the arts world
- Regional Leaders – heads of some of the world's most dynamic and successful regions.

A body of this scope clearly has not existed ever before. It is a true International of capital, the first identifiable forum in which concepts of control are debated and if need be, adjusted, on a world scale. Until well into the 1990s, the WEF was a pivot of neo-liberal hegemony, bringing together the ascendant buccaneers of the privatising contender states with the established ruling class of the heartland. At this point, the celebration of the 'lean and mean' world corporation went hand in hand with the declared commitment of, say, an entrepreneur from India to sweep his country clean of its 'Soviet-based model' (A. Gulabchand of Hindustan Construction, quoted in *NW*, 24 June 1991). Indeed, if 'in every region of the world, states, economies, and political processes are being transformed under the guidance of a class-conscious transnational bourgeoisie' (Robinson 1992: 8), the WEF can certainly be credited with synchronising and unifying this process. The guaranteed absence of the wider public or critics ('participation in the activities of the WEF is reserved for its members and constituents . . . special guests [can be proposed] if their presence creates additional value for other members', *World Link*, July/August 1994) ensures that outsiders must either conform or accept isolation. This works at the Davos summits as well as in regional meetings, of which often, there are several in a single month. Here the process of hegemonic integration is most pronounced. Thus the Prague meeting in April 1994 was chaired by Carl Hahn of Volkswagen, the biggest investor in the Czech Republic (Hahn incidentally had warned against 'the excesses of the European welfare state' at the Davos summit earlier in the year – *NRC*, 1 February 1994). At the Southern Africa summit in Cape Town, 9–10 June 1994, President Mandela exhorted those present to join forces in 'attracting significant investment flows to the region'. In Moscow twelve days later, First Deputy Prime Minister O. Soskovets restated the priority accorded to a favourable investment climate while warning against neo-liberal dogma being pressed too far at the Middle East summit jointly prepared with the Council on Foreign Relations, etc. (all examples from *World Link*, July/August 1994).

The comprehensive concept prevailing in the WEF through these debates would seem to be solidly neo-liberal, enhancing competition to the full and eliminating whatever niches remain protected from the full impact of the discipline of capital. The annual 'World Competitiveness Report' it prepares jointly with the IMD management institute in Lausanne, and the emphasis the WEF places on the global consultancy phenomenon as the breeding ground of the 'manager of the future: rootless and versatile', and so on (*FT*, 16 December 1996), would all seem to work in the same direction. The WEF perspective is on a global *network society*, which in the words of Schwab and his managing director, Claude Smadja, results from 'economic globalization and the information-technologies revolution' and represents 'a quantum leap from what we are used to. . . . It tests to the limit the ability of political and economic leaders to manage repercussions of the changes' (*IHT*, 30 January 1997; see also the Morse quote at the beginning of this chapter).

However, this 'management of repercussions' precisely allows us to refer back again to the paradigmatic example of the Rhodes–Milner group. For in this case, too, transnational planning groups prove to be not a conspiratorial world government, but class organisations constantly adjusting to the real balance of forces confronting them. Especially after the surge of class struggles in France in December 1995, which as we argued before, may mark a historic limit to the ongoing neo-liberal drive, the WEF, too, has begun to reflect a shift to a more cautious attitude. At the 1994 summit, CEOs and government leaders still had been bidding up to each other as to who was applying the harshest economic 'reform' programme and firing the largest number of employees (*NRC*, 1 February 1994; *Vk*, 2 February 1994), and even the 1996 summit 'celebrated business and trade globalization' (*IHT*, 30 January 1997). But on the eve of the 1997 meeting, the financier, George Soros, unexpectedly denounced 'the destruction of those values which do not produce commercial return' and 'the totalitarian tendency of unregulated market capitalism'.

At the WEF in Davos, the new mood was expressed in a project on 'human social responsibility', to be studied by prominent theologians and the new head of the AFL–CIO, John Sweeney, among others (*IHT*, 30 January 1997). Indeed in the view of Schwab and Smadja, the emerging network society by the elusiveness of the 'intangible e-dimension', and the 'virtual communities' created by it, exerts a downward pressure on wages that remain unrelated to 'knowledge-based value addition', and widens the gap between 'knows and know-nots' if there is no countervailing education effort. Discontentment reveals that 'capital markets are more and more perceived as dictating the course of events, forcing or tying the hands of policy-makers, and fostering a mood [of] . . . "share value feti[s]hism" '. 'A perception is already wide-spread that the benefits of the changes so far have gone to shareholders and financiers, while workers were left to bear the costs' (*IHT*, 31 January 1997). As states are less and less capable of dealing with the challenges of a globalised network society on their own, the authors propose a global tripartism between capital, states, and labour, which should rein in the 'pressure for instant shareholder gratification' and restore the longer-term view and some sustainable format of social cohesion.

But the question – which new pattern would support a shift away from this exhaustive and ultimately, self-destructive form of capitalist discipline – cannot be answered any longer with reference to a newly emerging mode of accumulation, because not one is in sight. Also, transnational forces associated with deregulated neo-liberalism have come to include increasingly powerful networks of organised crime. These networks, often interlocked with regular business and politics (Scott and Marshall 1991; Kaplan and Dubro 1987), will not be tamed simply by a shift in economic policy. It may be, therefore, that a new synthesis can only be established beyond capitalist relations of production – that is, by radically reversing the priority of the economy over society. This in our view will prominently involve a stratum of functionaries which has so far been implied in our analysis – the professional–managerial stratum active both in the private and public spheres, the cadres. To this stratum we turn in our final chapter.

5 Cadres and the classless society

The need, from a socialist standpoint, is for a critique of scientific management not dissimilar in intention for our epoch of transition from Marx's critique
of political economy for the classical epoch of capitalism.

Alfred Sohn-Rethel

In this chapter we will develop the notion of a cadre function that is created
by the process of *Vergesellschaftung*. 'The connection of the individual with all,
but at the same time also the independence of this connection from the individual', by which Marx denotes the moment of socialisation in the development
of the world market (1973: 161; emphasis deleted), is not sustained spontaneously. As socialisation proceeds in conjunction with commodification or by
other modes of alienation (e.g. by state formation), the need for control and
direction of collective labour, and the task of maintaining social cohesion
under conditions of advanced division of labour, brings forth a specific stratum
of functionaries.

The second part of the above quotation from the *Grundrisse*, as will be
remembered, claimed that the condition of universal, impersonal interconnection engendered by the world market 'at the same time contains the
conditions for going beyond it'. This implies that if there exists a definite
social stratum which is associated with socialisation, it cannot be left out of
an analysis of the transformation of capitalist society.

Such an argument of course ascribes a role to this social group quite beyond
established notions of its function in a 'service' economy. But then, the familiar
view of an agricultural society giving way to a 'secondary' sector (industry),
and an industrial society to 'tertiarisation', contains an important flaw. For
'tertiarisation' occurs also *within* the 'primary' and 'secondary' sectors, as well
as between the three. 'All the land, labor, and capital in the world won't meet
consumer needs if they cannot be integrated at a far higher level than ever
before,' observes Alvin Toffler, quoting the assessment of a French think-
tank that

service economies '. . . are not characterised by the fact that people have
suddenly begun to fulfill their needs through non-tangible consumption

but rather by the fact that activities pertaining to the economic realm are increasingly integrated' (Toffler 1991: 78).

The result is a proliferation of administrative interfaces between particular activities. As the sociologist, Amitai Etzioni, writes, there have always been organisations, but in modern times there are so many of them 'that a whole set of second-order organisations is needed to organise and supervise organisations' (quoted in Hirszowicz 1980: 15).

The people performing this role of organising and supervising are the subject of James Burnham's *The Managerial Revolution* (1960 [1941]), or have been called, alternatively, 'new petty bourgeoisie' (Poulantzas 1971), 'surplus class' (Nicolaus 1970), 'intellectuals' (Konrád and Szelényi 1981), 'professional élites' (Perkin 1996), 'experts' (Benveniste 1972), 'professional–managerial class' (Ehrenreich and Ehrenreich 1979) or simply 'new middle class' (Wright 1978 uses the notion of 'contradictory class locations' in this connection). We will prefer, however, the term *cadre* used by French authors Gérard Dumenil (1975), Luc Boltanski (1982) and Alain Bihr (1989), who to varying degrees link the existence and orientation of the cadres explicitly to the process of socialisation.[1]

Hegel (1972: 182–3) already coined the notion of a universal class or estate, an *allgemeine Stand* entrusted with defending the general interests of the 'social condition'. But he could not yet envisage a social condition beyond the single state. Marx's argument for an ultimate triumph of the proletariat was projected on a global scale, but the concrete class structure leading the way to a classless society was not worked out. The French authors mentioned, on the other hand, have in our view provided the sociological–historical material to arrive at such a concrete analysis. Partly based on a critical elaboration of their theses, it will be our claim that the cadres represent the social class equivalent of 'the transcendence of capital within the limits of the capitalist mode of production itself' (*MEW* 25: 452), which Marx sees exemplified in e.g. the joint stock company. The cadres would then represent something like 'the class representing classless society within the limits of class society' – which they, under certain circumstances, have developed into a historic social consciousness.

As we will argue in this chapter, the cadres already several times in the twentieth century, have developed into a conscious class. This always happened under the conditions of a severe crisis of the bourgeois order, and in our view cannot fail to do so again in light of their objective role in sustaining social cohesion. As before, however, their political orientation in such a crisis will depend on whether they will seek to uphold the privileges of the ruling class or, under the impetus of popular movements, feel compelled to circumscribe and look beyond capitalist discipline.

The class of socialisation

In chapter 1, we already indicated what we mean by socialisation: the planned or otherwise normatively unified interdependence of functionally divided social activity. Planning functions have to be executed and normative coherence upheld at every level of socialisation, in each of its structures. Under the discipline of capital and the commodity form, the real subjects cannot execute the planning/normative function for themselves; alienation and exploitation imply the negation of autonomy to begin with. Therefore, planning and the propagation and monitoring of social norms have historically evolved into a special task of a special category of functionaries subordinate to the ruling class – the cadres.

As a result we may hold that every unit of socialisation requires a specific sub-category of cadres who 'run' this unit on account of a delegated authority. Since their operation as cadres presupposes *control*, we will see that this concept plays a central role in the class consciousness of the cadres. Planning always derives from the need to reduce uncertainty and this, Benveniste writes, is 'the source of the experts' power' (1972: 29; see also Boguslaw 1965: 32–3).

Planning extends to the world of experience and overall behaviour. Here Habermas's concept of the socialisation of internal nature into normative structures is particularly relevant. Socialisation in its various forms incompletely compensates for the destruction of the community and its values. The cadres therefore typically perform functions which are meant to restore a degree of cohesion, technically and ideologically, to the fragmented social substratum of capital accumulation. The imagined community which results from this constitutes, in the cadre perspective, a terrain of social engineering rather than an authentic 'commons' to be protected in its own right. Instead, the cadres effectively integrate the various moments of alienation into an integral world of rules and norms, so that people subject to the dislocating effects of commodification and exploitation are surrounded by functionaries and organisations 'taking care' of their drives, aspirations, and fears (Greven 1974: 47–8). This helps to sustain the inverted world of society seeking to adjust to the requirements of the market and capital.

Marx still assumed that initially, the workers as a consequence of exploitation and accumulation would be reduced to a dumb mass in the face of ever-'smarter' machinery (a perspective also adopted by Braverman 1974); later they would gradually develop into a new type of 'polytechnic' worker due to their capacity to handle various applications of what we today would call 'user-friendly' machinery. Socialisation of labour/external nature thus would shape a new type of worker alongside ever-more sophisticated machinery (see also Gorz 1982: 35). While this is a recurring phenomenon (see also our reference to Elger's notion of new autonomies created by technology itself in chapter 2), Gorz rightly argues that capital is capable of reclaiming the terrain lost by separating organisational and technical advantages resulting from socialisation into special tasks. This precludes their being incorporated into the workers' competences, so that their capacity to contest this appropriation by capital is correspondingly reduced (1982: 36).

But it is not only the original proletariat from which tasks are taken and turned into moments of exploitation and domination. The ruling class, too, pays a price for making sure that socialisation remains subject to its class domination. This price is the increase in number of paid functionaries and intermediaries, the cadres. The ruling class, in other words, *cedes* aspects of its rule to the cadre stratum with every advance in the complexity of production and social organisation generally. 'Modern technological societies are vastly complex sets of interacting subunits and no modern Prince can comprehend the complexities of his domain,' Benveniste writes (1972: 3). Therefore, just as capital has to continually renew its hold on the working class by deepening its control of the labour process, so it continually faces the task to discipline the cadres it relies on to realise this control in the innumerable concrete situations created by advanced socialisation.

Functional mediation and the social labour process

The cadres are a product of capitalist development, more specifically of the process of socialisation; sociologically, however, they will often have a petty bourgeois background. But even if their mass emergence in the third quarter of the twentieth century amounted to a metamorphosis of an old middle class into a new one, certain ideological reflexes of this background have persisted. Among these are a weakly developed sense of class solidarity, an adherence to notions of abstract individual judgement, and a sensitivity to individual social status and privilege (see also Bourdieu 1979: 465). As we will see, these reflexes have been subsumed under certain new dispositions which can be ascribed to the cadres as a social stratum, but it will be obvious that there exists no a priori unity in a class sense here.[2] The coherence of the cadre stratum instead develops historically, often in the context of class struggles in which the cadres are assigned tasks of mediation, arbitration, and imposing discipline out of which emerge routinised planning and normative coherence functions.

The intermediate position, as 'middle' class, can be argued as follows. If we take the process of production as our point of departure, the planning function assigned to the cadres by capital is made possible by the expropriation of skills and knowledge from the workers, just as capital expropriates the material product of labour in exchange for wages. As Sohn-Rethel writes (1976: 39),

> The terms upon which the managerial science is founded, have first to be extracted from the live labour before they become the mental possession of the management. The study men [of Taylorism] themselves, who do this extraction, do not descend from a sphere of pure intellect like Platonic spirits into the nether regions of the labour process to cast it into

their inconvertible measures. *These time-study men are mere doubles of the workers themselves.* (Emphasis added)

The Ehrenreichs write that the professional–managerial class exists 'only by virtue of the expropriation of the skills and the culture once indigenous to the working class' and hence explain the relation between the cadres and the actual workers as 'interdependent yet antagonistic' (Ehrenreich and Ehrenreich 1979: 17). Gorz instead argues that the 'non-commissioned officers of production' controlling technical and organisational skills expropriated from the originally skilled workers in spite of having a working class background are part of the employer hierarchy (Gorz 1982: 54). We shall see that this is never established once and for all, however.

Once the working class responds to the increasing scale of production by organising the sale of its labour power on a commensurate scale, it is faced with the same dynamic as capital itself: it must rely on a new, mediating executive stratum, the trade union bureaucrats. While representing the workers, they do so as labour market specialists committed by necessity to this specialism. Since the power of the trade union resides in its capacity to mediate, this presupposes its relative independence also from the workers (Gorz 1982: 57). Having no 'work' experience or technical industrial knowledge, the union cadres usually seek 'to perpetuate and intensify the era of agreements, work contracts, social legislation, in order to enlarge their sphere of competence' (Gramsci 1977: 107). The natural interlocutors of the union cadres here are the bureaucrats of the employers' organisations, labour relations managers inside the company, as well as state functionaries responsible for monitoring collective bargaining or dealing with related terrains such as labour legislation, social insurance, and so on.

To the degree socialisation advances and the scale and intricacy of social organisation increases, as expressed in standardisation and regulation, the cadre stratum which embodies this infrastructure of advanced capitalist society grows into a distinct social force. Committed ideologically to bourgeois society, but practically representing a force of their own in social development on account of their function in socialised production, the cadres under certain circumstances have deployed as a class for itself – albeit under highly diverse political banners.

This brings us to the question of where precisely the supposed cadres' perspective on things differs from the bourgeois perspective of which we have discussed some determinants in previous chapters.

Modalities of cadre social consciousness

Even beyond the petty bourgeois heritage, one reason for the weakly developed sense of collective identity among the cadres resides in their function as specialists assigned with sectoral planning tasks. 'Ignorance of the political sociology of their own role tends to orient the new experts to conventional role definitions,' Benveniste writes (1972: 12). The technically qualified manager or the professional engineer, according to one of the founders of modern managerialism in the US, W.E. Wickenden, 'is rarely class-conscious. When he is, it is usually a sign of defeatism and disillusionment' (quoted in Noble 1979: 49).

Critics of the cadres' political aspirations, from both the right and the left, have often attacked them precisely on account of their sectoral, or otherwise particularistic orientation. Thus Hayek (1985: 69) has argued the neo-liberal critique of state intervention by pointing out that sectoral specialists have unduly sought to extend their planning functions to society at large; while democratic critics (Konrád and Szelényi 1981) claim that experts, if left unchecked, will tend towards extreme solutions in any direction. Therefore, although there is not a ready class consciousness among the cadres, certain typical dispositions can be ascribed to them which add up, under specific conditions, to a class perspective. By way of organising the argument, let us take Alain Bihr's analysis of cadre class consciousness as our point of departure, even though Bihr's definitions of cadre class dispositions (1989: 255f) tend to be generalisations of the situation of the 1970s when newly-recruited cadres joined the existing managerial–technocratic stratum in force and radicalised previous ideological propensities of that class in a generally democratic direction.

The first element discussed by Bihr is the cadre preference for *modernity*. The cadres tend to view themselves as being associated with the most developed forms of production and social organisation, such as the giant corporation and the modern welfare state apparatus, where all traces of the anarchic 'robber baron' capitalism have been removed. In the 1970s, society was actually seen by them as having moved beyond capitalism altogether. There is a general fascination with change; the idea that if there is no rapid change, there is stagnation (Hirszowicz 1980: 6). Generally, the orientation of the cadres is future oriented. As Greven (1974: 265) argues, the very idea of technocracy suggests a type of administration in which society is steered away in advance from any malfunctions and inefficiencies which might arise in the future.

Now all of this supports the modernity thesis. And of course, since the cadres develop with socialisation and since socialisation represents a moment of the development of the mode of production and even of its potential transformation, there is no need to be amazed if cadres are self-consciously in the vanguard of the development of a given order. But then, cadres have also been part of the *shifting coordinates* of modernity, which, after all, is a rather empty and relative concept by itself. Thus, the cadres were prominent when in the early twentieth century and especially in the 1930s, liberalism in crisis was confronted by a state monopoly tendency and the welfare nationalist state; likewise, they represented a critical factor in establishing and sustaining corporate liberalism in the *Pax Americana* (Boltanski, in this connection, expounds at large on the French cadres' 'fascination with America' (1982: ch. 2)). But while their role in these constellations can still be explained from the socially protective aspects of the respective concepts of control, this cannot be said of course of neo-liberalism. Yet, here we find cadres, too – this time in the role of shaping, in sectoral, national etc. settings, the new pattern of class relations defined from the neo-liberal vantage point.

In other words, the cadres represent modernity, but the definition of what modernity is, the momentary code of normalcy inscribed in a hegemonic concept, derives from the balance of class and fractional forces deciding the thrust of overall development rather than any inherent outlook of the cadres (except in a very superficial sense).

This brings us to the second characteristic given by Bihr, the cadres' *rationality*; more specifically, their orientation towards rationalising social and economic development. This largely coincides with their 'modern' self-image. Rationality here comes in such shapes as the application of science, as scientific management (or scientific socialism for that matter), or more broadly, a preference for planning and regulation in the name of the wider social interest, what Whyte calls (1963: 11) their 'social ethic'. Such planning for society would then be based, of course, on 'hard data', mathematics allowing hard-headed, value-free analysis, etc. 'Measurement and quantitative analysis are the basis of the knowledge which differentiates [the cadres],' Benveniste notes (1972: 57). This approach is maintained as long as possible to postpone overt political conflicts hidden by figures and other scientific symbols, and reserve the terrain for the experts rather than politicians or actual representatives of the ruling class (ibid.: 58).

What we have said above on modernity, also goes for rationality. It is always the specific, historic rationality represented by the configuration of forces and hegemonic concept through which the bourgeoisie rules, to which the cadres adhere. Rationality, since Max Weber stands for stripping the capitalist order from the remnants of the past (Funke 1978; see also Kolko 1959), is practically a synonym for modernity to begin with. Hence while Bihr is right to stress this element of the cadre self-image, we must go further to be able to really understand what it is that in various circumstances directs the action of the cadres other than the directives from above (and occasionally, from below). We will come to the connection with rational*ism*, which is relevant in the cadres' collective consciousness in relation to systems analysis, in the next section.

The third, and most directly problematic characteristic of cadre class consciousness according to Bihr is its preference for *democratisation*. This in his view is necessary for the cadres to allow their rise through the ranks which otherwise might be impeded by ascriptive, restrictive patterns of élite recruitment by the ruling class. To gain access to education, to positions of power, to wealth, all require that the cadres circumvent the hereditary structures of ruling class social status. Given that education is their only capital, free access to it for 'all' is a logical line for the cadres to favour. But already in the managerial literature there is sufficient ground to question the conclusion that this would hence result in a general democratic attitude. Rather, it would seem that the scientific/technocratic orientation also can make the cadres, when confronted with a lack of responsiveness and understanding on the part of politicians or the social groups which they are supposed to direct, 'increasingly impatient with democratic politics' (Benveniste 1972: 15). Or as Boguslaw notes, the illusion of full control which is implicit in many administrative doctrines such as cybernetics, tends to overlook the problems inherent in communication between people and the reality of unreliable performance of human beings (Boguslaw 1965: 32–4).

The basic assumption of technocracy, namely that social problems can be solved, like mechanical ones, by technicians, experts, or administrators, in general feeds a professional arrogance towards the mass of the population (Hirszowicz 1980: 6; Grundstein 1981: 1). While it is certainly appropriate to describe the cadres, as Boguslaw does (1965), as 'utopian', the utopia is the *ideal state of existing reality*, rather than an ideal reality fundamentally different from the existing one.

A second problem compounding the democratic attitude of the cadres is the fact that their access to power takes place typically outside the political process. The experts are 'called in', advance by bureaucratic methods and in fact derive their authority from remaining aloof from explicit politics (Benveniste 1972: 65). Also, there is an entire spectrum of political techniques involved in the cadres' contribution to decision-making: 'leaking' of documents instead of publication, maintaining closed circuits of experts, and so on.

Therefore we should try to probe deeper for what actually organises the cadre mind. This specific frame of reference and mode of analysis, in our view is constituted by *systems* analysis.

Socialisation and systems analysis

If we look for the deeper and more general aspects of the cadre perspective, class consciousness, and cadre social practice, we inevitably stumble upon fragments and aspects of the larger body of thought that comes under the heading of systems analysis. More particularly, it can be argued that it is the socialisation of labour (planned co-operation, use of science, collective use of means of production, etc.) which lends social substance to systems analysis; a given 'system' would then conform to a unit of socialised labour or any other unit of socialisation along the ramifications of socialised production, reproduction, and normative cohesion beyond the actual labour process.

Systems analysis, we would claim, can be viewed as the comprehensive language of the cadre stratum and a common thread in its historical functions and interventions. It also lends cohesion to the forms of cadre class consciousness offered by Bihr. A historically concrete discussion of systems analysis very soon stumbles upon the cadre stratum, its history, and its relationship to the bourgeoisie and the working class and their respective theoretical universes, i.e. liberalism and historical materialism (of course the latter connection is one by default at best, which we will not argue here). The systems approach can be said to be the typical technocratic, expert perspective, the perspective of social engineering. From this perspective, both liberalism (individual choice, etc.), and spontaneity or democratic initiative from below tend to be appreciated negatively, as problems, potentially disruptive and certainly dysfunctional.

Let us briefly trace the history of the systems idea to substantiate our claim that it constitutes a cornerstone of cadre thinking. Systems analysis is the science of organised entities, defined in terms of their maintenance, rules of operation, and ways of dealing with other organised entities. The idea of optimal states of organised entities dates from early Enlightenment rationalism. Especially the 'covering science' projected by Leibniz's *scientia generalis* may be mentioned in this connection.

However, since ideas only achieve coherence once the historical setting for their actual or potential application comes into existence, the history of systems analysis may be said to begin with the French Revolution. As Rosenstock-Huessy argues (1961: 353), the French Revolution faced the task of directly organising and administering a vast land mass (previous revolutions either affected smaller units and a less sophisticated level of administration or were, as in the English case, protected by an island geography). In the French Revolution, the term *organisation* became a general password, especially once the actual transformation gave way to the stage of consolidation and administration. The Hobbesian state/society complex and its revolution from above (in this case, 'Thermidor' and the Napoleonic consolidation), as well as restoration and the passive revolution in Europe, constitute the setting in which problems of administration and planning posed themselves, before the same perspectives could develop among cadres throughout the developed capitalist world including the English-speaking heartland.

In early nineteenth-century France, Saint-Simon expressed the prevailing configuration of forces with his conception of society as a giant factory run by engineers (Fennema 1995: 88, 93). In reaction to this technocratic, engineering approach to organisation, the conservative classes in Germany coined a rival concept – *organism*. These two derivatives of 'organ', one administrative–technical, the other biological, constitute the twin sources of systems analysis as we know it. Both can be used, albeit in a different philosophical frame of reference, to describe the processes of planned division of labour and normative coherence we denote by socialisation, including the way they develop, deal with failures, etc.

The adoption of the notions of organisation and organism into a philosophical–methodological concept of 'system' had been pioneered by Kant (Greven 1974: 232, 323n; see also Rosenstock-Huessy 1961: 353). In the section entitled 'The Architecture of Pure Reason', in part two of the *Critique of Pure Reason*, Kant writes that by 'system', he means the 'unity of manifold knowledge under an idea', in which the *goal* and the *form* of the totality are both contained. In Kant's view, organisation is implied in the form of the human being as an organism (Grundstein 1981: 119). Both serve 'The unity of the goal, to which all parts are directed and in the idea of which, are also mutually connected . . .'

> The totality hence is articulated and not simply thrown together; it can grow within itself, but not by external addition, just as the growth of an animal body does not add limbs, but makes each of them stronger and more fit for its purpose, without a change of proportion (Kant 1975: 839–40; Latin explanations omitted).

While other authors developed the system notion by either elaborating the organisation or the organism metaphor (see also Spencer's famous formula of evolution from 'indefinite, incoherent homogeneity to definite, coherent heterogeneity', quoted in Broom and Selznick 1970: 46; see also Boguslaw 1965: 41), there runs a straight line from Kant's synthesis to Ludwig von Bertalanffy, the Austrian-Canadian biologist who in 1954 launched the Society for General Systems Theory.

For Bertalanffy, the differentiating criterion of systems analysis is that it deals with living wholes (cybernetics is considered to remain at the level of mechanistic machine theory; Bertalanffy 1968: 23). Gurwitsch's and Lewin's Field Theory (from 1921 on) with its claim of an organic formative principle, followed a decade later by Weiss's generalisations drawn from embryo development (functional differentiation and growth), prepared the terrain for *General System Theory* (GST) which Bertalanffy himself dates as of 1945 (Bertalanffy 1968: viii; 1962: 113–20, 138).

All living organisms and collectivities of living organisms according to GST function roughly along the same lines.

> Whether we consider nutrition, voluntary and instinctive behaviour, development, the harmonious functioning of the organism under normal conditions, or its regulative functions in cases of disturbances of the normal, we find that practically vital processes are so organised that they are directed to the maintenance, production, or restoration of the wholeness of the organism (Bertalanffy 1962: 8).

Here we encounter all the functional roles which hold a complex organisation together; and the appeal of what is essentially a metaphor to anybody facing planning and administrative tasks involving organisations would seem obvious.

'History' from the GST perspective becomes *development*, defined as the 'increase of the degree of visible complexity from internal causes' to which external factors contribute, although the essential impulse is endogenous. This leads to the more comprehensive definition of development as 'a gradual rise in the level of organisation' (Bertalanffy 1962: 68). Although 'life' is the differentiating factor, and the elements of which a system is composed are supposed to be active (a system is a complex of interacting elements, a 'spatially and temporally well-defined material and energetic state' being guided to a final state, Bertalanffy 1968: 55; 1962: 179), the subjects are not considered to be literate as to where the system is heading for. Accordingly, systems-thinking leads to a distinct 'impatience with "human error"'' which results from the fact that those who think in terms of systems tend to have in mind not real people but 'people-substitutes' (Boguslaw 1965: 2; see also 20). The philosophy of management, Grundstein notes (1981: 1), 'draws upon the fundament of human regulativeness.' This is a characteristic of rationalism generally, and the fact that a system can be written as a mathematical set of equations in which changes in one element induce changes in others and in the whole (Bertalanffy 1968: 56) approximates Leibniz's ideal that in his covering science, errors in thinking could be reduced to errors in calculation.

Of course Bertalanffy and other systems thinkers dealt with the obvious criticisms of their approach, but this does not concern us here. Our claim is that a structure of socialisation is equal, from the perspective of its management, to a system in the sense of GST. Thus, whether we are speaking about a department of a factory or office, a state or any other unit of socialisation, GST offers a perspective for its maintenance as a functional whole. As Greven (1974: 223) has noted, systems analysis is a technical instrument which equates rationality with the control of external stimuli and the correction of malfunctions. The inherent tendency of a systems picture of any real, concrete configuration of socialised labour, therefore, is to put aside the human reality and project an abstract image of idealised efficiency and fail-safe operation. Since socialisation represents a contradictory aspect of capitalist development – contradictory both in relation to commodification and in the sense that it contains the elements for surpassing its capitalist frame – the systems way of looking at units of socialised labour is obviously a way of obscuring this moment of transformation. On the other hand, the systems approach allows the cadres to address problems created by socialisation of labour in all its ramifications, because it is a *general* theory which can be applied to any organisational problem anywhere. Since the cadres, if abstractly defined in terms of their function, view society neither as a terrain for individual self-realisation, nor as an oppressive structure to be resisted, let alone revolutionised, but as a complex totality to be managed, the systems perspective offers the most congenial mode of thinking.

There is no question that this would imply a conservative position, on the contrary: systems are not fixed orders, but living organisms reacting to disturbances, developing towards optimum states, etc. In other words, they react dynamically to their environment (all other systems). The same goes for the cadres. They are not like the bourgeoisie, which cannot retreat beyond the principle of private property. But since their role as experts is to provide, in a *given political situation* (that is, in a situation where the overall goals are already set), *coherence* to often unconnected and disparate processes and, once the systemic relationships (intra-systemic and relationships between systems) are known, to offer *optimisation* strategies to realise the goals defined beforehand (Benveniste 1972: 71–2), the question of changing the basic pattern of social relations simply is not part of the tasks assigned to them. In developed capitalist society, therefore, ruling class power thus is routinely wielded by observing rules and practices which apparently are only intended to maintain social cohesion. In the words of Horkheimer and Adorno (1990: 31), 'by subjecting the whole of life to the demands of its maintenance, the dictatorial minority guarantees, together with its own security, the persistence of the whole'.

In the final analysis, Bertalanffy's central claim that systems management differs from mechanistic interpretations of human behaviour becomes problematic, since the systems perspective by its exalted rationalism a priori restricts humanity's fundamental historic capacity for creative intervention. The system determines people's behaviour; to enter an organisation implies 'the surrender of control of personal conduct' (Ch. Barnard quoted in Grundstein 1981: 65). Below, we will see that the cadres actually were able to turn system requirements and functionalism against the ruling class in specific crisis conditions (and will do so again – one needs only to think of the 'system maintenance' requirements and functional needs deriving from the exhaustion of the natural substratum). But then, the systems perspective as such has usually facilitated their renewed subordination as well.

Let us conclude this section by summing up the key elements of systems analysis that are constitutive of the cadre perspective and actually point to their social role.

First, *functionalism*. All behaviour, relations, and goal setting are defined from the need of system maintenance, or else rejected as dysfunctional. The connection with planned division of labour and the mechanism of rule attached to it was already referred to.

Second, *equilibrium*. A system aims at a future equilibrium, not as straight teleology in the sense of an anthropomorphous projection, but as a growth process in which purpose enters the objective tendency. Equilibrating functions can be static (a fur meant to keep warm) or dynamic (homeostasis, thermoregulation) (Bertalanffy 1968: 75–8). The equilibrium concept corresponds to the mediating functions of the cadres, their role in sustaining balances of class forces, and 'thermoregulating' disruptions of such balances.

Regulation is a third key concept. Malfunctioning from a systems perspective is not only a matter of a single part not functioning, but also can be a result of the state of the whole organism (Bertalanffy 1962: 49). This of course has become standard management knowledge. The question is, where do we look for the regulators? In biological systems, there is self-maintenance/self-regulation (Bertalanffy 1962: 184) but never without a central regulating element, which, while part of the entire set of interacting elements, functions as the regulator (like a central nervous system). Again, the relation to socialisation and the role of the cadres is clear: for if regulation were a spontaneous process of adaptation and anticipation, cadres would not be necessary to begin with (in the Lockean setting, where the idea of self-regulation is paramount, there has been a corresponding distrust of the cadre role, highlighted again in the rise of neo-liberalism).

Centralisation, therefore, is the fourth key concept of systems analysis.

The fifth concept relevant here is *hierarchy*. Hierarchy refers to different states of the system in terms of progressive conditions towards a fully grown end state. This also explains the moment of development in a system: as long as a biological system has not yet reached its potential level of organisation, it tends towards it (Bertalanffy 1962: 186). Here we encounter an element which can lead to cadre autonomy: i.e. from the perspective of the cadres, the requirements of optimisation of the functioning of a unit of socialised labour may imply changes that modify the relations of production, suspend/circumscribe property rights, etc.

The final concept pertinent to our discussion is *growth by differentation and specialisation*. Bertalanffy makes much of the distinction between organisms and merely physical wholes. While in the latter, there is a union of pre-existing elements (atoms, molecules), in a living organism the whole takes shape by 'differentiation of an original whole which segregates into parts' (Bertalanffy 1968: 69). This for him was not just a theoretical difference. Mechanical, physical explanations in his view were the product of a *Zeitgeist* characterised by commercialisation and mechanisation (Bertalanffy 1968: 191); whereas the system approach understands the reality of organisation. Organisation can in fact degenerate into mechanic interconnection if the process of segregation, or functional differentiation, leads to individual causal chains which are no longer part of the system. The creative, 'formative' power of the organism then is reduced to the machine's 'motive' power which Kant distinguishes from it (see also Grundstein 1981: 120). Bertalanffy in this case speaks of 'progressive mechanisation' and indicates that it implies a loss of regulability, also because centralisation no longer works (Bertalanffy 1968: 69–74). This example again underscores the correspondence of a system with a structure of socialisation: here, too, the need to keep the component parts together in a single, functioning organism and not allow parts of it to harden into life-less appendices, is central to its fulfilling its tasks.

When we discuss the instances of cadre class formation further below, these elements of systems analysis will be seen to have worked, implicitly or explicitly, in the cadres' outlook, both under routine and emergency conditions.

Historical instances of cadre class formation

In the course of the twentieth century, cadres can be said to have been galvanised into a class of their own at several crisis junctures. Capital at an advanced level of development (the notion 'monopoly capital' brings out precisely this aspect) rests on an intricate complex of structures of socialisation; the bourgeoisie in turn relies on a stratum of cadres to manage these structures, and all structures in combination. The centralisation of capital and the involvement of the state allow large parts of the mass of profits to be reserved for the payment of the cadres (Nicolaus 1970). In this constellation of forces we can see, on the one hand, the moment of transformation (the social logic potentially overtaking the private one); on the other, the limitation of the freedom of action of the cadres, dependent as they are on capital for their reproduction as a class.

The emergence of technocracy

The contours of the cadre phenomenon were already visible in the nineteenth century. The early French sociologists (Saint-Simon and Comte), Herbert Spencer, and the Italian élite theorists Pareto and Mosca all contributed elements of its definition as a regulative instance in the new mass society – if not actually as a bulwark *against* the masses (Therborn 1980). The Bolshevik revolution in Russia, among other things, precipitated the creation, in 1919, of the International Labour Organisation (ILO) which was intended to equilibrate different patterns of capital/labour relations internationally. The ILO offered a structure in which the cadre function of mediation could be defined outside the structures of the national state. The European trade union and Social-Democratic traditions of class compromise in this way were mobilised to ensure that exploitation would not be pursued to extremes that would expose the capitalist world to further revolutionary breakthroughs (Haas 1964: 140).

In the national settings with their complex class balances directly imbricated with state power, such a laboratory experiment with a mediating cadre role at the time was impossible – certainly once the Russian revolution politicised the conflict between the ruling classes and the proletariat. In fact, the term 'cadre' obtained its specific connotation in France under the Popular Front. At that time, amidst severe class struggles, the middle classes old and new moved towards unification in order not to be excluded from capital–labour compromise. They acted in the name of the 'nation', referring to themselves as its 'sane' and 'stable' component; a 'third way' between the left and the right (Boltanski 1982: 77, 63). At this point, the 'cadres' still were an amalgam of a majority of small owners and self-employed notaries and doctors, and a minority of engineers and salaried managers. Together they hardly qualified as the 'new middle class' which the Belgian socialist turned corporatist H. de Man called 'the articulators of the general interest'. The Catholic Church took an active interest in the cadre movement. A Jesuit priest, father Desqueyrat, even provided the movement with an ideology of its own, which centred on the personality, 'Personalism' (ibid.: 83; Wijmans 1987: 121, 133).

Critics on the left warned against the authoritarian implications of the cadres' role under these conditions. Thus Simone Weil argued in 1934 that the essence of bureaucratic control lay in the enterprise and consisted of the centralisation of knowledge ('including the secrets') formerly possessed by the workers (Weil 1978: 123). The expropriation of the capitalists would in her view not lead to working class power, but turn the administrative (managerial–technocratic) element into a dictatorial bureaucratic caste, as had happened in the USSR (van der Linden 1992: 68–9). The big French 'technocrats', men like Mercier, Tardieu, and Laval, indeed were authoritarian élitists who rejected democracy. They stood in the tradition of Saint-Simon, favouring growth, science-based modernisation, and a transfer of power from the politicians to the 'experts' (Kuisel 1967: vii-ix; Granou 1977: 36–7). Economically, they were in favour of a modernisation of capitalist relations of production rather than their abolition; hence their predilections were shared by some of the scions from the Fordist growth industries such as Louis Renault who encouraged the organisation of the middle classes to provide anti-communism with a mass basis (Boltanski 1982: 76). Eventually, in the Vichy regime, the mixture of backward- and forward-looking cadres became discredited. It degenerated into a form of fascism, 'the celebration of the union of spiritualism and rationalism which in the field of social classes is incarnated and realised not only by objectively proclaimed "class collaboration", but also, more profoundly, by the alliance, *within each class, of fractions in decline and ascendant fractions*' (ibid.: 102; emphasis added).

The specific context in which the cadres emerged in France, converged in important respects with conditions in neighbouring countries. The actual Nazi order in Germany mobilised, in the exact sense indicated by Boltanski, declining and ascendant fractions within each single class – in this case united behind a violent, racist revanchism ignited by Versailles, and with incomparably greater economic power. As Aly and Heim (1993) have argued, modern technocracy was an integral part of the Nazi state, complementing the geopolitical and racist designs of the movement's leadership. The planning of a new European order, and the demographic and social–geographic calculations which in conjunction with Nazi racism would find their apogee in Auschwitz, were largely the result of the 'systematic' thinking of a whole class of young, highly qualified engineers, geographers and administrators (most of whom would continue their work in the Federal Republic after the war). Here even more so than in France, the cadres moved to take the place of a bourgeoisie in crisis, radicalising in the context of a process of class formation towards the right, which ultimately proved self-destructive.

In the United States, in the absence of an old middle class of European dimensions, the cadre element developed under different auspices. Integrating the large-scale economy in the sense of socialisation at the end of the nineteenth century here produced the 'system-builder', men who 'linked separate American railroads together into a single comprehensive network' (Murphy 1994: 64). As state involvement in the US was secondary to private enterprise, the rise of these engineers and managers occurred largely under the auspices of capital. New industries such as chemicals and electrical engineering fostered polytechnical education and the number of professional engineers trained at the new technology institutes increased from 45,000 in 1900 to 230,000 in 1930 (Noble 1979: 39). The hegemony of capitalist enterprise was much stronger than in Europe, and there was no basis for a 'third way'.

In the Progressive Movement of 1890–1920, the transition to a large-scale economy (including scientific management and a degree of state intervention) had already been assimilated ideologically by the ruling class, among others through the National Civic Federation mentioned in chapter 4. 'The emphasis upon management responsibility . . . as the mark of professional success,' writes David Noble, 'undercut whatever support there might have been for trade-union activity by engineers' (1979: 41; see also Ehrenreich and Ehrenreich 1979: 27).

Hence, whereas in Europe, the cadres would remain relatively aloof from big capital and form into a class as state personnel and independent professionals, in the US they can best be described as the new breed of corporate officers committed to rational economic management. In the New Deal period, this view was expressed by the concept of 'managerial revolution' by A.A. Berle, Jr. and G. C. Means (*The Modern Corporation and Private Property*, 1932) and James Burnham (*The Managerial Revolution*, (1960 [1941]). 'Mid-twentieth-century capitalism,' Berle later wrote (1954: 35) 'has been given the power and the means of more or less planned economy, in which decisions are or at least can be taken in the light of their probable effect on the whole community.'

Clearly, this unreflected conclusion alone would have made the capitalist class look with due distrust upon the ideologues of managerialism notwithstanding their red-baiting zeal (as in the case, at a later stage, of authors such as Daniel Bell and J.K. Galbraith). But the 'more or less planned economy' implied more than communitarian benevolence. The Keynesian notion of assuming control of the investment process by suppressing the *rentier* aspect of the capitalist mode of production envisaged suspending the private operation of a fraction of capital, implicitly replacing one class of private owners by paid functionaries. Immediately following the famous comment on the euthanasia of the *rentier* in his *General Theory*, Keynes wrote that 'we might aim in practice . . . at an increase in the volume of capital . . . and at a scheme of direct taxation which allows the intelligence and determination and executive skill of the financier, the entrepreneur [and this entire species], . . . to be harnessed to the service of the community on reasonable terms of reward' (1970 [1936]: 376–7; passage in brackets in Latin in the original). Since Keynes was everything but a revolutionary, this shows how strongly the *logic* of socialisation itself points to fundamental transformation, new class perspectives, and a different mode of production. This was not missed on the ruling class in such countries as Italy and Germany, where the balance of class forces was too fragile to allow a comparable reordering of private and public power. In the US, however, the transformation of the New Deal from its initial state monopolistic to a corporate liberal stage made the sustained experiment with state intervention possible. It inscribed both Keynesianism and managerialism into the transnational expansion of big corporations, thus extending the 'managerial revolution' abroad and prolonging its lease on life in a Cold War context (see also Noble 1979: 61).

Cadres and corporate liberalism

The extrapolation of the New Deal synthesis to Western Europe under the Marshall Plan terminated the specifically European incorporation of retrograde small business and professionals' concerns in the political concept of the cadres. As Boltanski notes (1982: 152), after the war the situation was reversed in that the real cadres, the technocratic and managerial element, became the dominant force.

> One cannot understand the transformations which after the war have affected the social representation of the "cadres" if one ignores to which extent these changes derive from the importation of systems of values, social technologies and models of excellence of American origin which have accompanied and sometimes preceded the realisation of the Marshall Plan (ibid.: 155).

In the Marshall Plan, this watershed in terms of social restructuration was accompanied, in the shape of the Cold War, by an element of restoring cadre discipline. For however functional the cadres may be in holding society together in a crisis, guiding the class structure to its new configuration and articulating the new concept of control (a task which the bourgeoisie at large cannot perform because its short-term interests by definition are tied to the old situation), their tendency to autonomise into a class-for-itself risks unsettling the capitalist order. Therefore, in the immediate postwar years and the Truman doctrine/Marshall Plan period, the discipline of capital was reaffirmed by Cold War rhetoric and political surveillance. More particularly, the interpenetration which in the New Deal, the wartime Grand Alliance, and the European resistance had occurred between the cadres and working class and their respective political universes, unravelled in a frenzy of Free World orthodoxy.

In Europe, postwar Social Democracy became the vehicle by which the social changes mentioned were both expressed and contained. As Rudolf Bahro has argued (1980: 157),

> Social Democracy in power is the party of the compromise between the layer of specialists susceptible to "transcendence of the system" and the part of management oriented to "system reform", especially in the public sector; although always respecting the limits imposed by the long-term interests of the monopoly bourgeoisie. But these two tendencies of course only find their common language when they enter into confrontation with the conservative fraction of the bourgeoisie.

The Marshall Plan reinforced the managerialist and technocratic orientation of Social Democracy (Carew 1987: 240–1), although 1930s ideologies such as personalism, corporatism and de Man's ideas on planning lingered on in the movement. In the 1950s and early 1960s, programmatic reformulations replaced whatever anti-capitalist rhetoric had remained in Social Democratic political vocabulary (the Godesberg Programme and its equivalents in other continental European countries). Echoes of systems-thinking were traceable in notions that a conflict-free development path was possible, that society could be self-regulating, that the end of ideology could be declared, and that society had actually moved beyond being capitalist (Greven 1974: 186). Whereas previously, the socialist and communist parties, and the trade unions, had been led by party and union bureaucrats, in the course of the later 1950s, the managerial, technocratic and general intellectual elements within the cadre stratum rose to prominence on account of their growing functional role in society at large. Their culture, qualifications, and self-consciousness clashed with the idea of representation and pointed to self-organisation and autonomy instead. In the Communist parties, where traditional working class leaders continued in power until the late 1970s, the same shift would occur later.

The student movement of the 1960s was a watershed here. This movement, in its 'New Left' posture, overwhelmingly reaffirmed the independence from both capital and the working class. Although radicalised to the point of insurrection in 1968–69, the new generation eventually was absorbed into the existing left-wing party and welfare state structures. The 'Long March through the institutions', helped along by the popularisation of positivistic and anti-voluntaristic versions of Marxism such as Althusser's, thus channelled the radicalised post-war generation into the expanding ranks of the managerial–technocratic stratum. The 'New Left' take-over of Social Democracy is illustrated in Table 5.1.

Although the data on which this table is based, are heterogenous, and a category 'cadre stratum' can be constructed only tentatively due to different definitions used in sources, the trend away from the working class and towards the new middle strata is clear.

Table 5.1 Cadres and workers in Social Democratic parties and in the Italian Communist Party (percentages)

	Party members	MPs			Congress delegates	
	FRG 1977	Sweden 1968	GB 1977	Denmark 1975	France 1973	Italy PCI 1975
Working class	28	12	28	1.5	3.2	36
(previously)	(45)[a]	(38)[b]	(35)[c]			
Cadre stratum*	34	58	32	76	63.9	58.2
(previously)	(22)[a]	(5)[b]	(20)[c]			

[a]1952; [b]1945; [c]1959

*Managers, civil servants/state bourgeoisie/bureaucrats, scientific–technical intelligentsia, teachers.

Sources: (France) Granou 1977: 218; Other countries, calculated from data in Raschke 1981, country tables.

Higher education and cadre reproduction

Here we should perhaps briefly pause and assess the role, dramatised in the events of 1968–69, of higher education in the transformation of the old into the new middle classes. More generally, universities, polytechnics, business schools, and all other higher and by implication, secondary education, in combination, can be argued to constitute the *reproductive apparatus* of the cadres. While the ruling class of course receives education as well, the overwhelming majority of students, especially since World War II, have been recruited from the middle and lower classes to be trained for cadre roles.

Education provides the cadres with their 'capital', knowledge. By obtaining knowledge and gaining expertise, and subsequently, like all salaried employees, trying to win a degree of autonomy and a corresponding negotiating position, cadres can translate their education into extra income; Bihr calls this a 'knowledge rent' (1989: 203). University education is the critical mark of distinction here. Much more than other forms of (vocational) education, the university creates an atmosphere of pure science, sustaining the image of expertise as a social force distinct from the state and capital. And although these have become more prominent in higher education, too, important distinctions remain between various disciplines in this respect. Thus in the natural sciences, partly due to the technical outlays like laboratories, partly due to the direct functionality of scientific advance to industrial application and capital accumulation (science parks etc.), a stage has been reached where we can speak of *real subordination* of scientific labour (both teachers and students) to capital.

In the humanities and social sciences, by contrast, this picture is contradictory. While there are applied fields such as industrial psychology and other aspects of labour relations studies in which the requirements of capital accumulation dictate the curriculum fairly directly, other fields still remain the province of the traditional intellectual. The organisation of work in all cases is based on autonomy, and the discipline of capital is exerted essentially as a social ideological force. Therefore, we can speak of the persistence in the social sciences of a pattern of only *formal* subordination of labour to capital. The arts and social science departments constitute one of the enclaves in advanced capitalist society where the (intellectual) worker is still an artisan controlling his/her own means of production (comparable to other professions such as lawyers and notaries, pharmacists, etc.); the results of social scientific work are exchanged as in simple commodity exchange (Kijne 1978: 30). However, pressures to impose the discipline of capital *directly* by separating teaching from research, introducing additional levels of management and bureaucratic ways of defining curriculum content, while making research dependent on outside financing, continue and may be succeeding where they still stumbled on mass protest in the late 1960s.

The difficulty of imposing discipline here is that it should not compromise the necessary functional autonomy of the future cadres. They must assume their professional tasks with conviction and determination, 'freely' considering options for social equilibration and yet restricting those options to strict limits. In the words of Eliot Freidson:

> Unlike craft or industrial labour . . . most professions produce intangible goods: their product, in other words, is only formally alienable and is inextricably bound to the person and the personality of the producer. It follows, therefore, that *the producers themselves have to be produced* if their products or commodities are to be given a distinctive form (quoted in Feltes 1986: 43).

It is this task which is complicated by the prevailing condition of merely formal subordination of the humanities and social science teachers who should do the 'producing' and who today mostly hail from the radicalised, postwar generation themselves.

Now the student movement of May 1968 was also a reaction of students whose parents were self-employed (small shopkeepers and artisans marginalised by industrialisation) to attempts by the state to advance real subordination to the entire university. In West Germany, two-thirds of the dramatically expanded student population of 1967–68 were from parents who had no higher education (Weber 1973: 27–9), and in other countries, the same pattern prevailed. Although they were inevitably destined to be absorbed as cadres into the world of advanced socialisation, a catalogue of progressive, yet 'petty bourgeois' values (direct democracy, equal chances, individual self-realisation, rejection of the division of labour) predisposed them to a democratised version of the traditional university with its humanistic ideals, rather than to the mass education factories of advanced capitalist society. The institutional autonomy of the university was and is congenial to this attitude, and as John and Barbara Ehrenreich observe (1979: 33–4), in the aspiring cadres' consciousness conforms to what they see as their future autonomy relative to capital.

The notion entertained by observers of the student movement and the 'new worker', i.e. the salaried technician, that the new mass-produced intelligentsia would assume a revolutionary vanguard role, could be dismissed in advance on account of the values in which most of them had been reared at home and which had been reproduced in the course of their training (Hortleder 1973: 33). Often the fact that the students were studying Marxism was taken as a sign of their radical intentions. But even allowing for the insurrectionary momentum in the 1968–69 period, the actual curricula should not, of course, be composed exclusively of liberal doctrine if the cadres' future role as *mediators* between capital and labour, and in the entire architecture of socialisation constructed around this polarity, is taken seriously. Although this is dependent on the balance of class forces in society at large and the hegemonic concept which expresses it, theories taught at universities should, from a perspective of 'system maintenance', ideally include liberal, individualist theories; theories typically reflecting the cadre role of managing units of socialised labour, reproductive structures, and ideological processes aimed at integrating society; and even allow for the odd instance of historical materialism. Systems analysis accordingly is prominently represented in the syllabus of most social science fields.[3]

Autonomisation of the cadres and planned interdependence in the 1970s

One target of the 1960s student movement was US involvement in Vietnam. This intervention had been undertaken in a spirit of technocratic arrogance that characterised the period and the incoming Kennedy administration in particular. Dubbed alternatively 'the best and the brightest' by journalist David Halberstam (1973), and 'the New Mandarins' by Noam Chomsky (1969), the president and his ministers and advisers considered behavioural social science and management expertise the key props in dealing with the unprecedented challenge of a Third World revolting against European colonialism and looking to the rising power of the USSR for help. Kennedy's Secretary of Defense and future World Bank president, Robert McNamara, epitomised the cadre profile in this respect. He 'brought to the Pentagon a brilliant, systematic mind and high confidence in his own judgment. Once he had analyzed the data and come to a conclusion on an issue, his style was to never acknowledge doubt; he always acted decisively and with an aura of total certainty' (Stubbing 1986: 265).

This attitude (especially after Kennedy's assassination had removed the reformist, Wilsonian element from US foreign policy) led to a carnage in South East Asia which in its systematic, managerial thoroughness evoked comparisons with the Nazi extermination machinery. Student leaders denouncing imperialist atrocities in the Third World, such as Rudi Dutschke, spoke of the 'anonymous terrorism of the state-societal machinery' (1969: 248). Such sentiments spilled over into the bureaucracies of all sorts which in the early 1970s were absorbing the radicalised students. Hence, against the background of sustained working class militancy and power, pervasive 'tertiarisation' of the social structures throughout the heartland including Japan (Hagelstange 1987: 155; Morioka 1989: 144–5), and a succession of profound international defeats for the West culminating in the US retreat from Vietnam, the cadres again veered to a position of relative autonomy from bourgeois hegemony and control. But where in the 1930s, the cadre perspective had focused on national planning, this time the cadres' frame of reference tended towards democratic, equitable *inter*-nationalism, or what we will term *planned interdependence*.

The Club of Rome, the transnational planning group already mentioned in the last chapter, became the focal point of discussions which soon revealed that the orientation of the cadres was beginning to abandon the framework imposed on it by capitalist discipline. The crisis of corporate liberalism was interpreted in these discussions as one of exhaustion and spreading disorder, for which only integrated global planning would offer a solution (Alexander King interview in *Vk*, 21 November 1987; see also Braillard 1982). The first Club of Rome report, the 1971 Meadows/Forrester MIT study *The Limits to Growth* (Meadows *et al.* 1972), was a systems projection of the exhaustion of the natural substratum of the current regime of accumulation. It was almost immediately overtaken by an even more dramatic report, *Blueprint for Survival* (by a group of British scientists including Julian Huxley) which expressly blamed the capitalist nature of development as the source of what the report saw as the impending 'breakdown of society and of the life support systems on this planet possibly by the end of this century and certainly within the lifetime of our children' (*Time*, 24 January 1972). This position was then echoed by a 1974 Club of Rome report, *Reshaping the International Order*. It was written by a team headed by the Dutch Social Democratic economist Jan Tinbergen and stressed the need for the entire political and economic overhaul of a world thrown into disarray by 'the relentless operation of market forces' (Tinbergen 1977: 15). This report amplified the Third World demands for an NIEO – even emphasising that such an order could not remain 'economic' but would have to include the political structures of world order as well, hence the absence of the 'E' in its title abbreviation. The specific measures proposed in the Reshaping report were mostly phrased in standard cadre vocabulary and aimed at reinforcing, on a world scale, 'the criteria of a broadened social rationality' (ibid.: 314).

The existing infrastructure of international organisation configured around the United Nations at this juncture began to function as a relay of Third World demands for stable raw material prices and related measures to assist them in their attempt to industrialise and feed their populations (Krasner 1985). The fact that support for the NIEO idea in the West 'arose mainly among international officials concerned with aid and specialists associated with them' (Cox 1979: 204), and resonated most strongly at the level of international organisation, also brought to light the inherent internationalism of the cadres and their susceptibility to planning. The international integration philosophy of 'functionalism' has been congenial to the cadres ever since they became associated with international organisation. 'The functional logic,' Ernst Haas observes (1964: 153), 'relies heavily on the use of dispassionate inquiries, based on value-free modes of research, to expose problems and lay the groundwork for eventual policy compromises. Experts, not politicians, are singled out as the agents for defining the limits of accommodation, preferably along lines of pure computation and problem-solving' (see also Cox 1977: 407–8). Craig Murphy (1994: 63) in this connection points out that the terrain of international organisation so attracted the 'expert' because 'disciplinary communities have always been transnational, voluntary associations linked by norms other than service to the national interest' – and we could add, 'or private interests'.

The cadre drift towards planned interdependence which reciprocated demands put forward by the state classes of the Third World had a strong

West European focus in post-Godesberg Social Democracy (see also above). Willy Brandt, West German Chancellor until 1974, was an exponent of the cadres' drive to develop corporate liberalism towards what was seen as its optimal state. Brandt favoured a stabilisation of capitalist society by infrastructural supports and regulation, *Ordnungspolitik*. Following his ouster by a spy scandal, he embarked on a project to revamp the Socialist International (SI) together with Austrian and Swedish party leaders Kreisky and Palme. They more specifically envisaged that the new SI would work with bodies such as the OECD to develop elements of *Ordnungspolitik* on the international plane (Günsche and Lantermann 1977: 143). When in 1977, Brandt was asked by World Bank president McNamara to head a Commission to investigate the persistence of the North–South gap, the rather timid result yet again radiated the cadre frame of mind. The basic idea was that modern/rational/democratic social relations ultimately reflect a technical imperative to which the entire world must by necessity conform. Convergence theory (with Tinbergen one of its most prominent advocates) and concretely, Brandt's *Ostpolitik*, had been based on this very assumption (Braunmühl 1973).

All along, the same Social Democrats had taken care to cover their left flank, true to the cadre preoccupation with holding the middle ground in the class structure. This was brought out most clearly in the German *Berufsverbote* campaign launched by the Brandt government. But there were also attempts to create a privileged fraction of the cadres and encourage corporatist class organisation so that they could be accommodated separately, playing to their lingering susceptibility to privilege. In West Germany under Brandt's successor Schmidt, a new co-determination law was enacted in 1976 which prescribed a mandatory representation of 'managing employees' *(leitende Angestellte)* in the company (Briefs 1979: 1353–4). A comparable development took place in the Netherlands, another country with a Socialist-led government. Here, also in 1976, the fast-growing union of higher employees finally was admitted into the collective bargaining framework.

The prevailing mood was captured in the February 1978 issue of *International Management* which illustrated an article on 'the Militant Managers' with a quasi-revolutionary poster illustration carrying the slogan 'Managers of the World, Unite'. Indeed, even among big corporate managers in the US, the argument that it was mandatory to move from the corporate liberal synthesis to full-fledged planning could be heard until well into the 1970s. Thus Th. Bradshaw, president of Atlantic Richfield, argued that state intervention should be rationalised by moving towards coherent planning, as in the government-led war production effort of the 1940s (*Fortune*, February 1977). However, out of alarm over the proliferation of plans for placing private capital under public surveillance (see my 1993), a movement for restoring discipline was well under way at this juncture.

Deregulation and the dilemmas of global governance

The neo-liberal restructuring away from the corporate liberal class configuration has clearly undermined the situation in which the cadres functioned to maintain what Bihr (1989: 283) calls the 'equilibrium of compromises' – between industry and labour, productive and financial capital, and the private and public sectors. To break the deadlock engendered by state-centred socialisation and planned interdependence, capitalist strategies, from the 1970s onwards, aimed at raising the level of commodification of social relations by privatisation, flexible labour relations, up to outright attacks on the trade union movement and on the socially protective state and international quasi-state roles. In due course, the entire configuration of management and collective bargaining practices built into the giant corporation, which was linked to national, Keynesian demand management, began to unravel in what we have elsewhere called the 'Second Glorious Revolution' (see also my 1995).

The cadre stratum as a whole has been profoundly affected by this restructuring. The return of the owners in an entrepreneurial role in the US and subsequently, in Europe as well (whether by 'raiding', shareholders' revolts, or otherwise) entailed a reduction of management power and presence at all levels (Useem 1989: 14, 16). This was reflected, among other things, in the rise of white collar unemployment over the decade 1982–93 from less than one-quarter to one-third of total US unemployment (*BW*, 28 February 1994). As the bastions of cadre power (trade unions, managerial bureaucracies, states, the UN system) have been severely damaged and knowledge/information monopolies have disintegrated, the autonomy of the cadres in society has been reduced dramatically. This once again has made them more subservient to the ruling classes, since these after all can hire and fire the experts/planners and managers in a thoroughly shaken labour market segment. The hegemony of international finance and its institutional mode of operation (IMF dictates, OECD 'recommendations', etc.), summed up in Gill's concept of the new constitutionalism, among other things works by 'removing many areas of domestic policy debate from the political arena, and to undermine radical intellectual elites, as a new form of intellectual orthodoxy becomes the dominant framework in which policy issues are cast' (Sinclair 1994: 153).

Yet the thrust of neo-liberalism, which consists of attacking the cumulative structures of social protection and planning, matured under corporate liberalism, cannot as such undo the process of socialisation. As Costello writes (1989: 3, 5), 'When the micro-computer was first being introduced, the typical form of innovation, promoted by the media and right-wing ideologists, was the small-scale isolated start-up company . . .':

> Now the emphasis of technical advance is shifting back towards global efficiency, integration of systems, networks, compatibility and

standardisation ... As production becomes increasingly advanced, and the development of new production techniques, products and services requires more use of science and high-level skills, success is less and less a matter of chance and more and more a product of conscious policy.

The inevitable reintegration/socialisation of labour has a technical side in the growth of information technology under the impetus of virtual accumulation, such as integration between electronics and telecommunications. Already in the context of the neo-liberal drive, we may discern the historically specific form of the cadre role here in the activities of *consultancy firms*.

The consultancy phenomenon

In the process of restoring the discipline of capital and the necessary degree of socialisation of labour on a world scale, management consultancies have become prominent channels for creating the basis for control and transmitting the norms of profitable management among both private and public establishments. 'Consultants are in many ways the advance guard of the globalising trend in world business,' observes the *Financial Times* (24 February 1995). Andersen Consulting, the biggest in the field, has no world headquarters – staff may live where they like, if only near an airport; they use laptop and modem to access both the company's database and clients. Epitomising the type of manager engendered by virtual accumulation,

> Consultants are the perfect type of what Robert Reich ... used to call "symbolic analysts" – workers who make their living from manipulating abstract concepts. Being rootless and highly mobile, they can amass experience and information across continents and industries in ways that corporate executives find increasingly hard to duplicate (*FT*, 24 February 1995).

The cadre role in neo-liberal deregulation has been facilitated by historic defeats of the organised working class. On a terrain redefined by globalisation of the discipline of capital, one segment of the cadres again are acting as agents of capital against the workers and society at large. As the same newspaper notes, 're-engineering will normally mean job losses ... To that extent, the [consultancy] profession will be paid out of the wages of the victims'.

Likewise reinforcing the neo-liberal thrust are the *rating agencies* we have referred to before. They are an example, like the consultants, of 'non-state forms of international authority' (Sinclair 1994: 133). Both rating agencies and consultancy firms serve to develop international norms of behaviour derived from the requirements of virtual accumulation and the hypertrophy of money capital. In the 1980s, they had become globally operating forces working to generalise norms of profitability and viability around the globe. Clients of consultancies include business but also non-business institutions such

Table 5.2 Clientele of major management consultancies, early 1990s

	Clients	
Consultancy firm	Private capital	(Former) state/ semi-public institutions
Andersen	Astra/Merck, Constr. Aeronauticas SA	London Stock Exchange, British Rail, Komercní Banka (Cz.);
McKinsey	Hewlett-Packard, Pepsi Co, AT&T, GE, GM, AmEx, IBM	UN Secretariat;
Booz Allen & Hamilton	Chevron, GE, Caterpillar	US government, NASA, Civil Aviation Authority, Russian Railways;
Boston Consulting	Reuters	Harvard Business School, Karolinska Hospital (Swe.), Save the Children Fund;
A.T. Kearney	General Motors	Treuhand (Ger.), Olympic Games;
Bain & Co	Guinness, Dun & Bradstreet	Russian government, Polish government.

Source: adapted from *World Link*, July/August 1994: 15–9; communication from Professor Craig N. Murphy.

as states and semi-public institutions. In Table 5.2, the potential transfer of micro-economic rationality across regions as well as between private/public bodies is illustrated.

What Table 5.2 suggests is that a wide variety of non-business institutions become subject to a discipline primarily designed for capitalist enterprise. For as the *FT* notes (19 June 1997), management consultants increasingly converge on recommending behaviour that turns 'the stock market [into] the final arbiter of value':

> In some cases, boards of directors need help in grasping the principle of shareholder value in the first place. In almost every case thereafter, they need help in explaining it to the rest of the organisation and creating structures to deliver it.

Another effect of socialisation, the universalisation of polytechnical labour processes, or what Marx called 'abstract labour' (1973: 104) is precisely what consultancies aim at. 'Technology is removing constraints of time, place, and form' so that, in the words of an A.T. Kearney director, 'technology convergence . . . provides for process convergence, which in turn will enable industrial convergence' (*FT*, 19 June 1997).

It is our thesis that in this process of synchronising socialisation and institutional behaviour under the discipline of capital, consultancies and their equivalents are in effect laying the groundwork for a system of *global governance* (see also

Sinclair 1994). By this term, we understand the world-wide integration of economic, social and political organisation into a mediated complex of state and quasi-state authority. At first sight diametrically opposed to the drift of 1970s planned interdependence, global governance under the discipline of capital in fact *also* signifies a further advance in global planning. Here it is necessary to see that management consultancies and rating agencies are not alone in the field of synchronising behaviour and outlook along common lines. In reality, a whole range of Non-Governmental Organisations (NGOs), often with a background in the planned interdependence experience, also increasingly function as consultancies. Thus in the area of forest conservation and World Bank monitoring of it, such NGOs, Ans Kolk writes (1996: 286), 'have been involved in consultancy, negotiations and the implementation of projects, and cooperate intensely with governments and international organisations.' This cannot but draw them into the same orbit as the management consultancies proper (see also Table 5.2). For the idea that NGOs, or 'civil society' with which they are often equated, constitute a contemporary form of political opposition, overlooks the fundamental limitation of non-political forms of organisation. As Kolk points out with respect to forest conservation NGOs,

> A major dilemma has been the question of representation and accountability. Although NGOs frequently claim to speak on behalf of (sectors of) civil society and strive for an important, generally supported cause, it is often unclear whether they are truly representative and to whom they are accountable (ibid.).

Hence there is little guarantee against all kinds of co-optation by the much more powerful state, international quasi-state, and corporate actors in the international political economy. After all, a concept of control (here the neo-liberal one) works to demarcate an area of possible solutions and define legitimate courses of action for the cadres most directly.

It would seem that only a re-articulation with the level of politics, either at the national state level or, in novel forms, at the level of regional/sectoral or universal international organisation, can ensure that global governance becomes transparent in terms of the interests represented in its concrete manifestations. The discipline of capital can operate through progressive NGOs as easily as it does, much more expressly of course, in the recommendations of management consultancies. If that discipline is to be constrained and the destructive consequences of today's exploitation of society and nature averted, the sphere of civil society must be recognised as a terrain of capitalist socialisation, that is, a global commons parcellised by private property. Likewise 'expertise', whether Left or Right, 'globalising' or dedicated to preserving humankind and nature, should be decoded as the alienated form of collective knowledge. In this sense we should read, and extend, Sohn-Rethel's claim that we need a critique of scientific management in the spirit of Marx's critique of political economy quoted at the head of this chapter.

Cadres, democracy, and the classless society

Let us conclude this chapter with a note on the cadres' possible role in a resurrection of democracy that would build on the (still private, 'civil') structures of global governance.

As we saw before, it is a general tendency of the cadre stratum to adopt a radical, 'utopian', and potentially totalitarian attitude towards the operation of a social constellation. McNamara had Vietnam bombed and defoliated, but as World Bank president after 1968, geared that institution towards a comprehensive planning orientation, commissioning the Brandt report, etc. (see also Benveniste 1972: 41–2). If the neo-liberal concept of control after the collapse of the Soviet bloc and the general abandonment of the Hobbesian contender state posture has assumed a certain totalitarian quality, this in our view can at least in part be related to the cadres' propensity to work towards the ideal state of existing reality.

As in the previous experiences with this characteristic, however, the cadres' zeal in reaching the optimum state of a given 'system' of political economy and class relations is historically finite. It necessarily remains locked in the balance of forces between on the one hand, capital, and on the other, people resisting original accumulation, exploitation, and the exhaustion of the reproductive context at large. The evolution of class struggles in these arenas, relayed to the field of international relations, also decides the orientation of the cadres.

Now especially since the 'class struggles in France' of November/December 1995, which capped a longer series of revolts against neo-liberalism on a global scale, resistance to the discipline of capital not only has prompted a rethinking of neo-liberal precepts in the context of the World Econonomic Forum and other transnational planning groups of the ruling class. Also, it has mobilised a rival orientation to neo-liberalism *within* the cadre stratum itself (the upper crust of which of course also is represented in WEF and comparable networks). The cadres are oriented, by definition, to sustaining social cohesion and the integrity of the social (and by implication, natural) substratum exploited by capital. Even if, as in neo-liberalism, the dominant orientation is towards deepening the discipline of capital, the function of providing cohesion cannot be abandoned. As the limits to what the people can bear in terms of imposing the market logic on their lives, and the limit to what nature can sustain, are becoming manifest, a segment of the cadres is accordingly mobilised against yesterday's prescriptions.

The reduction of trade union influence over the traditional working class, one crucial result of the neo-liberal reimposition of discipline, has in fact worked to obliterate the dividing lines between manual workers and hitherto privileged cadres. The latter are engaging in struggles modelled on workers' union action, but largely autonomously and with union cadre this time in a consultative role. This has resulted in common battles which Alain Lebaube in *Le Monde* (26 February 1997) has called 'social conflicts of a new type', to distinguish them from the corporatist, trade-union-led workers' struggles against redundancies that ended in working class and union defeat in the 1980s. The cadres have joined the struggle for survival of workers but also of the unemployed, struggles which mark 'the end of resignation' (ibid.). A comparable conclusion is drawn by a Morgan, Stanley economist (*FT*, 3 July 1997), who observes that on a world scale, 'corporate restructuring has stretched the fabric of the social contract that had long held in check the power struggle between workers, managers and elected politicians,' and notices a mounting tide to put an end to the unrestrained profit bonanza.

A report of the French organisation of young managers (Centre des Jeunes Dirigeants d'Entreprise), coming a year after the social explosion of late 1995, illustrates how the demands of this mass movement against neo-liberal globalisation reverberate among the ranks of the most enlightened of the cadre stratum (excerpts in *FT*, 13 November 1996). Keeping its distance from the 'temptation to enslave man to the economy' engendered by competition, the report concludes that society is in danger of collapsing from the demands made by 'unregulated capitalism'.

> Today, in submitting to excessive constraints of productivity, in downsizing without limit, in seeking to make gains at the expense of society, business is in the process of breaking the social links which it used to build. We are convinced that unregulated capitalism will explode just as communism exploded, if we do not seize the chance to put man back at the centre of society.

Already, the equilibrating, 'systemic' function of the cadres has been reactivated also at the political level, as testified by the resurgence of Social Democracy in Europe. The 'Socialists', representing the fraction of the cadres with a background in the state and international organisation (and were it not for the structural corruption of US politics, the Clinton/Gore presidential team would have to be counted among this tendency), are seeking to contain the untrammelled forces of private capital spearheaded by the management consultants, in order to maintain a degree of social cohesion. However timid, in the present context of revolts against the discipline of capital on a global scale, even the slightest reduction of this discipline is meaningful. Indeed, once the cadre stratum reorients its perspective towards social goals, prioritising (however superficially at first) survival over profitability, this enlarges the space for a deepening of democracy, a reappropriation of the public sphere by the population, and eventually, a more fundamental transformation away from class society.

Marx's concept of the transformation of the capitalist mode of production (apart from the specific course of political revolutions anticipating or clearing the way for such a transformation), was that the new society matures in the context of the old.[4] However, the notion of the working class taking over from capital has not been warranted by twentieth-century experience. In every revolutionary situation, the cadres, as Alain Bihr (1989) writes, immediately seized the reins of power from the faltering bourgeoisie, either to 'lead' the workers or to repress their aspirations, and always terminating working class autonomy. But then, Bahro points out (1982: 60), history has not produced one single example of a subordinate class proper to the structure of a given type of society simultaneously embodying a new order: 'One oppressed class cannot carry the fate of humanity in its entirety.'

The rise of a cadre stratum expressing the socialisation dynamic, if necessarily in an alienated fashion, and the fact that it already several times has followed a course different from the one desired by the ruling class (however erratic, or even disastrous, this course may have been), highlights a fault-line in the structure of advanced capitalist society which is of crucial significance for its transformation. What these experiences (including the Soviet experience which in important respects and in the specific circumstances of a contender state role, forms part of it) teach us is that the cadre stratum requires a reunification with the working class to merge into the 'proletarian' historic subject, humanity reclaiming its alienated self. In the confrontation between a capitalist class which has no existence beyond privilege and private property, and a working class resisting the discipline of capital, the cadres have all along tended to adopt positions which look beyond the straight class antagonism. In terms of their historic role they represent what Gorz calls (but unnecessarily restricts to the marginalised and rejected) the *non-class*. For even if the general interest which they claim to represent, is always the idealised special interest of a specific ruling class constellation at the same time, the drift of their intervention is to overcome this constraint. As we have argued above, the cadres are the *class which historically performs the role of shaping the structures for a classless society in the context of class society*.

Humanity will be able to survive only if such a classless society, a planetary community of fate, replaces the capitalist one, allowing people the world over 'to gain, in a common effort, control over their own productive capacity' (van Erp 1982: 304). The May 1968 events in this respect retain a crucial meaning as a laboratory of social experimentation – just as the December 1995 revolt in France stands out as a major turning point in more recent experience. But the concrete history of our present world and the development of its ruling classes to global unification under a neo-liberal concept, teach us that such a community cannot come about in a single act. Only through the cumulative momentum of a series of particular, largely contingent episodes can we hope that the forces capable of imposing limits on the capitalist exploitation of people and nature can prevail, and the suicidal drive of neo-liberalism reversed.

Notes

Introduction

1   One aspect of an adequate understanding of the contemporary political economy, Marx argues (1973: 460–1), is that it must reveal the past hidden behind its present self-evidence. The presentation hence can concentrate on those moments of historical development that have been critical in the making of the present. In the present study, this warrants why we deal at some length with the origins of the Lockean state in England, but largely leave out the origins of other states; or discuss Freemasonry, but not Protestantism, etc. In longer historical studies, this can of course be balanced better – e.g. my work on the Atlantic ruling class (1984, 1989a) and on the social history of International Relations theory (1992, 1996a); Henk Overbeek's study of British capitalism in the global context (1990), Otto Holman's *Integrating Southern Europe* (1996), or our edited collection on neo-liberalism (Overbeek 1993).

1 Commodification, socialisation and capital

1   The modern economy continues to relate to such primal activities, in that capitalist management, trade and finance, continues to evoke and stimulate the reflexes associated with hunting and war-making. This goes so far as commando training for securities traders organised by the US Department of Defense. However, although human instincts are mobilised in such endeavours (as are, in advertising notably, sexual instincts), the commodity form emerges as something impinging on the life of a community, rather than from its biological substratum as an innate characteristic of the species. While hunting is species-related, trading is *historical*, and accordingly is subject to a different life-cycle. In contrast to innate qualities of the species and in spite of Adam Smith (who counted the supposedly natural propensity to 'barter, truck and exchange' among these), commodification develops from the outside in; it has a social, not a biological origin. This is of central importance to our understanding of economic forms in general. Only because commodification grows on the prior community from the outside in, penetrating and transforming its internal forms of householding, it can have a dialectical counterpart, socialisation; a parallel process which from an external and historically contingent point of departure, develops to maturity (cf. Ilyenkov 1982: 83).

2   Brand names here play a crucial role. Flaubert, the father of the psychological novel, could still describe an actual shop in his *L'Education sentimentale* of 1869 by detailing the goods on display in terms of their physical properties only (Saisselin 1984: 28). A quintessential novel of 1960s America, Saul Bellow's *Herzog*, on the other hand uses brand names throughout the narrative to evoke aesthetic associations and atmosphere. Thus not a single car remains unidentified, and we also

get the brand names of bread (p. 7 in the 1965 edition); pharmaceuticals (pp.35, 225); liquor (pp.50, 218, 325, 333); candy (pp.154, 338); a typewriter (p.129); an anti-perspirant (p.225); a photo frame (p.227); and even a road map (p.401). This is but one illustration of the degree to which commodities enter our contemporary experience as marketable items first.

3   These self-styling acts are a way of establishing one's standing, too; Bourdieu's concept of *habitus* is used by its author to show that there is a relatively self-conscious hierarchy of such style patterns, turning 'taste' into a criterion of class distinction (Bourdieu 1979: vi, 190).

4   World-wide standardisation actually is an accelerating process today, concentrated in three Geneva-based organisations, the International Standards Organization (ISO), the International Electrotechnical Commission (IEC) and the International Telecommunications Union (ITU), which account for 96 per cent of all published standards. Although the ISO and IEC are non-governmental institutions while the ITU is a UN-specialised agency, the three increasingly work together as trade barriers are removed and the need for world-wide standardisation becomes mandatory (*FT*, 14 October 1994).

5   This perspective of 'market economy' exhausting society and nature is found also in Polanyi and may explain the renewed popularity of this author. Among Marxists, Rosa Luxemburg perhaps deserves a rereading because she does both in her book on imperialism: underconsumptionist and related theses, and the awareness that capital feeds on a prior social/natural basis (1966).

2 Capital accumulation and class formation

1   Hence, in Gramsci's view (1971: 52, 54–5), 'the subaltern classes, by definition, are not unified and cannot unite until they are able to become a state . . . their history is necessarily fragmented and episodic.'

2   Within European Christianity, Roman Catholic and Lutheran denominations still expressed the negative sentiment of agricultural society against trade and usury, *anti-chrematism* (from *chrema*, Greek for money), while Calvinism on the contrary helped it to respectability (Tawney 1952: 93). Anti-Semitism, as much as its equivalents outside the Christian/European world affecting other people performing the role of 'living money' in agrarian/traditional society (Chinese in Asia, Lebanese in the Mediterranean, South Asians in East Africa, Parsees in India, etc.) in one key respect can be understood by reference to anti-chrematism.

3   The imposition of the commodity form also takes place when, broadly within capitalist society, new products or services are developed outside the direct reach of capitalist enterprise. Thus many life-style products, but even the personal computer, which resulted from 1960s inventiveness and often were meant to be part of an imaginary, unalienated sphere of life celebrated in the May 1968 movement, found their way to corporate production, organisation and exploitation within a decade (Caute 1988: 49). (Something like it is occurring with the Internet before our eyes.) Of course, buying up or buying out the inventors here at most involves a court struggle; but for the users of such facilities, the conditions of access may be fundamentally transformed and this change does represent a moment of class formation.

4   By way of illustration, and to indicate the proportions involved: US foreign securities transactions rose from 9 per cent of GDP in 1980 to 93 per cent in 1990 (the corresponding figures for West Germany were 8 per cent and 58 per cent; Japan, 7 per cent and 119 per cent; in the case of Britain, securities transactions already stood at 360 per cent of GDP in 1985, doubling to 690 per cent in 1990). Derivatives markets grew explosively in the same period to a global stock of $6.9 trillion in 1991, daily turnover in foreign exchange stood at $900 billion a day in 1992, etc. (*Ec*, 19 September 1992). Marx, incidentally, considered the hypertrophy

of merely financial accumulation, by becoming an obstacle to real production, as a moment of capital's transformation towards a regulated, 'associated' mode of production (*MEW* 25: 454).

3 The Lockean heartland in the international political econamy

1 The terms Lockean and Hobbesian can be understood as *ideal types* in Max Weber's sense. Ideal types are analytical constructs which sum up those characteristics of a series of concrete configurations which have a logical inner unity, are 'sense-adequate' (Weber 1976: 10). This tool of Weber's is especially useful if we want to classify phenomena which cannot be explained from the analysis of capital but have a prior existence of a more historically contingent nature; roughly, a phenomenon that belongs to the category which we called 'social topography' in chapter 2.
2 These were kindly made available to the author by Professor Hans van Zon.

4 Transnational class formation and historical hegemonies

1 The rise of state monopolism to such an extent coincided with the ascent of Germany that in his *Road to Serfdom*, Hayek could argue that after liberal internationalism had radiated from England for more than two hundred years, German notions of planning and organisation held centre stage during the next sixty (1985: 36). The national epicentres were merely the nodal points in broader processes of class formation, though, and the concomitant concepts of control likewise pertained to social structures first.
2 The attempt to write an American equivalent to Quigley's 1949/1981 study, Sutton's *America's Secret Establishment* (1986), turns a plausible analysis of the influence of the Yale 'Skull & Bones' fraternity in the US ruling class (connecting the Whitney, Perkins, Taft, Lord, Harriman, and other families) into a classical example of a conspiracy theory, in which the Bonesmen are also presented as the force behind . . . the Russian revolution and the Nazis. On this strand of right-wing conspiracy theory, see Domhoff 1971.
3 The ICC still today functions as the most comprehensive business forum committed to liberalisation, actually contemplating a transformation to a 'World Business Organisation' parallel to the WTO but still continuing the heartland tradition of a behind-the-scenes role in that 'much of its . . . work is low-profile because it involves lobbying, the results of which are never very clear or public – and technical commissions, whose conclusions tend sometimes to reach only a small circle of experts' (*FT*, 8 November 1995). In a 1976 report by Rupert Murdoch to an ICC Committee headed by Ian McGregor (two men who would play key roles in Margaret Thatcher's attack on the British working class), it was stated that unless a massive campaign to highlight the virtues of the capitalist system was undertaken, 'the attitude of government and society towards the business community, already highly critical in many nations, could become downright hostile. And that might mean the end of the free economic system as we know it today' (quoted in Van der Pijl 1993: 52).
4 To illustrate the TC's continuing prominence, let us note that in the first Clinton Administration alone, the President, the secretaries of state (and eight under and assistant secretaries), interior, housing and urban development, and health; the Federal Reserve chairman, budget director, as well as the ambassadors to Britain, Japan, and Mexico, have been TC members, in addition of course to a cross-section of the US, European, and Japanese ruling class with a token presence of press figures and 'relevant' academics and professional politicians including some from what we might conveniently call 'Her Majesty's opposition' (TC Membership, 1994).

5 Cadres and the classless society

1 The literature on the cadres has been explored by Marcel van Maastrigt as part of his studies. I owe him a debt for bringing to my attention several of the titles used here.

2 In terms of internal stratification, data on Britain may give an indication of the structure of the cadre stratum: level A (higher managerial, administrative or professional), who in Britain represent 3.1 per cent of the adult population; B (intermediate managerial, administrative or professional), 17.7 per cent; and C1 (supervisory or clerical, and junior managerial, administrative or professional), 27 per cent; C2 (being the skilled manual workers), 23.5 per cent (*FT*, 13 February 1995).

3 We cannot substantiate this here, but if one looks at the 'systems' content of a few current IPE theories, it may become clear what is intended. Apart from integration theory, which all along was part of the cadre/systems complex both sociologically and theoretically, there is of course *world systems* theory – although Jan Nederveen Pieterse has argued in a critique of Wallerstein that 'we are dealing here with an untheorized use of "system" . . . a systems rhetoric . . . rather than a systems theory' (Nederveen Pieterse 1990: 30). *Regime* theory (Krasner 1985; see also Strange 1982), too, comes straight from David Easton's systems analysis of the 1960s (Nicholson and Reynolds 1967: 23). It is a matter of debate, finally, whether we can classify *regulation* theory, too, as a systems theory. The idea of regulation suggests it and the main proponents have insufficiently reflected on the functionalist implications (Jessop 1989: 36; see also 11) – although it was pointed out to me by Stephan Raes that this does not hold for Alain Lipietz (see for instance Lipietz 1985: 17).

4 'In conjunction with the material conditions and the social combination of the process of production, the rule of capital ripens the contradictions and antagonisms of its capitalist form, and with it, simultaneously, it creates the constructive elements of a new society and the moments of transformation of the old' (*MEW* 23: 526).

References

Aalders, G. and Wiebes, C. (1990) *Zaken doen tot elke prijs. De economische collaboratie van neutrale staten met Nazi-Duitsland* (The Hague, SDU).

Abraham, D. (1981) *The Collapse of the Weimar Republic. Political Economy and Crisis* (Princeton, NJ, Princeton University Press).

Aglietta, M. (1979) *A Theory of Capitalist Regulation. The US Experience*, transl. by D. Fernbach (London, New Left Books). Originally published in 1976.

Albert, M. (1992) *Kapitalisme contra kapitalisme*, transl. by H. Firet (Amsterdam and Antwerpen, Contact). Originally published in 1991.

Alletzhauser, A. (1990) *The House of Nomura* (London, Bloomsbury).

Althusser, L. and Balibar, E. (1975) *Lire le* Capital (Paris, Maspero), 2 vols. Originally published in 1968.

Aly, G. and Heim, S. (1993) *Vordenker der Vernichtung. Auschwitz und die deutschen Pläne für eine neue europäische Ordnung* (Frankfurt, Fischer). Originally published in 1991.

Amin, S. (1977) 'Universality and Cultural Spheres', *Monthly Review* 28 (9).

Anderson, B. (1983) *Imagined Communities. Reflections on the Origins and Spread of Nationalism* (London, Verso).

Andreff, W. (1976) *Profits et structures du capitalisme mondial* (Paris, Calmann-Lévy).

—— (1982) 'Régimes d'accumulation et insertion des nations dans l'économie mondiale', in J.L. Reiffers (ed.), *Economie et finances internationales* (Paris, Dunod).

Archibugi, D. (1995) 'Immanuel Kant, Cosmopolitan Law and Peace', in *European Journal of International Relations* 1 (4).

Armstrong, H.W. (1980) *The United States and Britain in Prophecy* (Pasadena, CA, Worldwide Church of God), 8th edn. Originally published in 1942.

Arrighi, G. (1991) 'World Income Inequalities and the Future of Socialism', *New Left Review* 189.

van Baaren, Th. P. (1960) *Wij Mensen. Religie en wereldbeschouwing bij schriftloze volken* (Utrecht, Bijleveld).

Bagwell, P.A. and Mingay, G.E. (1987) *Britain and America. A Study of Economic Change 1850–1939* (London, Routledge & Kegan Paul). Originally published in 1970.

Bahro, R. (1980) *Die Alternative* (Reinbek, Rowohlt). Originally published in 1977.

—— (1982) *Elementen voor een nieuwe politiek*, transl. by M. Polman (Amsterdam, Van Gennep). Originally published in 1980.

Baran, P.A. and Sweezy, P.M. (1968) *Monopoly Capital. An Essay on the American Economic and Social Order* (Harmondsworth, Penguin). Originally published in 1966.

Barratt Brown, M. (1988) 'Away with all the Great Arches: Anderson's History of British Capitalism', *New Left Review* 167.

Bartels, J. (1991) 'Filosofisch avontuur of filosofische impasse?' *Kritiek. Jaarboek voor social-istische discussie en analyse* 1 (Utrecht, Toestanden).

Basso, L. (1975) *Gesellschaftsformation und Staatsform. Drei Aufsätze*, transl. by Ch. Schenker (Frankfurt, Suhrkamp). Originally published in 1968.

Beard, C.A. (1957) *The Economic Basis of Politics and Related Writings*, compiled and annotated by W. Beard (New York, Vintage).

Bellant, R. and Wolf, L. (1990), 'The Free Congress Foundation Goes East', *Covert Action Information Bulletin* 35.

Bellow, S. (1965) *Herzog* (Greenwich, CT, Fawcett-Crest). Originally published in 1964.

Bendix, R. (1969) *Nation-Building and Citizenship. Studies of Our Changing Social Order* (Garden City, NY, Doubleday). Originally published in 1964.

de Benoist, A., (1983), *Aus rechter Sicht* (Tübingen, Grabert), two vols. Originally published in 1977.

Benveniste, G. (1972) *The Politics of Expertise* (Berkeley, Glendessary Press; London, Croom Helm).

Berend, I.T. and Ránki, Gy. (1982) *The European Periphery and Industrialization 1780–1914*, transl. by E. Pálmai (Budapest, Akad. Kiadó).

van den Berg, M.H.J. (1995) 'Culture as Ideology in the Conquest of Modernity: The Historical Roots of Japan's Regional Regulation Strategies', *Review of International Political Economy* 2 (3).

Berle, A.A. Jr (1954) *The 20th Century Capitalist Revolution* (New York, Harcourt, Brace & World).

Berle, A.A. Jr and Means, G.C (1968) *The Modern Corporation and Private Property* (New York, Harcourt, Brace & World). Originally published in 1932.

von Bertalanffy, L. (1962) *Modern Theories of Development. An Introduction to Theoretical Biology* (New York, Harper). Originally published in 1928.

—— (1968) *General System Theory. Foundations, Development, Applications* (New York, Braziller). Originally published 1940–68.

Bettelheim, C. (1972) 'Theoretical Comments by Charles Bettelheim', Appendix I to Emmanuel, A., *Unequal Exchange. A Study in the Imperialism of Trade*, transl. by B. Pearce (New York and London, Monthly Review Press). Originally published in 1969.

Bichler, S. and Nitzan, J. (1996) 'Putting the State in Its Place: US Foreign Policy and Differential Capital Accumulation in Middle East "Energy Conflicts"', *Review of International Political Economy* 3 (4).

Bihr, A. (1989) *Entre bourgeoisie et proletariat. L'encadrement capitaliste* (Paris, L'Harmattan).

Bode, R. (1979) 'De Nederlandse bourgeoisie tussen de twee wereldoorlogen', *Cahiers voor de Politieke en Sociale Wetenschappen* 2 (4).

Boguslaw, R. (1965) T*he New Utopians. A Study of System Design and Social Change* (Englewood Cliffs, NJ, Prentice Hall).

Bologna, S. (1976) 'Class Composition and the Theory of the Party at the Origin of the Workers Councils Movement', in R. Panzieri *et al.*, *The Labour Process and Class Strategies* (London, CSE). Originally published in 1972.

Boltanski, L. (1982) *Les Cadres. La formation d'un groupe social* (Paris, Editions de Minuit).

Bourdieu, P. (1979) *La Distinction. Critique sociale du jugement* (Paris, Editions de Minuit).

Boxer, C.R. (1965) *The Dutch Seaborne Empire 1600–1800* (London, Hutchinson).

Braillard, Ph. (1982) *L'imposture du Club de Rome* (Paris, PUF).

von Braunmühl, C. (1973) *Kalter Krieg und friedliche Koexistenz. Die Aussenpolitik der SPD in der Großen Koalition* (Frankfurt, Suhrkamp).

Braverman, H. (1974) *Labor and Monopoly Capital. The Degradation of Work in the Twentieth Century* (New York and London, Monthly Review Press).

Brenner, R. (1977) 'The Origins of Capitalist Development: A Critique of Neo-Smithian Marxism', *New Left Review* 104.

Briefs, U. (1979) '"Leitende Angestellte" als Potential für eine neoautoritäre Politik', *Blätter für deutsche und internationale Politik* 24 (11).

Broom, L. and Selznick, P. (1970) *Principles of Sociology*, 4th edn (New York, Harper & Row). Originally published in 1955.

Brownstein, R. and Easton, N. (1983) *Reagan's Ruling Class*, 2nd edn (New York, Pantheon).

de Brunhoff, S. (1976) *Etat et capital. Recherches sur la politique économique* (Grenoble, Presses Universitaires de Grenoble; Paris, Maspero).

Bukharin, N. (1972) *The Economic Theory of the Leisure Class*, transl. International Publishers (New York and London, Monthly Review Press). Originally published in 1927.

Burch, P.H. (1980) *Elites in American History* (New York and London, Holmes & Meier), 3 vols.

Burnham, J. (1960) *The Managerial Revolution* (Bloomington, Indiana University Press) Originally published in 1941.

Burnham, P. (1990) *The Political Economy of Postwar Reconstruction* (Basingstoke, Macmillan).

—— (1994) 'Open Marxism and Vulgar International Political Economy', *Review of International Political Economy* 1 (2).

Carew, A. (1987) *Labour under the Marshall Plan. The Politics of Productivity and the Marketing of Management Science* (Manchester, Manchester University Press).

Carr, E.H. (1964) *The Twenty Years' Crisis 1919–1939* (New York and Evanston, Harper & Row). Originally published in 1939.

Carstairs, G.M. (1957) *The Twice-Born. A Study of a Community of High-Caste Hindus* (London, Hogarth).

Caute, D. (1988) *Sixty-Eight. The Year of the Barricades* (London, Hamish Hamilton).

Chambers' Biographical Dictionary (1984), ed. by J.O. Thorne and T.C. Collocott (London, Chambers).

Charnley, A.H. (1973) *The EEC. A Study in Applied Economics* (London and Aylesbury, Ginn).

Chattopadhyay, P. (1974) 'Political Economy: What's in a Name?', *Monthly Review* 25 (11).

Chomsky, N. (1969) *American Power and the New Mandarins* (Harmondsworth, Penguin).

Clarke, S. (1978) 'Capital, Fractions of Capital and the State. "Neo-Marxist" Analysis of the South African State', *Capital and Class* 5.

Clarke, W.M. (1967) *The City in the World Economy* (Harmondsworth, Penguin).

Claude, H. (1969) *Histoire, réalité et destin d'un monopole. La Banque de Paris et des Pays-Bas et son groupe 1872–1968* (Paris, Editions Sociales).

—— (1972) *Le Pouvoir et l'argent* (Paris, Editions Sociales).

Clawson, P. (1976) 'A Review of Ernest Mandel's Late Capitalism', *The Review of Radical Political Economics* 8 (3).

Cockett, R. (1995) *Thinking the Unthinkable. Think-Tanks and the Economic Counter-Revolution, 1931–1983* (London, Fontana).

Cohen-Tanugi, L. (1987), *Le Droit sans l'état. Sur la démocratie en France et en Amérique* (Paris, PUF).

Collectif PCF (1971) *Le Capitalisme monopoliste d'état* (Paris, Ed. Sociales), 2 vols.

Costello, N. (1989) 'Planning the Digital Economy', paper, Kaldor Memorial Lectures, Budapest, September (mimeo).

Coston, H. (1963) *L'Europe des banquiers* (Paris, Documents et Témoignages).

Cox, R.W. (1971) 'Labor and Transnational Relations', *International Organization* 25 (3).

—— (1977) 'Labor and Hegemony', *International Organization* 31 (3).

—— (1979) 'Ideologies and the New International Economic Order: Reflections on some Recent Literature', *International Organization* 33 (2).

—— (1986) 'Social Forces, States and World Orders: Beyond International Relations Theory', in R.O. Keohane (ed.), *Neorealism and Its Critics* (New York, Columbia University Press).

—— (1987) *Production, Power, and World Order. Social Forces in the Making of History* (New York, Columbia University Press).

—— with T.J. Sinclair (1996), *Approaches to World Order* (Cambridge, Cambridge University Press).

Crozier, M., Huntington, S. and Watanuki, J. (1975), *The Crisis of Democracy* (New York, New York University Press).

Curtin, P.D. (ed.) (1971) *Imperialism* (London and Basingstoke, Macmillan).

Debord, G. (1967) *La Société du spectacle* (Paris, Buchet/Chastel).

Deppe, F. (ed.) (1975) *Europäische Wirtschaftsgemeinschaft* (Reinbek, Rowohlt).

Desai, R. (1994) 'Second-Hand Dealers in Ideas: Think-Tanks and Thatcherite Hegemony', *New Left Review* 203.

Dobb, M. (1963) *Studies in the Development of Capitalism* (New York, International Publishers). Originally published in 1947.

Domhoff, G.W (1971) 'Dan Smoot, Phyllis Schlafly, Reverend McBirnie, and Me' in *The Higher Circles. The Governing Class in America* (New York, Vintage).

—— (1978) *The Powers that Be. Processes of Ruling Class Domination in America* (New York, Vintage).

Doob, L.W. (1964) *Patriotism and Nationalism. Their Psychological Foundations* (New Haven and London, Yale University Press).

Doorewaard, H. (1988) 'Kantoorautomatisering in Nederland: Management by seduction', *Te elfder ure* 29 (3).

Dorril, S. and Ramsay, R. (1992), *Smear! Wilson and the Secret State* (London, Grafton).

Dumenil, G. (1975) *La Position de classe des cadres et employés* (Grenoble, Presses Universitaires de Grenoble).

Dutschke, R. (1969) 'On Anti-Authoritarianism', in C. Oglesby (ed.), *The New Left Reader* (New York, Grove Press).

ECE (UN Economic Commission for Europe) (1959) *Long-Term Trends and Problems of the European Steel Industry* (Geneva, UN).

Economic Report of the President (1977) (Washington).

Ehrenreich, B. and Ehrenreich, J. (1979) 'The Professional–Managerial Class', in P. Walker (ed.), *Between Labour and Capital* (Brighton, Harvester).

Elger, T. (1979) 'Valorisation and "Deskilling". A Critique of Braverman', *Capital and Class* 7.

Elsenhans, H. (1991) *Development and Underdevelopment. The History, Economics, and Politics of North–South Relations*, transl. by M. Reddy (New Delhi, Sage). Originally published in 1984.

Encyclopaedia Britannica (1959 edn).

Eringer, R. (1980) *The Global Manipulators. The Bilderberg Group, The Trilateral Commission.*

Covert Power Groups of the West (Bristol, Pentacle).

van Erp, H. (1982) *Het kapitaal tussen illusie en werkelijkheid. Dialektiese begripsontwikkeling en histories realisme in Marx' analyse van het kapitalisme* (Nijmegen, SUN).

Estall, R.C. and Buchanan, R.O. (1966) *Industrial Activity and Economic Geography* (London, Hutchinson).

Faulkner, H.U. (1968) *The Decline of Laissez-Faire 1897–1917*, vol. VII of *The Economic History of the United States* (New York, Harper & Row). Originally published in 1951.

Feltes, N.N. (1986) *Modes of Production of Victorian Novels* (Chicago and London, University of Chicago Press).

Fennema, M. (1976) 'Vermaatschappelijking van produktie en reproduktie in het staatsmonopolistisch kapitalisme', unpublished paper, Marxisme Seminar Valkenburg 2–6 August.

—— (1982) *International Networks of Banks and Industry* (Den Haag, Nijhoff).

—— (1995) *De moderne demokratie. Geschiedenis van een politieke theorie* (Amsterdam, Het Spinhuis).

Ferguson, T. (1984) 'From Normalcy to New Deal: Industrial Structure, Party Competition, and American Public Policy in the Great Depression', *International Organization* 38 (1).

—— (1995) *Golden Rule. The Investment Theory of Party Competition and the Logic of Money-Driven Political Systems* (Chicago and London, University of Chicago Press).

Ferguson, T. and Rogers, J. (1986) *Right Turn. The Decline of the Democratic Party and the Future of American Politics* (New York, Hill & Wang).

Fernández Jilberto, A.E. (1985) *Dictadura Militar y Oposición Política en Chile 1973–1981* (Dordrecht and Cinnaminson, NJ, Foris).

—— (1988) 'El debate sociologico-politico sobre casi dos siglos de estado nacional in America Latina: un intento de reinterpretacion', *Afers Internacionals* 12/13.

Foucault, M. (1981a) 'Discipline', ch. 3 of *Surveiller et Punir: Naissance De La Prison*, 1975, transl. by G. van den Brink and T. Hol, *Te elfder ure* 25 (3).

—— (1981b) 'Twee typen macht', transl. by H.C. Boekraad, *Te elfder ure* 25 (3).

Frank, A.G. (1975) *On Capitalist Underdevelopment* (Oxford, Oxford University Press). Originally published in 1963.

—— (1981) *Crisis in the Third World* (London, Heinemann).

Fukuyama, F. (1989) 'The End of History', *The National Interest* 16.

—— (1992) *The End of History and the Last Man* (Harmondsworth, Penguin).

Funke, R. (1978) 'Sich durchsetzender Kapitalismus. Eine Alternative zum spätkapitalistischen Paradigma', in *Starnberger Studien*, vol. 2 (Frankfurt, Suhrkamp).

Gallagher, J. and Robinson, R. (1967) 'The Imperialism of Free Trade', in E.C. Black (ed.), *European Political History, 1850–1870. Aspects of Liberalism* (New York, Harper & Row). Originally published in 1953.

Garaudy, R. (1971) *Niets dan de waarheid. Krisis in de internationale communistische beweging mei 1968–februari 1970*, transl. by H. Hom (Amsterdam, De Bezige Bij).

Genovese, E.D. (1989) *The Political Economy of Slavery. Studies in the Economy and Society of the Slave South*, 2nd edn (Middletown, CT, Wesleyan University Press). Originally published in 1961.

Gentles, I., Morrill, J. and Callinicos, A. (1994) 'Review Symposium: Merchants and Revolution', *New Left Review* 207.

Gerbier, B. (1987) 'La Course aux armements: l'impérialisme face au nouvel ordre international', *Cahiers de la Faculté des Sciences Economiques de Grenoble* 6.

Gerstenberger, H. (1973) *Zur politischen Ökonomie der bürgerlichen Gesellschaft. Die historischen Bedingungen ihrer Konstitution in den USA* (Frankfurt, Athenäum Fischer).

Geyl, P. (1969) *Orange and Stuart 1641–72* (London, Weidenfeld & Nicolson). Originally published in 1939.

Giddens, A. (1973) *The Class Structure of the Advanced Societies* (London, Hutchinson).

— (1992) *The Nation-State and Violence* (Cambridge, Polity).

Gifford, P. (1988) *The Religious Right in Southern Africa* (Harare, Baobab Books and University of Zimbabwe Publications).

Gill, S. (1991) *American Hegemony and the Trilateral Commission* (Cambridge, Cambridge University Press).

— (1993) (ed.) *Gramsci, Historical Materialism and International Relations* (Cambridge, Cambridge University Press).

— (1995) 'The Global Panopticon? The Neoliberal State, Economic Life, and Democratic Surveillance', *Alternatives* 20 (1).

Gill, S. and Mittelman, J.M. (1997) (eds) *Innovation and Transformation in International Studies* (Cambridge, Cambridge University Press).

de Goede, M. (1996) 'Ideology in the US Welfare Debate: Neo-Liberal Representations of Poverty', *Discourse and Society* 7(3).

Gorz, A. (1982) *Afscheid van het proletariaat*, transl. by M. Roelofs (Amsterdam, Van Gennep).

Gossweiler, K. (1975) *Großbanken, Industriemonopole, Staat. Ökonomie und Politik des staatsmonopolistischen Kapitalismus in Deutschland 1914–1932* (Berlin, DEB).

Gramsci, A. (1971) *Selections from the Prison Notebooks*, transl. and ed. by Q. Hoare and G.N. Smith (New York, International Publishers).

— (1977), *Selections from Political Writings 1910–1920*, transl. and ed. by Q. Hoare (New York, International Publishers).

Granou, A. (1977) *La Bourgeoisie financière au pouvoir et les luttes de classes en France* (Paris, Maspero).

Greenbaum, J. (1976) 'Division of Labor in the Computer Field', *Monthly Review* 28 (2).

Gregg, P. and Wadsworth, J. (1996) *It Takes Two. Employment Polarisation in the OECD* (Paris, OECD).

Greiner, B. (1980) *Amerikanische Außenpolitik von Truman bis heute. Grundsatzdebatten und Strategiediskussionen* (Köln, Pahl-Rugenstein).

Greven, M.Th. (1974) *Systemtheorie und Gesellschaftsanalyse* (Darmstadt/Neuwied, Luchterhand).

Grundstein, N.D. (1981) *The Managerial Kant. The Kant Critiques and the Managerial Order* (Cleveland, OH, Case Western Reserve University).

Günsche, K.-L. and Lantermann, K. (1977) *Kleine Geschichte der Sozialistischen Internationale* (Bonn, Neue Gesellschaft).

Haas, E.B. (1964) *Beyond the Nation-State. Functionalism and International Organization* (Stanford, Stanford University Press).

— (1968) *The Uniting of Europe*, 2nd edn (Stanford, Stanford University Press). Originally published in 1958.

Habermas, J. (1973) *Legitimationsprobleme im Spätkapitalismus* (Frankfurt, Suhrkamp).

Hagelstange, Th. (1988) *Die Entwicklung von Klassenstrukturen in der EG und Nordamerika* (Frankfurt and New York, Campus).

Halberstam, D. (1973) *The Best and the Brightest* (Greenwich, CT, Fawcett-Crest).

Hall, H.D. (1971) *Commonwealth. A History of the British Commonwealth of Nations* (London, Van Nostrand Reinhold).

Halliday, F. (1986) *The Making of the Second Cold War* (London, Verso).

Hampden-Turner, C. and Trompenaars, F. (1994) *The Seven Cultures of Capitalism. Value Systems for Creating Wealth in the United States, Britain, Japan, Germany, France, Sweden, and the Netherlands* (London, Piatkus).

Harvey, D. (1995) *The Condition of Postmodernity. An Enquiry into the Origins of Cultural Change* (Cambridge, MA. and Oxford, Blackwell).

Hayek, F.A. (1985) *De weg naar slavernij*, transl. by H.L. Swart (Amsterdam, Omega). Originally published in 1944.

Hegel, G.W.F. (1961) *Vorlesungen über die Philosophie der Geschichte* (Stuttgart, Reclam). Originally published in 1837.

—— (1972) *Grundlinien der Philosophie des Rechts*, introd. by H. Reichelt (Frankfurt, Ullstein). Originally published in 1821.

Helleiner, E. (1997) 'Braudelian Reflections on Economic Globalisation: The Historian as Pioneer', in S. Gill and J. Mittelman (eds), *Innovation and Transformation in International Studies* (Cambridge, Cambridge University Press).

Hesse, R. (1984) 'AirLand Battle 2000 und deutsche Interessen', *Blätter für deutsche und internationale Politik* 29 (1).

Hexner, E. (1943) *The International Steel Cartel* (Chapel Hill, University of North Carolina Press).

Hickel, R. (1975) 'Kapitalfraktionen. Thesen zur Analyse der herrschenden Klasse', *Kursbuch* 42.

Hilferding, R. (1973) *Das Finanzkapital* (Frankfurt, Europäische Verlagsanstalt) Originally published in 1910.

Hill, C. (1975) *Reformation to Industrial Revolution.* (Volume 2 of the *Pelican Economic History of Britain.*) (Harmondsworth, Penguin).

Hinkelammert, F.J. (1985) *Die ideologischen Waffen des Todes. Zur Metaphysik des Kapitalismus* (Freiburg, Exodus; Münster, Liberación).

Hirsch, J. (1973) 'Elemente einer materialistischen Staatstheorie', in C. von Braunmühl *et al., Probleme einer materialistischen Staatstheorie* (Frankfurt, Suhrkamp).

Hirszowicz, M. (1980) *The Bureaucratic Leviathan. A Study in the Sociology of Communism* (Oxford, Martin Robertson).

Hobson, J.A. (1968) *Imperialism, A Study*, 3rd edn (London, Allen & Unwin). Originally published in 1902.

Hofstadter, R. (1955) *The Age of Reform. From Bryan to F.D.R.* (New York, Vintage).

Holliger, C.M. (1974) *Die Reichen und die Superreichen in der Schweiz* (Hamburg, Hoffmann and Campe).

Holman, O. (1987/88) 'Semi-Peripheral Fordism in Southern Europe. The National and International Context of Socialist-Led Governments in Spain, Portugal and Greece in Historical Perspective', *International Journal of Political Economy* 17 (4).

—— (1996) *Integrating Southern Europe. EC Expansion and the Transnationalisation of Spain* (London and New York, Routledge).

—— (1997) 'Integrating Eastern Europe. EU Expansion and the Double Transformation in Poland, the Czech Republic and Hungary', paper for the 38th Annual Convention of the International Studies Association, Toronto, 18–23 March.

Homer, S. (1963) *A History of Interest Rates* (New Brunswick, NJ, Rutgers University Press).

Hoogvelt, A. and Yuasa, M. (1994), 'Going Lean or Going Native? The Social Regulation of "Lean" Production Systems', *Review of International Political Economy* 1 (2).

Horkheimer, M. (1970) *Autoriteit en gezin*, transl. by H. Bos and J. van Nieuwstad (Den Haag, NVSH). Originally published in 1936.

Horkheimer, M. and Adorno, Th.W. (1990) *Dialectic of Enlightenment*, transl. by J. Cumming (New York, Continuum). Originally published in 1944.

Hortleder, G. (1973) *Ingenieure in der Industriegesellschaft* (Frankfurt, Suhrkamp).

Hough, J. (1990) *Russia and the West. Gorbachev and the Politics of Reform* (New York, Simon & Schuster).

Houweling, H.W. (1996) 'Destabilizing Consequences of Sequential Development', in L. van de Goor, K. Rupesinghe, and P. Sciarone (eds), *Between Development and Destruction. An Enquiry into the Causes of Conflict in Post-Colonial States* (Basingstoke, Macmillan; New York, St. Martin's Press).

Houweling, H.W. and Siccama, J.G. (1993) 'The Neo-Functionalist Explanation of World Wars: A Critique and an Alternative', *International Interactions* 18 (4).

Huntington, S.P. (1997) *The Clash of Civilizations and the Remaking of World Order* (New York, Touchstone).

Ikenberry, G.J. and Kupchan, Ch.A. (1990) 'Socialization and Hegemonic Power', *International Organization* 44 (3).

Ilyenkov, E.V. (1982) *The Dialectics of the Abstract and the Concrete in Marx's Capital*, transl. by S. Syrovatkin (Moscow, Progress). Originally published in 1960.

Inosemzew, N.N., Menschikow, S.M., Mileikowski, A.G. and Rumjanzew, A.M. (1972) *Politische Ökonomie des heutigen Monopolkapitalismus*, transl. by S. Görbert *et al.* (Berlin, Dietz).

Jane's Major Companies of Europe 1971 (New York, McGraw-Hill).

Jessop, B. (1983) 'Accumulation Strategies, State Forms, and Hegemonic Projects', *Kapitalistate* 10/11.

—— (1989) 'Regulation Theories in Retrospect and Prospect', in *After The Crisis. Current Research on Capital and Strategy* (University of Amsterdam), Working Paper 5/6.

Jordan, R.S. (1971) 'The Influence of the British Secretariat Tradition on the Formation of the League of Nations', in R.S. Jordan (ed.), *International Administration* (New York, Oxford University Press).

Kant, I. (1953) *Zum ewigen Frieden. Ein philosophischer Entwurf* (Stuttgart, Reclam). Originally published in 1795.

—— (1975) Kritik der reinen Vernunft (Stuttgart, Reclam). Originally published in 1781.

Kaplan, D.E. and Dubro, A. (1987) *Yakuza. De onbekende Japanse onderwereld*, transl. by H. Kuipers (Utrecht and Antwerpen, Veen).

Kaviraj, S. (1989) 'On Political Explanation in Marxism', in K. Bharadwaj and S. Kaviraj (eds), *Perspectives on Capitalism. Marx, Keynes, Schumpeter and Weber* (New Delhi, Sage).

Kennedy, P. (1987) *The Rise and Fall of the Great Powers. Economic Change and Military Conflict from 1500 to 2000* (New York, Random House).

Kenwood, A.G. and Lougheed, A.L. (1971) *The Growth of the International Economy 1820–1960* (London, Allen & Unwin; Sydney, Australasian).

Keohane, R.O. (1984) *After Hegemony. Cooperation and Discord in the World Political Economy* (Princeton, NJ, Princeton University Press).

Keohane, R.O. and Nye, J.S. (1973) *Transnational Relations and World Politics* (Cambridge, MA, Harvard University Press).

Keynes, J.M. (1970) *The General Theory of Employment, Interest and Money* (London and Basingstoke, Macmillan). Originally published in 1936.

Kiernan, V.G. (1972) *The Lords of Human Kind. European Attitudes to the Outside World in the Imperial Age* (Harmondsworth, Penguin).

Kijne, H. (1978) *Geschiedenis van de Nederlandse Studentenbeweging 1963–1973* (Amsterdam, SUA).

Kindleberger, Ch.P. (1965) *Economic Development*, 2nd edn (New York, McGraw-Hill; Tokyo, Kogakusha).

Klaus, V. (1993) 'Interplay of Political and Economic Reform Measures in the Transformation of Postcommunist Countries', *The Mont Pèlerin Society Newsletter* 46 (2).

Knieper, R. (1976) *Weltmarkt, Wirtschaftsrecht und Nationalstaat* (Frankfurt, Suhrkamp).

Knight, S. (1985) *The Brotherhood. The Secret World of the Freemasons* (London, Grafton).

Kolk, A. (1996) *Forests in International Environmental Politics. International Organisations, NGOs and the Brazilian Amazon* (Utrecht, International Books).

Kolko, G. (1959) 'A Critique of Max Weber's Philosophy of History', *Ethics* 70 (1).

—— (1968) *The Politics of War. The World and United States Foreign Policy 1943–1945* (New York, Vintage).

—— (1976) *Main Currents in Modern American History* (New York, Harper & Row).

—— (1997) 'Privatizing Communism. Politics and Market Economics in Russia and China', *World Policy Journal* (Spring).

Kolko, G. and Kolko, J. (1972) *The Limits of Power. The World and United States Foreign Policy 1945–1954* (New York, Harper & Row).

Konrád, G. and Szelényi, I. (1981) *Die Intelligenz auf dem Weg zur Klassenmacht* (Frankfurt, Suhrkamp).

Koszul, J.-P. (1970) 'American Banks in Europe', in Ch.P. Kindleberger (ed.), *The International Corporation* (Cambridge, MA, MIT Press).

Krasner, S.D. (1985) *Structural Conflict. The Third World Against Global Liberalism* (Berkeley, University of California Press).

Krims, A. (1985) *Karol Wojtyla. Paus en politicus*, transl. by H. Lemmens (Haarlem and Brussels, In de Knipscheer).

Krippendorf, E. (1973) 'Staatliche Organisation und Krieg', in D. Senghaas (ed.), *Friedensforschung und Gesellschaftskritik* (Frankfurt, Fischer).

Kristol, I. (1971) '"When Virtue Loses All Her Loveliness". Some Reflections on Capitalism and "the Free Society"' in I. Kristol and D. Bell (eds), *Capitalism Today* (New York, Mentor).

Kuisel, R.F. (1967) *Ernest Mercier. French Technocrat* (Berkeley and Los Angeles, University of California Press).

Lamounier, B. (1989) 'Brazil, Inequality Against Democracy', in L. Diamond, J.J. Linz, S.M. Lipset (eds), *Democracy in Developing Countries – Latin America* (Boulder, CO, Reinner; London, Adamantine Press).

Landes, D.S. (1972) *The Unbound Prometheus. Technological Change and Industrial Development in Western Europe from 1750 to the Present* (Cambridge, Cambridge University Press).

Lasch, C. (1967) 'The Cultural Cold War', *The Nation*, September 11.

Lasswell, H.D. (1965) *World Politics and Personal Insecurity* (New York, Free Press; London, Collier-Macmillan). Originally published in 1935.

Lefebvre, G. (1967) *The Coming of the French Revolution*, transl. by R.R. Palmer (Princeton, NJ, Princeton University Press). Originally published in 1939.

Lefebvre, H. (1976) *De l'état* Vol. II, *Théorie marxiste de l'état de Hegel à Mao.* (Paris, 10/18).

—— (1977) *De l'état*, Vol. III, *Le Mode de production étatique* (Paris, 10/18).

Leigh, D. (1989) *The Wilson Plot. The Intelligence Services and the Discrediting of a Prime Minister* (London, Heinemann).

Leithäuser, Th. (1976) 'Kapitalistische Produktion und Vergesellschaftung des Alltags', in Th. Leithäuser, W.R. Heinz (eds), *Produktion, Arbeit, Sozialisation* (Frankfurt, Suhrkamp).

Lenin, V.I. *Collected Works* (Moscow, Progress).

Lennhoff, E. and Posner, O. (1932) *Internationales Freimaurer-Lexikon* (München, Amathea Verlag).

Levy, C. (1987) 'Max Weber and Antonio Gramsci', in W.J. Mommsen and J. Osterhammel (eds), *Max Weber and his Contemporaries* (London, Allen & Unwin).

van der Linden, M. (1992) *Von der Oktoberrevolution zur Perestroika. Der westliche Marxismus und die Sowjetunion*, transl. by K. Mellenthin (Frankfurt, Dipa).

Lions Clubs International History and Fact Sheet (no date, club documentation).

Lipietz, A. (1982) 'Towards Global Fordism?', *New Left Review* 132.

—— (1985) *Mirages et miracles. Problèmes de l'industrialisation dans le tiers monde* (Paris, La Découverte).

Lippmann, W. (1936) *Interpretations 1933–1935*, ed. by A. Nevins (New York, Macmillan).

Locke, J. (1965) *Two Treatises of Government*, introd. by P. Lasslet (New York, Mentor). Originally published in 1690.

Löwy, M. (1981) *The Politics of Combined and Uneven Development. The Theory of Permanent Revolution* (London, Verso).

Lundberg, F. (1937) *America's 60 Families* (New York, The Vanguard Press).

Luxemburg, R. (1966) *Die Akkumulation des Kapitals. Ein Beitrag zur ökonomischen Erklärung des Imperialismus* (Frankfurt, Neue Kritik). Originally published in 1913.

Maddison, A. (1971) *Twee modellen van economische groei*, transl. by P.J.J. Seebregts (Utrecht and Antwerpen, Spectrum).

Magdoff, H. and Sweezy, P.M. (1983) 'International Finance and National Power', *Monthly Review* 35 (5).

Malanczuk, P. (1993) *Humanitarian Intervention and the Legitimacy of the Use of Force* (Amsterdam, Spinhuis).

Mandel, E. (1972) *Der Spätkapitalismus* (Frankfurt, Suhrkamp).

Markov, W. (1989) *Napoleons Keizerrijk. Geschiedenis en dagelijks leven na de Franse Revolutie*, transl. by E. Thielen (Zutphen, Walburg Pers).

Martinelli, A., Chiesi, A.M. and Dalla Chiesa, N. (1981) *I Grandi imprenditori italiani. Profilo sociale della classe dirigente economica* (Milano, Feltrinelli).

Marx, K. (1971) *Un chapitre inédit du 'Capital'*, transl. by R. Dangeville (Paris, 10/18).

—— (1973) *Grundrisse*, Pelican/NLB edn, introd. and transl. by M. Nicolaus (Harmondsworth, Penguin).

Mattera, P. (1992) *World Class Business. A Guide to the 100 Most Powerful Global Corporations* (New York, Henry Holt).

Maurino, J.D. (1974) *Procès d'internationalisation et développement des luttes de classes* (Grenoble, CERES).

Mayall, J. (1990) *Nationalism and International Society* (Cambridge, Cambridge University Press).

McNally, D. (1995) 'Language, History and Class Struggle', *Monthly Review* 47 (3).

Meadows, D.H. et al. (1972) *The Limits to Growth. A Report for the Club of Rome's Project on the Predicament of Mankind* (New York, New American Library).

Menand, L. (1990) 'Pop Goes the Proletariat', *Esquire* (September).

Menshikov, S. (1973) *Millionaires and Managers. Structure of U.S. Financial Oligarchy* (Moscow, Progress).

MEW: Marx-Engels Werke (Berlin, Dietz). Vols. 23–25 are *Capital* vols 1–3.

Mills, C.W. (1959) *The Power Elite* (Oxford, Oxford University Press).

Monnet, J. (1976) *Mémoires* (Paris, Fayard).

Moore, B. Jr (1981) *Social Origins of Dictatorship and Democracy* (Harmondsworth, Penguin).

Morin, F. (1974) *La Structure financière du capitalisme français* (Paris, Calmann-Lévy).

Morioka, K. (1989) 'Japan', in T. Bottomore, R.J. Brym (eds), *The Capitalist Class. An International Study* (New York, Harvester Wheatsheaf).

Morton, F. (1963) *The Rothschilds. A Family Portrait* (Greenwich, CT, Fawcett-Crest).

Müller, L.A. (1991) *Gladio – das Erbe des Kalten Krieges* (Reinbek, Rowohlt).

Murphy, C. (1994) *International Organization and Industrial Change. Global Governance since 1850* (Cambridge, Polity).

Nairn, T. (1973) *The Left Against Europe* (Harmondsworth, Penguin).

Nederveen Pieterse, J. (1990) *Empire and Emancipation* (London, Pluto).

—— (eds) (1992) *Christianity and Hegemony. Religion and Politics on the Frontiers of Social Change* (New York and Oxford, Berg).

Nelson, J. (1993) 'Burston-Marsteller, Pax Trilateral, and the Brundtland Gang vs. the Environment', *Covert Action Quarterly 44*.

Nicholson, M.B. and Reynolds, P.A. (1967) 'General Systems, the International System, and the Eastonian Analysis', *Political Studies* 15 (1).

Nicolaus, M. (1970) 'Proletariat and Middle Class in Marx: Hegelian Choreography and Capitalist Dialectic', in J. Weinstein and D.W. Eakins (eds), *For a New America. Essays in History and Politics from "Studies on the Left" 1959–1967* (New York, Vintage).

Nima, R. (1983) *The Wrath of Allah. Islamic Revolution and Reaction in Iran* (London and Sydney, Pluto).

Nitsch, M. (1987) 'Das Management der internationalen Währungs- und Finanz-beziehungen in der Krise', in E. Altvater *et al.* (eds), *Die Armut der Nationen* (Berlin, Rotbuch).

Noble, D.F. (1979) *America by Design. Science, Technology, and the Rise of Corporate Capitalism* (Oxford, Oxford University Press).

Norman, E.H. (1940) *Japan's Emergence as a Modern State. Political and Economic Problems of the Meiji Period* (New York, Institute of Pacific Relations).

Novak, J. (1980) 'Trilateralism and the Summits', in H. Sklar (ed.), *Trilateralism. The Trilateral Commission and Elite Planning for World Management* (Boston, South End Press).

OECD (1980) *National Accounts of OECD Countries 1961–1978* (Paris).

—— (1986) *National Accounts of OECD Countries 1972–1984* (Paris).

—— (1990) *National Accounts of OECD Countries 1976–1988* (Paris).

—— (1997) *OECD, National Accounts 1983–1995* (Paris).

Ogburn, W.F. (1964) *William F. Ogburn on Culture and Social Change*, O.D. Duncan (ed.) (Chicago, University of Chicago Press).

OMGUS (Office of the Military Government for Germany, United States) (1985) *Ermittlungen gegen die Deutsche Bank* Greno). Originally published in 1946–47.

—— (1986) *Ermittlungen gegen die Dresdner Bank* (Nördlingen, Greno). Originally published in 1946.

O'Toole, G.J.A. (1991) *Honorable Treachery. A History of U.S. Intelligence, Espionage, and Covert Action from the American Revolution to the CIA* (New York, Atlantic Monthly Press).

Overbeek, H. (1980) 'Finance Capital and Crisis in Britain', *Capital and Class* 11.

—— (1990) *Global Capitalism and National Decline. The Thatcher Decade in Perspective* (London, Unwin Hyman).

—— (ed.) (1993) *Restructuring Hegemony in the Global Political Economy. The Rise of Transnational Liberalism in the 1980s* (London and New York, Routledge).

Overbeek H. and van der Pijl, K. (1993), 'Restructuring Capital and Restructuring Hegemony. Neo-Liberalism and the Unmaking of the Post-War Order', in H.W. Overbeek (ed.), *Restructuring Hegemony in the Global Political Economy. The Rise of Transnational Liberalism in the 1980s* (London and New York, Routledge).

Pakulski, J. and Waters, M. (1996) *The Death of Class* (London, Sage).

Palan, R. (1992) 'The Second Structuralist Theories of International Relations: A Research Note', *International Studies Notes* 17 (3).

Pallenberg, C. (1973) *Vatican Finances* (Harmondsworth, Penguin).

Palloix, C. (1971) 'Imperialismus und kapitalistische Produktionsweise', in S. Amin and C. Palloix, *Neuere Beiträge zur Imperialismustheorie* (München, Trikont).

—— (1973) *Les Firmes multinationales et le procès d'internationalisation* (Paris, Maspero).

—— (1974a) 'Impérialisme et mode d'accumulation international du capital', paper, CSE Conference, London, January.

—— (1974b) *Le Processus d'internationalisation dans la sidérurgie et les industries mécaniques et électriques*, vol. 1 (Grenoble, IREP).

—— (1976) 'The Labour Process: From Fordism to Neo-Fordism', transl. by J. Mepham and M. Soneuscher, in R. Panzieri *et al.*, *The Labour Process and Class Strategies* (London, CSE).

Palyi, M. (1960) *Währungen am Scheideweg. Lehren der europäischen Experimente*, transl. by E. Achterberg (Frankfurt, Knapp).

Parboni, R. (1981) *The Dollar and Its Rivals*, transl. by J. Rothschild (London, Verso).

Pastré, O. (1979) *La Stratégie internationale des groupes financiers américains* (Paris, Economica).

Perkin, H. (1996) *The Third Revolution. Professional Elites in the Modern World* (London and New York, Routledge).

Picciotto, S. (1989) 'Slicing a Shadow: Business Taxation in an International Framework', in L. Hancher, M. Moran (eds), *Capitalism, Culture, and Economic Regulation* (Oxford, Clarendon).

—— (1992) *International Business Taxation. A Study in the Internationalization of Business Regulation* (London, Weidenfeld & Nicolson).

van der Pijl, K. (1975) 'A Note on Internationalization of Capital as an Independent Variable in the Analysis of the International System', *Acta Politica* 10 (1).

—— (1978) *Een Amerikaans Plan voor Europa* (Amsterdam, SUA).

—— (1984) *The Making of an Atlantic Ruling Class* (London, Verso).

—— (1989a) 'Restructuring the Atlantic Ruling Class', in S. Gill (ed.), *Atlantic Relations: Beyond the Reagan Era* (Hemel Hempstead, Harvester; New York, St Martin's Press).

—— (1989b) 'Ruling Classes, Hegemony, and the State System. Theoretical and Historical Considerations', *International Journal of Political Economy* 19 (3).

—— (1992) *Wereldorde en machtspolitiek. Visies op de internationale betrekkingen van Dante tot Fukuyama* (Amsterdam, Het Spinhuis).

—— (1993) 'The Sovereignty of Capital Impaired. Social Forces and Codes of Conduct for Multinational Corporations', in H. Overbeek (ed.), *Restructuring Hegemony in the Global Political Economy. The Rise of Transnational Liberalism in the 1980s* (London and New York, Routledge).

—— (1995) 'The Second Glorious Revolution. Globalising Elites and Historical Change', in B. Hettne (ed.), *International Political Economy. Understanding Global Disorder*

(London and New Jersey, Zed).

—— (1996a) *Vordenker der Weltpolitik,* transl. by W. Linsewski (Opladen, Leske & Budrich).

—— (1996b) 'A Transnational Theory of Revolution. Universal History According to Eugen Rosenstock-Huessy and its Implications', *Review of International Political Economy* 3 (2).

Polanyi, K. (1957) *The Great Transformation. The Political and Economic Origins of Our Time* (Boston, Beacon). Originally published in 1944.

Post, K. (1996) *Regaining Marxism* (Basingstoke, Macmillan; New York, St Martin's Press).

Poulantzas, N. (1971) *Pouvoir politique et classes sociales,* 2 vols (Paris, Maspero).

—— (1976) *Klassen in het huidige kapitalisme,* transl. by S. Simonse (Nijmegen, SUN).

Pritzkoleit, K. (1959) *Das kommandierte Wunder. Deutschlands Weg im zwanzigsten Jahrhundert* (Vienna, Desch).

Quigley, C. (1966) *Tragedy and Hope. A History of the World in Our Time* (New York and London, Macmillan).

—— (1981) *The Anglo-American Establishment* (New York, Books in Focus). Originally published in 1949.

Raschke, J. (ed.) (1981) *Die politischen Parteien in Westeuropa* (Reinbek, Rowohlt).

Rebattet, F.X. (1962) *The European Movement 1945–1962,* Ph.D. thesis (St. Anthony's College, Oxford).

Reuveny, R. and Thompson, W.R. (1997) 'The Timing of Protectionism', *Review of International Political Economy* 4 (1).

Rey, P.-Ph. (1983) 'Klassentegenstellingen in verwantschappelijke maatschappijen', *Te elfder ure* 26 (2).

Rich, A. (1995) *Johann Sebastian Bach - Play by Play* (San Francisco, HarperCollins).

Rich, P.J. (1988) 'Public-School Freemasonry in the Empire: "Mafia of the Mediocre"?', in J.A. Mangan (ed.), *Benefits Bestowed? Education and British Imperialism* (Manchester, Manchester University Press).

Rich, P.J. and de los Reyes, G. (1997) 'Masonic and Other Secret Ritualistic Society Archival Sources – and Possibilities for International Studies', paper for the 38th Annual Convention of the International Studies Association, Toronto, 18–23 March.

Richelson, J.T. and Ball, D. (1990), *The Ties That Bind. Intelligence Cooperation between the UK/USA Countries,* 2nd edn (Boston etc., Unwin Hyman).

Ridgeway, G.L. (1938) *Merchants of Peace. Twenty Years of Business Diplomacy Through the International Chamber of Commerce 1919–1938* (New York, Columbia University Press).

Riesman, D. (1950), in collaboration with R. Denney and N. Glazer, *The Lonely Crowd* (New Haven, Yale University Press).

Rijkens, P. (1965) *Handel en Wandel. Nagelaten gedenkschriften 1888–1965* (Rotterdam, Donker).

Ritsert, J. (1973) *Probleme politisch-ökonomischer Theoriebildung* (Frankfurt, Athenäum).

Robinson, W.I. (1992) 'The São Paulo Forum: Is There a New Latin American Left?', *Monthly Review* 44 (7).

Rochester, A. (1936) *Rulers of America. A Study of Finance Capital* (New York, International Publishers).

Roobeek, A.J.M. (1987) 'The Crisis of Fordism and the Rise of a New Technological Paradigm', *Futures* 19 (2).

Rosenstock-Huessy, E. (1961) *Die europäischen Revolutionen und der Character der Nationen,* 3rd. edn (Stuttgart, Kohlhammer). Originally published in 1931.

Roy, A. (1994) 'New Interrelations between Indian Big Bourgeoisie and Imperialism', *The Marxist Review Occasional Letters* 16.

Ruigrok, W. and van Tulder, R. (1995) *The Logic of International Restructuring* (London and New York, Routledge).

Rupert, M. (1993) 'Alienation, Capitalism, and the Inter-State System: Towards a Marxian/Gramscian Critique' in S. Gill (ed.), *Gramsci, Historical Materialism and International Relations* (Cambridge, Cambridge University Press).

—— (1995) *Producing Hegemony. The Politics of Mass Production and American Global Power* (Cambridge, Cambridge University Press).

de Ste Croix, G. (1985) 'Class in Marx's Conception of History, Ancient and Modern', *Monthly Review* 36 (10).

Saisselin, R.G. (1984) *The Bourgeois and the Bibelot* (New Brunswick, NJ, Rutgers University Press).

Sampson, A. (1965) *Anatomy of Britain Today* (London, Hodder & Stoughton).

—— (1978) *The Arms Bazaar* (London, Coronet).

—— (1987) *Black and Gold. Tycoons, Revolutionaries and Apartheid* (London, Coronet).

Schama, S. (1990) *Citizens. A Chronicle of the French Revolution* (New York, Vintage).

Scheer, R. (1982) *With Enough Shovels. Reagan, Bush and Nuclear War* (New York, Random House).

Schor, J.B. (1992) *The Overworked American. The Unexpected Decline of Leisure* (New York, Basic Books).

Schumpeter, J.A. (1951) 'Social Classes in an Ethnically Homogeneous Environment', in *Imperialism and Social Classes* (New York, Kelley). Originally published in 1927.

Schwartz, H.M. (1994) *States versus Markets. History, Geography, and the Development of the International Political Economy* (New York, St Martin's Press).

Schweizer, P. (1993) *Friendly Spies. How America's Allies Are Using Economic Espionage to Steal Our Secrets* (New York, Atlantic Monthly Press).

—— (1994) *Victory. The Reagan Administration's Secret Strategy that Hastened the Collapse of the Soviet Union* (New York, Atlantic Monthly Press).

Scott, P.D. (1986) 'Transnationalised Repression: Parafascism and the US', *Lobster* 12.

Scott, P.D. and Marshall, J. (1991) *Cocaine Politics. Drugs, Armies, and the CIA in Central America* (Berkeley, University of California Press).

Seeley, J.R. (1962) 'The Americanization of the Unconscious', in H.M. Ruitenbeek (ed.), *Psychoanalysis and Social Science* (New York, Dutton).

Senghaas, D. (1982) *Von Europa lernen. Entwicklungsgeschichtliche Betrachtungen* (Frankfurt, Suhrkamp).

Shortall, F. (1986) 'Fixed and Circulating Capital', *Capital and Class* 28.

Shoup, L.H. and Minter, W. (1977) *Imperial Brain Trust. The Council on Foreign Relations and United States Foreign Policy* (New York and London, Monthly Review).

SIFI (1974) 'Internationalisation du capital et processus productif: une approche critique', *Cahiers d'Economie Politique* 1.

Silk, L. and Silk, M. (1981) *The American Establishment* (New York, Avon).

Sinclair, T.W. (1994) 'Passing Judgement: Credit Rating Processes as Regulatory Mechanisms of Governance in the Emerging World Order', *Review of International Political Economy* 1 (1).

Sklar, H. and Everdell, R. (1980) 'Who's Who on the Trilateral Commission', in H. Sklar (ed.), *Trilateralism. The Trilateral Commission and Elite Planning for World Management* (Boston, South End Press).

Sohn-Rethel, A. (1975) *Grootkapitaal en fascisme. De Duitse Industrie achter Hitler* (Amsterdam, Van Gennep).

—— (1976) 'The Dual Economics of Transition', in R. Panzieri *et al.*, *The Labour Process and Class Strategies* (London, CSE).

Soref, M. and Zeitlin, M. (1987) 'Finance Capital and the Internal Structure of the Capitalist Class in the United States', in M. S. Mizruchi and M. Schwartz (eds), *Intercorporate Relations. The Structural Analysis of Business* (Cambridge, Cambridge University Press).

Statistical Abstract of the United States 1984 (Washington, US Department of Commerce).

Stegmann, D. (1976) 'Kapitalismus und Faschismus in Deutschland 1929–1934', *Gesellschaft. Beiträge zur Marxschen Theorie* 6 (Frankfurt, Suhrkamp).

Stokman, F.N., Ziegler, R. and Scott, J. (eds) (1985) *Networks of Corporate Power* (Cambridge, Polity).

Stopford, J.M. and Strange, S. with J.S. Henley (1991) *Rival States, Rival Firms. Competition for World Market Shares* (Cambridge, Cambridge University Press).

Stover, E. (1975) 'Inflation and the Female Labor Force', *Monthly Review*, 26 (8).

Strange, S. (1982) 'Cave, hic Dragones: a Critique of Regime Analysis', *International Organization* 36 (2).

Stubbing, R.A. with R.A. Menzel (1986) *The Defense Game* (New York, Harper & Row).

Sutton, A.C. (1986) *America's Secret Establishment. An Introduction to the Order of Skull and Bones* (Billings, MO, Liberty House Press).

Sweezy, P.M. (1972) *Theorie der kapitalistischen Entwicklung*, transl. by G. Rittig-Baumhaus (Frankfurt, Suhrkamp). Originally published in 1942.

Tawney, R.H. (1952) *Religion and the Rise of Capitalism* (New York, Mentor). Originally published in 1926.

Teacher, D. (1993) 'The Pinay Circle Complex 1969–1989', *Lobster. Journal of Parapolitics* 26.

Therborn, G. (1980) *Science, Class, and Society. On the Formation of Sociology and Historical Materialism* (London, Verso).

Thomas, B. (1968) 'Migration and International Investment', in A.R. Hall (ed.), *The Export of Capital from Britain 1870–1914* (London, Methuen).

Thompson, E.P. (1968) *The Making of the English Working Class* (Harmondsworth, Penguin).

Thompson, P. (1980) 'Bilderberg and the West', in H. Sklar (ed.), *Trilateralism. The Trilateral Commission and Elite Planning for World Management* (Boston, South End Press).

Thompson, W.R. (1988) *On Global War: Historical–Structural Approaches to World Politics* (Columbia, SC, University of South Carolina Press).

Tiger, L. (1970) *Men in Groups* (New York, Vintage).

Tinbergen, J. *et al.* (1977) *Naar een Rechtvaardiger Internationale Orde* (Amsterdam and Brussels, Elsevier).

de Tocqueville, A. (1990) *Democracy in America*, transl. by H. Reeve, two vols (New York, Vintage). Originally published in 1835 and 1840.

Toffler, A. (1991) *Powershift. Knowledge, Wealth and Violence at the Edge of the 21st Century* (New York, Bantam).

Topitsch, E. (1971) 'Das mythologische Denken' in K. Lenk (ed.), *Ideologie. Ideologie und Wissenssoziologie* (Neuwied and Berlin, Luchterhand). Originally published in 1952.

Trevelyan, G.M. (1968) *Sociale geschiedenis van Engeland*, transl. by G.D.J. Blok (Utrecht/ Antwerpen, Aula). Originally published in 1944.

van Tulder, R. and Junne, G. (1988) *European Multinationals in Core Technologies* (Chichester, Wiley).

Useem, M. (1989) 'Revolt of the Corporate Owners and the Demobilization of Business Political Action', *Critical Sociology* 16 (2/3).

Veblen, T. (1994) *The Theory of the Leisure Class* (New York, Dover). Originally published in 1899.

Vieille, P. (1988) 'The World's Chaos and the New Paradigms of the Social Movement', in Lelio Basso International Foundation (eds), *Theory and Practice of Liberation at the End of the XXth Century* (Brussels, Bruylant).

Visser 't Hooft, W.A. (1971) *Memoires* (Amsterdam and Brussels, Elsevier; Kampen, Kok).

Waite, A.E. (1994) *A New Encyclopaedia of Freemasonry*, 2 vols (New York and Venel, NJ, Wings Books).

Wallerstein, I. (1974) *The Modern World System. Capitalist Agriculture and the Origins of the European World-Economy in the Sixteenth Century* (New York, Academic Press).

—— (1979) *The Capitalist World-Economy* (Cambridge, Cambridge University Press).

—— (1984) *Historisch Kapitalisme*, transl. by I. Claudius (Weesp, Heureka).

Weber, M. (1976) *Wirtschaft und Gesellschaft. Grundriss der verstehenden Soziologie* (Tübingen, J.C.B. Mohr). Originally published in 1921.

Weber, N. (1973) *Privilegien durch Bildung. Über die Ungleichheit der Bildungschancen in der Bundesrepublik Deutschland* (Frankfurt/M, Suhrkamp).

Weil, S. (1978) *Fabriktagebuch und andere Schriften zum Industriesystem*, transl. by H. Abosch (Frankfurt, Suhrkamp). Originally published in 1951.

Weinstein, J. (1970) 'Gompers and the New Liberalism, 1900–1909', in J. Weinstein and D.W. Eakins (eds), *For a New America. Essays in History and Politics from "Studies on the Left" 1959–1967* (New York, Vintage).

van Wesel, A. (1992) 'Catholics and Politics in Europe', in J. Nederveen Pieterse (ed.), *Christianity and Hegemony. Religion and Politics on the Frontiers of Social Change* (New York and Oxford, Berg).

Weston, R. (1980) *Domestic and Multinational Banking. The Effects of Monetary Policy* (London, Croom Helm).

Whatmough, J. (1956) *Language. A Modern Synthesis* (New York, Mentor).

Who's Who in the United States 1964–1965 (Chicago, Marquis).

Who's Who in the World 1982–1983 (Chicago, Marquis).

Whyte, W.H. (1963) *The Organization Man* (Harmondsworth, Penguin).

Wiebes, C. and Zeeman, B. (1983) 'The Pentagon Negotiations March 1948: The Launching of the North Atlantic Treaty', *International Affairs* 59 (3).

—— (1993) *Belgium, the Netherlands and Alliances 1940–1949*, Dissertation (University of Leyden).

Wijmans, L. (1987) *Beeld en betekenis van het maatschappelijke midden. Oude en nieuwe midden-groepen 1850 tot heden* (Amsterdam, Van Gennep).

de Wilde, J. (1991), *Saved From Oblivion. Interdependence Theory in the First Half of the 20th Century* (Aldershot, Dartmouth).

Willan, P. (1991) *Puppet Masters. The Political Use of Terrorism in Italy* (London, Constable).

Williamson, J.G. (1968) 'The Long Swing: Comparison and Interactions between

British and American Balance of Payments, 1820–1913', in A.R. Hall (ed.), *The Export of Capital from Britain 1870–1914* (London, Methuen).

Wright, E.O. (1978) 'Intellectuals and the Working Class', *The Insurgent Sociologist* 8 (1).

Yallop, D. (1984) *In God's Name* (London, Jonathan Cape).

Zaretsky, E. (1977) *Gezin en privéleven in het kapitalisme*, transl. by J. van Opzeeland and F. van Wel (Nijmegen, SUN).

Ziebura, G. (1984) *Weltwirtschaft und Weltpolitik 1922/24–1931* (Frankfurt, Suhrkamp).

Index

Note: page numbers in bold type denote figures; those in italics denote tables.